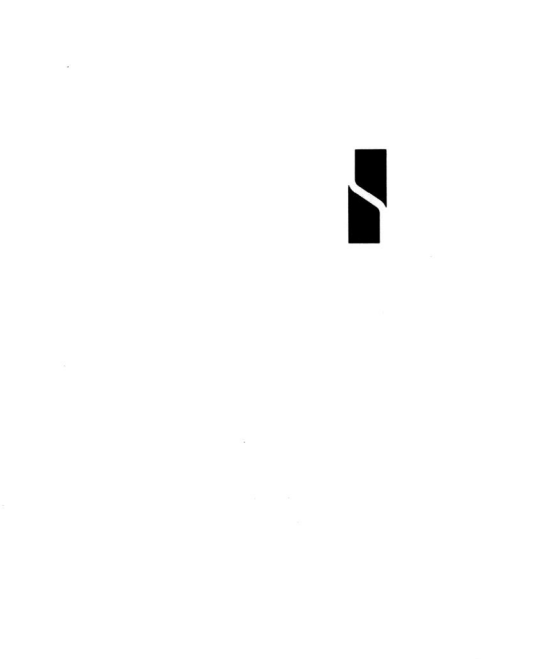

DANCE IN THE SHADOW OF THE GUILLOTINE

Judith Chazin-Bennahum
Foreword by Selma Jeanne Cohen

Southern Illinois University Press
Carbondale and Edwardsville

Copyright © 1988 by the Board of Trustees,
Southern Illinois University
All rights reserved
Printed in the United States of America
Edited by Teresa White
Production and design by Linda Jorgensen-Buhman

Library of Congress Cataloging-in-Publication Data

Chazin-Bennahum, Judith.
Dance in the shadow of the guillotine / Judith Chazin-Bennahum.
p. cm.
Bibliography: p.
Includes index.
1. Ballet—France—History—18th century. 2. Ballets—Stories, plots, etc. 3. France—History—1789–1815. I. Title.
GV1649.C48 1988
792.8'0944—dc19   88–12199
ISBN 0-8093-1487-8   CIP

The paper used in this publication meets the minimum requirements of American National Standard for Information Sciences—Permanence of Paper for Printed Library Materials, ANSI Z39.48-1984. ∞

CONTENTS

List of Illustrations ix
Foreword by Selma Jeanne Cohen xi
Acknowledgments xv
Introduction xvii
Select Chronology xxix

PART I. Prologue

1. The Ballet Livret, or the Moving Scenario 3
2. Ballet before the French Revolution 10
3. Theatres in Paris, or the Beset Stage 20

PART II. Mythology Survives the Century

4. Ballet's Love Affair with Antiquity 29
5. Ballets from Olympus, 1787–1801 35
   Maximilien Gardel, *Le Premier Navigateur, ou Le Pouvoir de l'Amour*
   Pierre Gardel, *Télémaque dans l'Isle de Calypso*
   Jean Georges Noverre, *Psyché et l'Amour*
   Jean Dauberval, *Psyché*
   Pierre Gardel, *Psyché*

Contents

Jean-Baptiste Hus, *Les Muses, ou Le Triomphe d'Apollon*
Louis-Jacques Milon, *Héro et Léandre*
6. An End to Suffering Psychés and Devilish Cupids   63

PART III. Revolutionary Spirit

7. Ballet as the Servant of Politics   69
8. Ballets of Political Passion, 1790–1796   82
La Fête de la Fédération
La Fête de l'Achèvement de la Constitution
Pierre Gardel, *La Contre-Révolution*
Pierre Gardel, *L'Offrande à la Liberté*
Pierre Gardel, *La Fête pour l'Inauguration des Bustes de Marat et Lepeletier*
Pierre Gardel, *Le Triomphe de la République, ou Le Camp de Grand Pré*
Pierre Gardel, *Le Siège de Thionville*
Pierre Gardel, *La Fête de l'Unité et de l'Indivisibilité de la République*
Joseph Lavallée, *La Constitution à Constantinople*
Coindé, *La Liberté des Nègres ou Sélico*
Planterre, *La Fête de l'Egalité*
Pierre Gardel, *La Réunion du Dix Août*
Pierre Gardel, *La Fête de l'Etre Suprême*
Chevalier Peicam de Bressoles, *La Fête Américaine*
Chevalier Peicam de Bressoles, *La Fête de l'Agriculture*
9. The Tree of Liberty   127

PART IV. Rediscovery of the Commonplace

10. Theatre Aesthetics and the Ballet   133
11. Realistic Ballets, 1787–1801   137
Maximilien Gardel, *La Chercheuse d'Esprit*
Maximilien Gardel, *La Fête du Sérail*
Maximilien Gardel, *Mirza*
Jean Dauberval, *Le Ballet de la Paille, ou Il n'est qu'un pas du Mal au Bien (La Fille Mal Gardée)*
Citoyen Beaupré, *Annette et Jacques, ou Les Semestriers Alsaciens*
Sebastien Gallet, *Les Circonstances Embarrassantes*

Contents

Jean-Georges Noverre, *Annette et Lubin*
Filippo Taglioni, *Le Jour de Noce, ou L'Enlèvement*
Pierre Gardel, *La Dansomanie*
Louis-Jacques Milon, *Les Noces de Gamache*
12. Bourgeois Sentiment on the Ballet Stage   163
    13. Bravo Ballet!   166

Notes   177
Bibliography   197
Index   205

vii

LIST OF ILLUSTRATIONS

1. Costume designs by Jean-Baptiste Martin   xix
2. Costume sketch by Jean-Baptiste Martin   xx
3. Costume sketch by Louis-René Boquet   xxi
4. Costume sketch by Louis-René Boquet   xxii
5. Marie-Madeleine Guimard   xxiii
6. Jean-Georges Noverre   7
7. Theatre of the Opéra   21
8. Performance of the *Machabées*   24
9. Forcing closure of the Opéra   25
10. The Gaîté and Ambigu-Comique theatres   26
11. Great Theatre of the Arts   30
12. Costume of a Bacchante   31
13. Mlle Guimard in *Le Premier Navigateur*   36
14. Pierre Gardel   39
15. Costume for Pierre Gardel   40
16. Mlle Clothilde as Calypso   42
17. Pierre Gardel as Telemachus   44
18. Marie Miller Gardel as Psyché   47
19. Jean Bercher Dauberval   48
20. Louis-Jacques Milon   58
21. Mlle Clothilde in *Judgment of Paris*   60
22. A revolutionary   71

Illustrations

23. Dancing to a revolutionary song 73
24. Illustration of "Heroic Deeds" 81
25. View honoring the storming of the Bastille 83
26. Night view of the *Fête de la Confédération* 85
27. Commemoration of the storming of the Bastille 97
28. *Le Triomphe de la Montagne* 99
29. *Hommage à la Liberté* 101
30. Mlle Maillard as Miss Liberty 102
31. Tragic end of Louis XVI 105
32. *La Fontaine de la Regénération* 107
33. *Fête Civique* document 109
34. A black woman from Santo Domingo 110
35. *The Freedom of French Women* 115
36. *Fête Célébrée en l'Honneur de l'Etre Suprême* 117
37. *Fête de la Raison* 118
38. "March of the Marseillaise" 122
39. *Vue de la Montagne Elevée au Champ de la Réunion* 124
40. Perspective view of the Panthéon 140
41. M. Beaupré in *La Dansomanie* 154
42. Costume design, early 1800s 159
43. Elisa Gougibus as Petite Nichon 171
44. Prison-set design 174

FOREWORD

This book comes as a most welcome antidote to a common weakness in much dance-history writing. Typical is the assertion: "During the revolution, there was a new production of *Giselle.*" But what "revolution"? How did it affect that production, its dancers, its audience? The author never tells us. Secure at the barre of a mirrored classroom or on the stage before a darkened auditorium, dance has been viewed in utter isolation from the world around it. What matter a revolution in the streets as long as a favorite ballerina is in command on the stage?

With *Dance in the Shadow of the Guillotine,* Judith Chazin-Bennahum tells us about that Revolution. Further, we learn that much of what happened to dance in late eighteenth-century France happened because of that Revolution and the changes it wrought in society. Here we discover a new audience, the people, who clamor for a new kind of popular entertainment. Disdainful of the ways of the old aristocracy and bored by idealized shepherds, they were eager to see on the stage their own counterparts—farmers and cobblers and merchants. The novel realism of Jean Dauberval's comedy of peasant life (now known as *La Fille Mal Gardée*) is shown here not merely as a personal choice but as a product of social and political forces. What has been passed over as an accidental aberration from a prevailing style is revealed as a sign of fundamental changes occurring not only in dance but in the much broader context of a national upheaval.

This fresh perspective opens before us a fascinating era that has long been neglected by dance historians. Framed by the zealous rhetoric of Jean-Georges Noverre that preceded, and by the glamorous Romantic ballet that followed, the years of the French Revolution have attracted little attention. But these very years, as Ms. Chazin-Bennahum shows, witnessed startling developments in theatrical dance—in its plots and characters, its decors and costumes, its techniques. We have long misconstrued the significance of Romanticism by ignoring its crucial forerunner. The late eighteenth-century's freeing of society from the bonds of royal power was reflected in the freeing of the body from the bonds of the corset. The way was paved for the advent of the melting, lyrical sylphide of the nineteenth century.

What kind of dancing did the audience see under the shadow of that guillotine? Readers might question applying the term "dance" to some of the fêtes and processions described by the author. But though devoid of what we now consider virtuosity, these pageants featured rhythmic movement designed to hold the attention of a rapt audience. There is evidence of the use of symbolic gestures and decidedly choreographed groupings. We long to know more, but the author is cautious. The era predates the invention of film. A system of notation existed, but it may well have been considered defiled, since it had been used to record the social dances of Louis' court.

Though lacking the documentation of movement, Ms. Chazin-Bennahum draws fully on the fortunately preserved *livrets* that tell the stories of the ballets. Thus, we can trace the evolution, beginning with mythological subjects and broadening out into the "rediscovery of the commonplace," having touched on exotic settings and sentimentally happy endings along the way. Despite their varied locales, most of the plots are simple—true love appears to be thwarted but wins in the end—and are easily made to serve what the author identifies as the revolutionary principles of concern for liberty, adventure, and free choice.

Although some of the ballets described are familiar, many have been quite unknown, even to a veteran dance-reader. And the familiar ones take on added significance when viewed as manifestations of this

Foreword

particular revolutionary fervor. We have needed an in-depth study of dance in this period of seminal importance. And such a fine study as this is a special treat.

But the time has come to read *Dance in the Shadow of the Guillotine*. Marchons, marchons . . .

Selma Jeanne Cohen

ACKNOWLEDGMENTS

I dedicate this first book to my husband and friend, David Alexander Bennahum.
  I would like to thank my children, Nina, Rachel, and Aaron; my mother, Mary Chazin; and my mother-in-law, Muriel Bennahum, for their enduring support of my flights into dance history. I also thank my father, Maurice Chazin, for his unerring and sympathetic recommendations from the very first to the last page of this study. I am indebted to Claude Marie Senninger for soliticously directing my dissertation from which this book was derived. I am deeply appreciative of the continuing and affectionate encouragement of Selma Jeanne Cohen who has been a good friend and mentor since my days at Performing Arts. I am grateful to Michaela Karni and Sarah Nestor for their thoughtful and accomplished editorial help, as well as my typists, Cheryl Dole, Dorothy Cunningham, and most especially Victoria Garcia from the University of New Mexico. I also thank James and Jennifer Linnell, Claude and Sharon Fouillade, Maurice and Lélie Kurtz, Shlomo Karni, David McPherson and Christena Schundt for their long-standing friendship and guidance.
  I am obliged to the following people who advised me in my search for materials in various libraries—Marie Françoise Christout and Sylvia Bleton from the Bibliothèque de l'Arsenal; Martine Kahane and

Acknowledgments

Marie Borel at the Bibliothèque de l'Opéra; and Ivor Guest and Sarah Woodcock in London. And I thank my editor, Teresa White, for her skilled advice to a neophyte in the publishing world.

Finally, I thank my ballet teachers and choreographers, notably Robert Joffrey, Lillian Moore, and Antony Tudor, as well as my colleagues in the dance world, with whom I share the most profound love of dance.

INTRODUCTION

What were the plots of ballets during the reign of reason that so quickly became the Reign of Terror? Who performed them? Where? And for whom? How did politics affect the choreographers of the time? Questions like these, concerning that crucial moment of transition—that missing link—between the court ballet of the 1700s and the flowering of the Romantic movement of the 1820s, have long been subjects of investigation. It can plausibly be argued that the seeds of change—in the technique, the themes, costumes, and especially scenic design—were already apparent before the Revolution. But their evolution and innovations were spurred on by the Spirit of the Revolution—to be realized fully in the nineteenth century. This book on French revolutionary ballet intends to explain why the period of the French Revolution was unique in the history of theatrical dance.

Let us begin by understanding a bit about the ballet as it existed prior to the Revolution. Because of the creation of a school of dance by Louis XIV in the late 1600s, we can presume that the dancers' performance techniques were by now highly developed, for we do know the training was rigorous. The dancers had to learn complex movement designs and subtle rhythmic patterns and had to work with a specific vertical sense of their bodies in space—in other words with a straight back. The arms were held simply but flowed lyrically, with

Introduction

wrists that gently mirrored the rising and bending of the knees. There was, no doubt, a strong emphasis on powerful feet and calves, a trademark of ballet today. This permitted the smooth, eloquent gliding and jumping through space by excellent control of the metatarsal and ankle. The eighteenth-century ballet dancers were serious and dedicated artists. They performed in theatres, in private showings at the court, and at the fairs and often traveled abroad for further money and fame. The orchestras the dancers worked with played compositions not always created especially for the dances. Their scenarios usually lacked the much-needed tight, serious plots around which all the scenes could revolve. Loosely knit divertissements characterized the dances, which were often inspired by mythology, lighthearted and fanciful. Dancers tended to perform only those dance forms in which they could excel—a gavotte, musette, or courante (the favorite of Louis XIV). And they would cajole the choreographers into letting them do those personal specialties their audience came to expect, even if they bore no relation to what preceded or came afterward. The scenery, costumes, and machines that were used to fly in the gods created extraordinary pictures, with a number of transformations in each ballet. All of these elements required not only great inventiveness in constructing movable machines but also substantial sums of money, which the king was not averse to spending. While ballet emphasized the legs and feet moving through space, pantomime accentuated the gesture, the facial expression, and the hands. Pantomimes were primarily conceived for the specific art of the *commedia* actor. The senior actor in a group would write the scenarios, while the troupe commonly improvised the various scenes. Improvisation was an inherent technique that stressed ingenious stage business. Pantomimes were commonly seen at the fairs, and they almost always told stories. The spectators understood what was going on by means of cards or roll-up signs that indicated what the action would be.

As for their costuming in the mid-eighteenth century, before and during the Revolution, ballet dancers were so weighed down with so much material—elaborate feather dressings, wigs, and masks—that their movement had certain restrictions. Their costumes were often those the aristocracy wore to their balls, with particular modifications and visual indications of the roles to be played onstage. The Roman

Introduction

1. *Eighteenth-century dancers, costume designs by Jean-Baptiste Martin (1659–1735), costume designer in chief of the Paris Opéra. The male dancer is the escort to Zephyr, the lady dancer is the escort to Flore. Gaston Vuillier,* History of Dancing *(London: Heinemann, 1898), p. 150.*

mythological tradition demanded feathers and masks. The skirt for female dancers that we now call the tutu resembles what was called a *tonnelet* for the male heroic dancer of the period. Heels were traditional, though they varied in height; female French dancers wore heels up to two and one-half inches high, whereas their English counterparts generally wore more practical ones one inch high.

An example of the exquisite fancy dress used in court ballets may be seen in figures 1–4. Dancers in court ballets moved within heavy, corseted confines and, according to the rules of Baroque dance, a style quite different from that of ballet as we know it today. Nevertheless, it is obvious that the torso in these figures has the same strong verticality associated with modern ballet technique, and that the feet and legs are turned out. Also, we see that the arms held to the side have a certain roundness, softness, and gently floating quality, but that they seem restricted to the position more in front of the shoulder. It is evident the elbows are not straight so that a spherical shape is main-

2. Jean-Baptiste Martin's costume sketch for La Silphide in the Ballet des Eléments. *Bibliothèque de l'Opéra.*

3. *Louis-René Boquet's costume sketch of Marie Allard (1742–1802), famous dancer with the Paris Opéra and mother of Auguste Vestris.* Gaston Vuillier, History of Dancing *(London: Heinemann, 1898), p. 160.*

Introduction

4. *Costume sketch by Louis-René Boquet. Bibliothèque de l'Opéra.*

tained while the arms move up, to the side, or down. If the left arm is in front, generally, the right foot is forward. That is a characteristic of all dancing, simply to maintain balance and harmony. One may ask how high the legs were lifted, how high dancers jumped, how swiftly they moved through their complex floor patterns of z's and s's, or how multiple were their turns or beats? The answers to these questions are beginning to emerge as the notation of eighteenth-century Baroque dance, the parent of ballet, is accurately read and reconstructed.

A comparison of these early illustrations with later ones reveals a remarkable change in costume in a very short time. Clearly, there was much more possibility for movement and freedom of gesture after

5. Marie-Madeleine Guimard (1743–1816), important featured dancer of the Paris Opéra in the ballet Le Premier Navigateur (1785). Bibliothèque de l'Arsenal.

Introduction

1789. Multiple pirouettes and a simpler path passage from a bent knee to a raised heel became possible with the change from the heeled shoe to the sandal. Interestingly enough, dancing on the tips of one's toes, without the assistance of a boxed shoe, in order to give the illusion of height and suspension was said to have begun as early as the 1790s. Jumps were more exciting and could travel more swiftly, and movements became more natural as a result of the new soft slipper and more flexible clothing—looser corsets and lighter, freer-flowing materials. The elimination of wigs and leather masks brought the head and face into a clearer focus, allowing facial expressions and emotive pantomime. This development was encouraged by a call for realism, the new aesthetic that expected a Greek Cupid to look Greek. The attempt to dress in the style of ancient Greece freed dancers from yards of excess satin and the limiting high heels of court fashion. Yet, even late eighteenth-century characters were lost within yards of material that had purposes other than the display of the human body.

In the course of this book, I describe some of the dramatic exigencies that may have contributed to changes in costuming, movement, gesturing, and technique. It is important to recognize the revolutionary period as the threshold of, and transition to, the Romantic era, which has been so appreciated in our century, and to see this nineteenth-century period of florescence and freedom as having its roots in the strict and rigorous theatre, court, and opera ballet of the eighteenth century. In the years before the Revolution, the French court ruled ballet because it was the source of patronage. Despite calls for change by men as influential as Denis Diderot, the philosopher; Pierre Augustin Caron de Beaumarchais, the playwright and author of *The Marriage of Figaro*; and Jean-Georges Noverre, the great choreographer of *ballets d'action*, or ballets with plots, change was slow in coming. The court tended to be conservative and held on to old ballet stories that flattered and displayed their opulence and heroic power. Certain dance forms remained in force not only because of tradition but also because the nobility insisted on an aristocratic coolness and effortlessness that was evident in such dances as the minuet, the chaconne, and the passepied.

Exciting movement and visual ideas increasingly occurred as audience and dancers came to accept the new stories, rhythms, and

Introduction

special conceptions that foreshadowed the innovations of the revolutionary period. These developments reflected the democratization of the audience as it moved toward the time of the Revolution. The growing wealth and prestige of the middle class had a gradual but irresistible influence on what had been the province of the court alone. Thus, popular preferences began to play a larger role in the production of a ballet, as they did in politics, and ever-quickening change was inevitable. The ideology that led to the swift political and economic developments of the Revolution also influenced the theatre and dance of the period—and with exhilarating directness.

Far from being shut down, the theatres of Paris during the turbulent years of the French Revolution offered a surprising number of ballets and pantomimes.[1] Dance historians mention these works and sometimes present a study of a single ballet, but there has been no detailed study of the genres, themes, and stories of the ballets of the period from approximately 1787 to 1801[2]—the gap this book intends to fill. By analyzing the printed scenarios, or *livrets*, of ballets from this time, I have discovered that while some of the ballets hearkened back to an old tradition, others were innovative and predicted themes that were to flourish during the Romantic movement.[3]

Following preliminary chapters on the *livret*, ballet, and theatres (part I), this book examines a few examples of the most interesting ballets in three categories, based on what I perceive as the period's main sources of inspiration: part II concerns classical mythology, which tended to look back toward Renaissance forebears; part III evokes the new politics, which I call "Revolutionary Spirit" (these pieces are unique to the period, as they rely on choral processions and movement positioning—hardly ballet but choreographed by famous choreographers of the time); and part IV explores middle-class themes from pastoral drama, traditional comedy, and exotic settings (these contain more realistic plots and exaggerated emotions that look both back to comic opera and Baroque theatre and forward to a new interest in bourgeois values). By placing the *livrets* in thematic and then chronological order, I am able to show the development in the approach of ballet to myth, revolutionary spectacle, and bourgeois drama.

Occasionally, I allude to political or newsworthy events that influenced the theatre. Specific moments recorded in the *Journal de l'Opéra*

Introduction

have a particular significance—for example, the times the Opéra had to close because of the riots, the "Prise de la Bastille," and after the arrest of the king. Often, one reads in the *Journal* that benefits were given to the poor or wounded. In part III, "Revolutionary Spirit," I demonstrate that political events of the moment, such as battles being waged on the frontiers of France or important disputes among political parties seeking control, take precedence over all other happenings. Whenever possible, box-office receipts and comments from contemporary critics are cited as testimony of the success or failure of a performance.[4]

The *Fêtes Révolutionnaires*, or Grand Festivals of Revolutionary Sentiment, often had large choral segments extolling the glories of the Revolution. They were intricately staged in dance, pantomime, and processions by important choreographers and, therefore, are appropriate to this study. I also chose to include a few revivals of ballets, as a reflection of the condition of ballet at the time and of the contemporary taste for certain kinds of stories. Though there is no question as to the significance of ballets created in cities other than Paris (especially London, Bordeaux, and Lyon), this book concerns itself with Paris; however, I have included a few of the ballets of Noverre and Dauberval in theatres outside Paris, because they were among the most daring and inventive eighteenth-century choreographers and strongly influenced what was performed on the stage in Paris.

Most histories of the theatre in Paris during the French Revolution begin in 1789 and go to 1800, but I have chosen to cover the years 1787 through 1801—not only to broaden the scope of this study but also to give it the precise historical and artistic setting. Political and social studies of the period by such eminent historians as Lefebvre, Cobban, Rudé, and Cobb emphasize the fact that the beginning of the Revolution was the calling together of the Notables, or Parlement, to meet the financial crises of 1787.[5] The Parlement traditionally saw its role as guardian of the people's rights in the contract between the king and the nation. The dismissal of the Assembly of Notables in May 1787 unleashed the *révolte nobiliaire*. This revolt should be seen as an intrinsic part of the Revolution, as it was the aristocracy and the Parlement—the *noblesse de robe*—that forced the king to convene the Estates-General. It was they who, by their open challenge to the

xxvi

Introduction

monarchy, drew into action the classes mainly engaged in the Revolution—the bourgeoisie, the peasants, and the urban masses. The second reason I chose 1787 as a year to begin was an artistic one. In that year, the choreographer of the Opéra, Pierre Gardel, took over for his brother who died, suddenly, of gangrene. Gardel held reign as *maître de ballet* of the Opéra until 1820—a remarkably long time, especially since he survived the Revolution, Napoleon, and the Restoration. The book ends at 1801 because the imperious influence of Napoleon countered revolutionary ideals. He was soon to be crowned, and his ideas on theatre and ballet had already been felt and expressed. The publication of Chateaubriand's *Atala*, a part of *Le Génie du Christianisme*, in 1801 was, in a sense, the culmination of those marvelous *livrets* of ballets and pantomimes with exotic settings.

One final word about my purpose and perspective. I have approached the *livrets* not only as a historian but also as a dancer. An important element of this study is the visualization of what I sense to be the action during a performance.

SELECT CHRONOLOGY

1787	February:	Meeting of the Notables
	May:	Dissolution of the Notables
		Edict of Toleration of Protestants
	August:	Exile of Parlement of Paris
	September:	Anglo-Prussian intervention in Dutch Republic
		Recall of Parlement
1788	May:	Suspension of Parlement
	August:	Convocation of States-General
	September:	Recall of Parlements
	December:	Royal council approves decree doubling Third Estate
1789	February:	Sieyès' *Qu'est-ce que le Tiers Etat?*
		Bread and grain riots in spring and early summer
	April:	Riots at Paris
	May:	Meeting of States-General
	June 17:	Third Estate adopts title of National Assembly
	June 20:	Tennis Court Oath

Chronology

	June 23:	Royal session
	June 27:	King orders first two orders to join third
	July 14:	Fall of the Bastille
	July–August:	Grand Peur (Great Panic)
	August 4–11:	Decrees abolishing feudal rights and privilege
	October 21:	Decree on martial law
	November–December:	Secularization of church lands and issue of *assignats* decreed
1790	July:	Civil Constitution of the Clergy
	November:	Burke's *Reflections on the Revolution in France*
1791	April:	Death of Mirabeau Papal bull condemns oath of Civil Constitution
	June 21:	Flight to Varennes
	July 17:	Meeting at Champ de Mars dispersed by National Guard
	August 27:	Revolt in St. Domingo
	September:	Constitution of 1791 voted Dissolution of Constituent Assembly
	October:	Meeting of Legislative Assembly
	November:	Pétion elected mayor of Paris
1792	April 20:	France declares war on Austria
	June 20:	Popular demonstrations in Paris
	July 11:	"La Patrie en Danger" Manifesto of Duke Brunswick
	August 10:	Attack on Tuileries
	August 19:	Flight of Lafayette
	September 2:	Fall of Verdun
	September 2–6:	September massacres
	September 20:	Valmy—retreat of Brunswick, first meeting of the republican forces

Chronology

September 21:	Meeting of Convention
September 22:	Abolition of monarchy
October:	Custine crosses the Rhine
November:	Dumouriez's victory at Jemmapes, occupation of Belgium
November 19:	Decree of the Convention offering help to all peoples wishing to recover their liberty
December:	Trial of Louis XVI
December 15:	Decree on treatment of occupied territories

1793

January 21:	Execution of Louis XVI
February 1:	French declaration of war on Great Britain
February–March:	Food riots
March:	French declaration of war on Spain
	Revolt of the Vendée
	Revolutionary Tribunal set up
	Dumouriez defeated, evacuates Netherlands
April:	Establishment of the Committee of Public Safety
May 31:	Riots in Paris
June 24:	Constitution of 1793 voted
July 13:	Assassination of Marat
	Robespierre enters Committee of Public Safety
	Suppression of remaining seigneurial rights without compensation
August:	Toulon delivered to English
	Levée en masse (national draft) declared
October 16:	Execution of Marie-Antoinette
	Execution of Girondins
	Dechristianization campaign

Chronology

	December:	Toulon retaken by Revolutionaries
	December 4:	Defeat of Vendeans
1794	March 24:	Execution of Hébertists
	April 5:	Execution of Dantonists
	June 8:	Fête of the Supreme Being
	June 10:	Law of 22 prairial reorganizing Revolutionary Tribunal
	June 26:	Reconquest of Belgium
	July 27–28:	9 Thermidor—fall of Robespierre
	September 1:	Billaud, Barère, and Collot leave Committee of Public Safety
	November:	Jacobin Club closed
1795	April:	Deportation of Billaud, Collot, and Barère decreed
		Peace of Basle between France and Prussia
	May:	Peace with Holland
	July:	Quiberon: defeat of émigrés
		Peace between Spain and France
	August:	Constitution of Year III voted
	October 5:	Dissolution of the Convention
	November:	Rule of the Directory begins
1796	November:	Victory at Arcola
1797	January:	French victory at Rivoli
	May:	Bonaparte occupies Venice
	September 4:	Coup d'état of 18 fructidor
1798	May:	Departure of French expedition to Egypt
	July:	French victory at Battle of the Pyramids
	August:	Aboukir Bay: Nelson destroys French fleet

Chronology

1799	March–July:	Austrian and Russian successes
	September–October:	Russian army defeated in Switzerland
	October:	Return of Bonaparte to France
	November 9–10:	Coup d'état of 18 brumaire
	December:	Constitution of Year VIII Bonaparte first consul
1800	June:	Marengo, Napoleon's victory
	December:	Royalist bomb plot
1801	August:	Armed neutrality French army in Egypt capitulates Chateaubriand's *Le Génie du Christianisme*
1802	April:	Concordat promulgated
	May:	Bonaparte consul for life

Part I
PROLOGUE

1
THE BALLET *LIVRET*, OR THE MOVING SCENARIO

It has been extremely difficult to develop a sharp picture of ballet-pantomime in Paris in the late eighteenth-century, since there is little available notation for theatrical ballet during that time.[1] Still, we are fortunate in the discovery of Gennaro Magri's *Trattato Teoretico-Prattico di Ballo*. The treatise offers notation for some theatrical dances prior to 1779 and discusses their relationship to music. It provides important clues in connecting the development of the formalized theatrical dance techniques with the pre-Romantic movement of the early nineteenth century. But we must pursue other areas in order to resolve this complex puzzle. Observers of the ballet, and well-known aestheticians of the late seventeenth and eighteenth centuries, such as Michel de Pure (1668), Le Père Menestrier (1682), Pierre Rameau (1725), Abbé du Bos (1733), Remond de Saint-Mard (1741), Charles Batteux (1746, Louis de Cahusac (1752), Giovanni Andrea Gallini (1762), and le Sieur Compan (1787), have given us some excellent descriptions and analyses. Incomplete newspaper articles that speak of dancers rather than choreography also aid in "looking at" the period. Paintings and musical scores help us to imagine the styles, shapes, and pictures that dancers created. But possibly one of the best ways to discover the ballets and pantomimes is an intense reading of the *livret*, or program of the performance.

Prologue

The *livret*, usually written by the choreographer, is a strange literary form because it was not an end in itself but a guide to something else. It is sometimes as long as forty pages, though more often only twenty-five, and usually lists the choreographer, composer, theatre, date of presentation, cast of characters, dancers, censor's stamp, publisher, summary of the story to be performed, and, occasionally, the set and costume designer. The latter were generally not listed simply because they were attached to the theatre and their names were assumed. The *livret* was printed and sold at the time of performance in order to help the audience understand the action and, also, to establish a kind of copyright for the choreographer. After all, any myth or known literary theme could be choreographed in an individual manner. To the dance historian, the scenario represents an invaluable source. Sometimes specific information may be given about movements and gestures, although this is unusual. Because of the research of twentieth-century dance scholars as well as the tradition in ballet of handing down information, both orally and by physical demonstration, it has become clear what nineteenth-century ballet looked like. We even know a bit about one prerevolutionary ballet, *The Whims of Cupid* (Galeotti, 1786), and one revolutionary ballet, *La Fille Mal Gardée* (Dauberval, 1789), as they are still in the repertoire of some major ballet companies. The original choreography is not known, however. The *livret* often begins with a prologue that provides key information about the setting of the ballet. It may explain certain problems met in the course of production, such as the lack of funds because of revolutionary strife. It may acknowledge a patron or teacher who helped the choreographer. There may be an aesthetic discussion. During the Reign of Terror, it was expeditious to tip one's hat to the *sans-culottes*, or Revolutionaries, who wore trousers rather than the breeches that were characteristic of the dress of gentlemen. In short, the prologue frequently offers a personal glimpse of the choreographer, even when he tries to mask himself behind the traditional eighteenth-century stylized, often involuted language. Censorship was commonly practiced in France before the Revolution. The censor was an appointee of the king who scrutinized all prospective scripts for plays, ballets, operas, and the like. He would stop any piece that criticized, questioned, or parodied the laws of the state, the king, or the activities of the court.

The Ballet Livret

The practice of giving out or selling printed programs at ballets and pantomimes has lasted for four hundred years. In 1668, in his *Idées des Spectacles*, de Pure mentions that in his time "it is easy to see the defects in these ballets where one knows nothing if not for the stories that are sung, or the programs that are distributed or the verses that are inserted in order to visualize the plot and to connect the plot with the scenery."[2] Often, the choreographers did not succeed in realizing the story, but this problem was compounded if the plot made no sense in the first place. Fortunately, some of the finest writers of the sixteenth, seventeenth, and eighteenth centuries were involved in writing the ballet *livrets*, so at least, the meanings of the ballets were clear.[3]

The early ballet *livrets* of the sixteenth and seventeenth centuries were accompanied by poetry that was recited or sung during the ballet. But as the dancing began to take precedence over the poetry, these verses were no longer spoken or sung, and the poets of quality stopped writing *livrets* for the court. According to French ballet historian Henry Prunières, "Malherbe, who for ten years wrote verses for all the ballets, does not hide his disdain for this kind of spectacle. He pretends to only collaborate on these divertissements because he is forced to do so."[4]

In the opinion of Prunières, these *livrets* contain little movement description and therefore have little merit: "The poetic text of the declaimed or sung scenes offers no technical details found in the court ballets."[5] The assumption of Prunières that poetry and literature are greater forms of art than ballet in the seventeenth century may be surmised from his saying that "the 'précieux' Bertaut, the rude and pompous Malherbe, the vulgar Sigognes, the heroic Pierre Corneille, the mediocre Bordier—all of these men put their talents to the same purpose: None of them tries to compose a ballet of the same high quality as a literary work."[6] He also notes disdainfully that important poets would not write programs for ballets, because the poetry would not be recited and learned. Thus, third-rate poets were employed by the court to fabricate plots for ballets.

What value do these *livrets* have for dance historians? Prunières discusses their importance as an indication of the taste of the times. In 1616, mention is made of the arrest of the Prince de Condé (the audience loved glimpsing newsworthy tidbits), hidden in the allegorical

Prologue

ballet *Damon et Sylvie*. Political figures of the time were often celebrated in court ballet, as were expressions of the trials and tribulations of their love affairs.[7]

But what disappoints the dance historian, even when looking at *livrets* composed by great writers such as Ronsard, Molière, and Benserade, is that what is written in the program does not necessarily tell us how the work is danced or moved. The story, with descriptions of scenery changes (costume changes are rarely indicated) and scene and act divisions, may give us some idea of the performance but not a full sense of it.

A *livret* that does contain several relatively specific movement directions is *Le Siège de Cythère* by Dauberval (pseudonym for Jean Bercher, a pupil of Noverre).[8] In the first act of *Le Siège*, there is a description of a festivity that is interrupted by Caliste, the favorite nymph of Venus. She announces that Scythians are approaching Cythère in order to destroy their celebration and to vent their fury on Adonis. Venus shivers and entrusts her lover, Adonis, to the Zephyrs and the tiny Loves who decide to hide in a labyrinth while Caliste and Venus think of ways to defend themselves against the Scythians' anger. A handwritten note written next to the scene gives this description:

> In the middle of this charming, fresh and voluptuous setting, Caliste, pale and disheveled arrives. . . . This creates a delightful and perfect contrast. Imagine the effect when after having seen all the adorable behinds of fauns, nymphs and cupidons, the Scythians enter, in all the severity of their costumes; their dances are truly barbaric and antique. Dauberval has the brilliant touch of creating all kinds of dances that take place in all periods of time; it seems, truthfully that this man has seen everything. Nothing is foreign to his art.[9]

This personal note not only gives a sense of the power Dauberval created by bringing in a mythological army of warriors but also demonstrates the deep respect his artistry commanded at the time of the ballet. In this scenario, there are eight brief handwritten notes of this sort. One, in particular, mentions that the person writing the notes

The Ballet Livret

6. Jean-Georges Noverre as portrayed in 1764, by
Jean-Baptiste Perronneau (1715–83), shortly after the Lettres had
appeared. Bibliothèque de l'Opéra.

is the dancer who played Caliste—that is, Mme Dauberval; she excuses herself for the praise she gives her husband and for the remarks she makes about her success as the Caliste of this performance.

A dance calls for movement, and in order to visualize the action, we must have a writing style that evokes the movement and clarifies

Prologue

the story. Rarely, at this period, do we find a *livret* that does that. Occasionally, some writers—or, I should say, choreographers—such as Jean-Georges Noverre (1727–1810), Dauberval (1742–1806), Pierre Gardel (1758–1840), and Charles Didelot (1767–1837) would create scenarios in language simple and direct, yet with that eighteenth-century flair for descriptive flourish that gave to the words a life of their own separate from the dance story. (Didelot is especially gifted in descriptive language.) But, for the most part, the possibility of creating a fine poetic narrative escaped most revolutionary-period choreographers.

During the mid-eighteenth century, ballet choreographers Gaspare Angiolini, Vicenzo Galeotti, Jean-Georges Noverre, and Franz Hilverding all tried to return the "story" to its former importance.[10] The *ballet d'action*, or ballet with a single plot, received its impetus from the decadence of the divertissements, or showy dances, that were strung together without any rhyme or reason and could in no way bring the audience to tears or laughter. Furthermore, the choreographer, usually a dancer, began to assume complete control over the music, the decoration, the *livret*—all the elements of the performance. He often took his story from a play or opera, carefully avoiding anything that would obscure the direction of events:

> In principle [said Noverre], one should eliminate accessory details and secondary plots for the sake of clarity. In the case of a faithful adaptation, the ambiance or spirit must be respected, not the letter. Vision replaces, in effect, description; sensations or feelings take the place of reflection. And sometimes scenic necessities impose their own limitations.[11]

No limitations hindered the majestic spirit of Noverre, who writes *livrets* and comments upon them with sincerity and flair. He emphasizes the need for clarity and intelligence in the writing of a *livret*. If the subject is guided by suspense, then new events must be used in order to further the mystery. He worked ceaselessly on structure, making certain that transitions from one scene to another and from one act to another were motivated and logical. He sought scenarios from the greatest playwrights, knowing that their work brought to the stage

The Ballet Livret

the truth of human emotion and "une peinture vivante des passions." Experiences are suggested and sentimentalized by the *livret* of the ballet-pantomime, and Noverre admitted that the language of dance is more allusive than directly expressive. With this in mind, he wrote that without the *livret*, the audience was in the dark. Nevertheless, the hope that the dance could stand alone, without a *livret*, obsessed late eighteenth-century aestheticians such as Karl Engel, who hoped that "it will not be necessary to have either a title or scenario for the ballet."[12]

2
BALLET BEFORE THE FRENCH REVOLUTION

The long and complex history of ballet in France since the sixteenth century is a fascinating study of manners, literary aspirations, and scenic splendor. Ballets occasionally had popular audiences, though they were created and nurtured for court consumption, and they tended to seek ideas from contemporary dramas, dances, operas, and fair theatres that played in Paris. Most popular were mythological and pastoral productions using giant machines to divert the eyes with strange and exotic settings.

Throughout the eighteenth century, ballet companies in France rarely supported themselves; they lived at the expense of the king or a patron and were usually connected to the most important opera house of the city. Ballets were often played in the presence of His Majesty at the court at Versailles (where the heart of political power rested before the Revolution). Quite a few ballets had their first performances at a chateau rather than an opera house. The theatres in these chateaus or hotels were grand ballrooms, the scenes of fancy-dress social affairs. In the seventeenth century before stages were constructed, a ballet performance offered loosely structured stories with people dancing in and out of whatever space seemed useful to the ballet; moving scenery was a usual feature. When stages became com-

Ballet before the Revolution

mon during the eighteenth century, the scene designer constructed amazing feats for the eye, with as many as twenty dancers moving in the myths or poetic tales. Important people who came to see the performance would be seated at a central point. Occasionally, tickets were sold to people who were not connected to the court, which allowed a more general-public audience to attend. The ballet was considered an important tool for entertainment, for the display of certain political persuasions, and most of all, for the exaltation of the king's power and that of the court. In some theatres, there were *parterres*, where the bourgeoisie and poorer individuals paid to stand and mill around.

When Louis XIV instituted the Academy of Dance in 1661 (this became the Academy of Music and Dance and then the Paris Opéra), a professional seriousness accompanied the royal backing of ballet. Although the ballet of the late seventeenth century was already a highly developed and skillful art, technique evolved rapidly in the eighteenth century, incorporating complex figures (patterns of design in space), jumps, beats, and pirouettes. The spectacle of movement, costume, song, and scenery took people out of the present into the exotic. In his *Mémoires* (1669), the Comte de Marolles gives his definition of the art at this time: "But what is a ballet of the type seen today? It seems to me that it is a dance of many masked persons dressed in dazzling clothes, composed of diverse entrées or parts which can be distributed into several acts and which relate agreeably to a whole, with some different airs [tunes] to represent an invented subject, where the pleasing, the unusual, and the marvelous are not forgotten."[1]

But reformers complained that a ballet dancer in the late eighteenth century was burdened with many unnecessary objects. He or she wore wigs, had heavy materials on the body that limited arm movements, forced feet into shoes with high heels, and often performed in the traditional masks associated with heroes, heroines, and other personages.

In the *Encyclopédie*, Louis de Cahusac (1700–1759), an opera and ballet librettist, wrote the definition of ballet as he saw it in 1752: "Every ballet is a dance with two or more people who perform. Only one dancer does not create a ballet; that would be a pantomime. The

Prologue

dance, the union of several people, the representation of an action by gestures, steps, the movement of the body are thus what constitute a ballet."[2]

According to Cahusac, sources for the ballets in France came from history, mythology, allegory, literature, and, of course, the imagination. The most important rule of ballet, according to Cahusac, was unity of design. The unities of time and place, however, did not have to be followed, although form remained foremost. This precept then led to the figures, or patterns of steps in space, the movements themselves integrated into the proper whole of the music, instrumental or vocal, and finally the decor and machine-moved sets. Poetry could be used for the sake of commentary and explanation. Cahusac describes what his readings from ballet historians Abbé du Bos and Père Menestrier taught him, but he accentuates a fairly new element, the importance of a plot and the requirement that it move the audience intensely:[3] "Anything that is without a plot is unworthy of being seen in the theatre. Anything that is not relative to the plot becomes an ornament without taste or depth."[4]

These ideas were favored and furthered by the choreographer and dancer Noverre,[5] who began his *Lettres sur la Danse et les Arts Imitateurs* in late 1757 after his return from his second season in London. Noverre, who is often called the "father of modern ballet," urged that choreographers write their *livrets* with structure and skill. He advocated the use of a variety of subjects, saying that the composer must look to life for his plots, not just myths and pastorals, and that peasants as well as kings had a place in the ballet. To accompany the widening range of permissible subjects, he also called for new movements for the expression of ideas. These, Noverre believed, were to be found in the art of pantomime, an art that had virtually become a fad in the mid-eighteenth century. Although the *livrets* of the time rarely had tragic endings, Noverre urged the use of horror, terror, and catastrophe. In these scenarios, we often find threats and menaces offering frightful conflict before the happy ending. For strong emotions to be communicated, Noverre felt there needed to be a simplification of virtuoso cabrioles and pirouettes, which told nothing about human psychology. (Noverre was a prophet, but his prophecies were not necessarily realized by his own work or by the subsequent work of Gardel or Dauberval.)

Noverre said, "Off with the masks so that the face and the body can become more expressive and less encumbered." He did not like the wide skirt, or *tonnelet*, on male dancers and felt that the constant use of masks for "heroic" roles put them at a disadvantage in front of the women, who often discarded their masks. Noverre stated that pantomime, which Cahusac had also praised for its expressive possibilities, could be the key to a good ballet drama. His scenarios freely utilized powerful feelings such as anger, jealousy, fear, and love. Acting techniques, which he had learned in London from the great English actor David Garrick, were integrated into his ballets. For Noverre, a gesture was worth a thousand words.

Noverre's ballet precepts were also found in the work of dramatic writers of the time, notably Denis Diderot, Sebastien Mercier, and Pierre Augustin Caron de Beaumarchais. Eighteenth-century theatrical reforms centered upon the intention of touching or profoundly moving the spectator by bringing the play closer to the experience of the audience.[6] Plots were to deal more authentically with the natural feelings of men, women, and children in real-life situations. The *drame bourgeois* acknowledged the presence of the emerging French middle class, with its money problems and class struggles. In Diderot's third *Entretiens sur le Fils Naturel* (ca. 1757), the *genre sérieux* was intended to reach the "people" and to provide an agency for social reform.[7]

Though the execution of Diderot's dramatic works fell far short of his aims, they contained a fermenting element not lost upon the choreographer Noverre and his pupils Dauberval[8] and Pierre Gardel;[9] for them, the frigid artificiality of mythical subjects and classical tragedy had to be metamorphosed into a new theatre. The theatre of the fairs and the pantomime of the Italian comedy contained dramatic elements that spoke more truthfully than did the ballet or stage drama in Paris. As Diderot said, "Let the subject be important, the plot simple, domestic and close to life"[10]—precisely the qualities of fair pantomimes and comic operas. From the end of the sixteenth century, it had been customary for strolling players to erect their booths at the fairs, or Théâtre de la Foire, in Paris in the winter (the Foire Saint-Germain) and in the summer (the Foire Saint-Laurent). Here they presented comic dialogues, ballets, and pantomimes that gradually developed

Prologue

into dramatic scenes after the Italian players were expelled in 1697. (The Italian players were a company of Italian actors [the Gelosi] who, in the seventeenth century were authorized to play Italian impromptus in Paris. They gradually introduced scenes in French, parodied tragedies, and, in general, exceeded the limits that had been assigned to their performances. They were expelled in 1697, ostensibly for indecency but in reality for ridiculing Mme de Maintenon (Louis XIV's consort) in a play called *La Fausse Prude*. They returned in 1716 after the death of Louis XIV.) To this invasion of its monopoly, the Comédie-Française offered opposition. But the Théâtre de la Foire established itself. It combined with the Italian players when they returned in 1716 and specialized in *opéra comique* (romantic comedy interspersed with song and dance) besides producing various other forms of comedy suited to popular audiences. Audiences paid a small fee to enter these temporary, small theatres.

When we examine the ballet *livrets* of the late eighteenth century, myths, pastorals, and bourgeois comedies abound. In fact, every sort of subject, including heightened moments of thrilling melodrama, is explored. What astounds the contemporary reader is the paradoxical struggle to sustain old traditions. Ballet could not let go of its original themes, as even today we continue to perform the nineteenth-century classics *Swan Lake* and *Giselle*. The reforms, influenced by the new popular audiences, which asked for simple plots, expressive gestures, and sentimental responses, were just beginning to be recognized.

The ballet vocabulary taught at the Opéra in Paris, with its conservative and formal training, absorbed influences from pantomime, the *commedia* tradition exemplified by the fair theatres and the English theatre, where David Garrick, the extraordinary English actor, experimented with an emotional and expressive manner of playing Shakespeare. In France, Noverre and his disciples were the messengers for these developments. Old ideas die hard, and choreographers only gradually sought new ways to move the dancers onstage. The *ballet d'action* demanded different movements that not only would employ ballet technique but also would tell a powerful story, with people acting and responding to dramatic situations. Pantomime, which tended

Ballet before the Revolution

to call upon real-life gestures, was a perfect medium for the revelation of personalities in the dance. The improvisational techniques, as well as the lighter acrobatic training of the *commedia* or Italian *comédiens*, also contributed to the changes in ballets, now called "ballet-pantomimes." The Italian comic tradition of parodying everyday life provided realistic stories, which Maximilien Gardel (1783–87) preferred to call upon when he was the chief choreographer at the Paris Opéra. Though later, his brother, Pierre Gardel, made his fame with the myth ballet, and these emotionally charged myth plots no doubt moved his adoring public. It is interesting that in 1800 he went back to the comic plot with his *La Dansomanie*, and that this was his most popular ballet in Paris as well as in other cities of Europe.

The people who wrote about ballet in the eighteenth century expected to see these hoped-for changes on the stage. As Patricia Murphy has said, "Their writings reflect the growing sense of militancy that had developed."[11] Increasing criticism of the dances as divertissements in opera became quite open, especially among the Encyclopedists. Richard Oliver reiterated that "the main defect of the ballet, according to Cahusac, Baron Grimm and other Encyclopedists, was that it presented a series of disconnected scenes which do not even have the interesting tonal relations of the danse suite."[12] This is not surprising, as at the Opéra, the ballets were brought in to cover the defects in the composition of French operas. But the dances themselves were also mediocre, since they were detached from the main line of dramatic action. Castil-Blaze later remarked, looking back to this period:

> Previously the music of ballets was restricted to the uniform framework of chaconnes, passepieds, sarabands, gigues, minuets and gavottes. The dance has been free for some time from the shackles that bad taste and the necessity to continuously reproduce the same figures and to execute the same steps that dancers without experience have imposed. This art has made tremendous progress since the end ot the eighteenth century. And although its revolution seems slower than music's, people like Milon, Gardel, Vestris and Paul have carried it to an unsurpassable point.[13]

Prologue

Baron Grimm, who wrote on the subject in the article "Poème Lyrique" in the *Encyclopédie* (1750s), describes a typical opera ballet:

The best dancers, however, are reserved to show off as soloists or in pas de deux; for important moments, they form pas de trois, quatre or cinq or six, after which the corps du ballet had stopped moving in order to make way for the masters to regroup, and finish the ballet. For all of these different divertissements, the composer furnishes chaconnes, loures, sarabands, minuets, passepieds, gavottes, rigaudons and contradances. If once in a while there is a moment of action, or a dramatic idea, it is a pas de deux or trois that executes it and then the corps du ballet immediately begins its insipid dances. The only real difference between one ballet and another is the way the tailor [costume designer] costumes the ballet, whether it be in yellow, white, green, red, following the principles and etiquette of fashion. Thus the ballet in French opera is only an academy of dance, where in public view, mediocre people exercise, make figures break apart and reform into groups and where the great dancers show us their most difficult moves by making noble, gracious and wise positions or poses.[14]

Grimm's analysis of the problems plaguing ballet was accurate enough. The questionable state of ballet may have been aggravated by the insolent behavior of principal dancers who had achieved public fame. Marie Sallé, who is said to have shared in the invention of the *ballet d'action* with her choreography for *Pygmalion* (1735 in London), La Camargo, La Guimard, Louis Dupré, and the Vestris family were very influential and, as a consequence, had control of the repertory, their working conditions, and vacations.[15] They displayed a general arrogance toward the audience and the administrations of the Opéra.[16] Unconcerned with the ego of the dancer and dedicated to theatrical reform, the great writer and Encyclopedist Jean Jacques Rousseau clearly understood many of these problems, both technical and artistic. None of the arts escaped Rousseau's creative mind; he, too, wrote ballet *livrets*.[17] In *Julie, ou La Nouvelle Héloise*, published in 1761, Rousseau writes in letter form of his impressions of the possibilities of

16

Ballet before the Revolution

dance and pantomime.[18] Criticizing the manner in which the ballets are gratuitously thrown into the operas, without dramatic reason or preparation, Rousseau admires the potential excitement that the dance can produce but deplores the thoughtlessness of opera choreographers. He notes that popular dances are included in a simple-minded manner. The audience watches the protagonists of the opera or dance watching the dancers. Is the king joyous? Yes? Well then, we will participate in his joy and dance with him. Is he sad? Well then, he must be cheered up, and so everyone dances again. Rousseau sees this mindless pretext for a ballet as distracting and unnecessary, but, he says, "The ballet can be so successful if created as . . . an integral part of the work. There are many subjects for a dance; the most serious experiences in life are done with dancing. Priests dance, soldiers dance, Gods dance, devils dance; people dance in the cemeteries and burials and any dance is appropriate to an event. Consequently, chaconnes are unworthy in a tragedy."[19]

During the years this book covers, 1787–1801, ballet became more and more separate from opera, which had usually dictated the subjects and types of dances and their rhythms. Ballet choreographers, trained in the subsidized ballet schools, were highly skilled dancers, often the composers of their own music, and quite literary. Pierre Gardel, for example, knew Latin and played the violin beautifully. In making a ballet separate from an opera and thus creating a twenty-or-thirty-minute piece, complete unto itself, the choreographer produced a more cohesive, coherent, and structured work. The unities, though they were argued about constantly, were used because they emphasized structure. There was also a tendency toward integrating pantomime or a gestural technique of expression with ballet. As a result, ballet developed into a larger, more identified, and self-important projection into space.

In eighteenth-century Paris, several theatres had ballet companies associated with them. In charge of the training and choreography for these companies was the *maître de ballet*, whose responsibilities developed rapidly with the evolving ballet techniques. Cities all over Europe cultivated the teaching and information of dancers in their preparation, first as great dancers, then as *maitres de ballet*. In addition, there was stiff competition among choreographers for rich patrons.

Prologue

Young girls and boys, often from families of dancers but sometimes without fathers, were enrolled at very young ages at the Opéra or theatre schools. There they learned the art of the dance and the repertoire. Sometimes, there were children's troupes that reflected the current trends in the theatre and ballet. One such company was Mme de Pompadour's Théâtre des Petits Appartements, all trained by the famous Jean-Baptiste de Hesse.[20] The Opéra had large numbers of children, who occasionally had to work the machinery at the tops of the stages, because their tiny bodies were small enough to fit on the rafters. In the boulevard theatres, the public nicknamed the *corps de ballet* "la grosse cavalerie," since on the battlefield it was the heavy cavalry, like the ballet corps, that finished off the action.[21]

As in the boulevard theatres, ballet dancers were extremely important at the fairs in Paris. In a letter of 1775 to David Garrick concerning a London engagement, Noverre mentions that. "it is necessary that you tell me how many male and female figurants you have, so that I can hire on your behalf those you lack and that I will need. The Saint-Laurent Fair is always well-provided with dancers and will facilitate my being able to furnish you with good ones all trained in my style of composition."[22]

When their run in the major cities ended, the fair dancers toured the provinces. They were well known for their fine and diversified technique, which displayed an expertise in acrobatics and ropedancing.[23] This talent was exemplified by Marie Sallé, whose father directed one of these *commedia* troups. As has been mentioned, she became one of the greatest early eighteenth-century opera dancers, her success due in part to the finesse of her gestures: "Of her debut performances in the Théâtre de la Foire where one is not accustomed to make a gesture without reason, and where, due to the persecutions of the Comédiens Français, she composes a spectacle with very few words and many movements and she has sustained her unique predilection for pantomime."[24] Sallé knew the value of a simple and meaningful gesture. Her talents were greatly appreciated by Voltaire, who sang her praises in a poem dedicated to another remarkable theatre person, Adriana Lecouvreur called *Epître sur la Mort de Mlle Lecouvreur*: "O you, young Sallé, daughter of Terpsichore, who is insulted in Paris, but whom all London honors, Receive my adoration with your new

Ballet before the Revolution

successes, and the applause of a respectable people."[25] As Dacier so aptly puts it, "One is never a prophet in one's own country."[26]

In a sense, Sallé embodied the call for change by Noverre and his Encyclopedist colleagues. In addition, Noverre's pupils, Pierre Gardel, Jean Dauberval, and Charles Didelot, listened well, employed his ideas as best they could within their limitations, and succeeded in developing a form of ballet that brought the spectator a production in tune with the artistic and literary excellence of the time.

The years of the Revolution unleashed possibilities in ballet for techniques that were never before realized. Dancers began to jump much higher and to move more freely, largely as a result of changes from heavy to lighter costumes, and to pirouette like tops, freed of the high heels that had interrrupted their flow of movement. These modifications allowed *maîtres* to develop a strong training technique that was reinforced by the dancers of the ballet schools. Choreographers increasingly wrote stories with tightly knit plots that were suspenseful and easy to understand. Though upstaged by political events during the years of the Revolution, choreographers were permitted to give freer expression to their imagination and greater variety to their movements than in the years dominated by the taste of the court.

3
THEATRES IN PARIS, OR THE BESET STAGE

The key to the history of ballet and pantomime is closely tied to the theatres in which they were performed. And the notion of *privilèges* given to different theatres by the king is essential to an understanding of the history of the theatres in Paris. A *privilège* was a monopoly authorized and enforced by the court for the purpose of limiting certain genres to specific theatres. But that control did not end with the death of Louis XVI. The practice of *privilèges* was an important form of censorship; the revolutionary government controlled significant aspects of any drama or musical. Some theatres could only let their performers do acrobatics or pantomime. Some had gauze curtains separating actors from audiences. Most of the theatres opened at 6:00 P.M., while some were forced to open at 7:00 P.M. Some could play music, and some could use mime or do ballet.

The Paris Opéra, having complete supremacy, created a considerable tax on ballets elsewhere in order to assure its continuing power and the prestige of the Théâtre Français and the Théâtre Italien, which were considered official theatres. The actors at the Comédie-Française could not play comic opera. The Italian actors were originally not allowed to play works without music, but eventually they obtained permission to do plays with Harlequin as the central character without music, in five acts—but no tragedies were allowed there. These plays

7. View of the theatre of the Opéra and of the library of the king. Bibliothèque de l'Opéra.

replaced the traditional Italian scenarios on Tuesdays and Fridays, and on those days the Opéra refused to permit the Italians to use any music. The Théâtre de Monsieur, supported by the king's brother, did only Italian operas or Italian parodies, but it skirted the law by saying that original operas were indeed parodies. The Variétés could perform only three-act plays; Nicolet was obliged to keep to ropedancers; Audinot could not let his marionettes talk for some time, until children replaced them. In some theatres, a ditty could not be sung even when it was necessary to the action; the actor had to recite the song to the tune of a violin. The Beaujolais actors mouthed the words (as they, too, were not allowed to sing) while the musicians in the wings sang for them. At the Associés, all types of plays were put on, but they had to be preceded by a marionette show. The Délassements-Comiques also had marionettes, but in order to be differentiated from the Associés, they were obliged to use a gauze curtain. In addition, they could have only three actors onstage at one time. Some theatres could use acrobatics, some could not use people in playing dramas, some could not play

Prologue

comedy. The Opéra-Comique was not allowed to play foreign works or translations; however, the Théâtre de Versailles of Marie-Antoinette had complete freedom. The Variétés Amusantes had to pay a sixty-thousand-franc fee to the Opéra as a tax. The actors of the Théâtre Français also scrutinized the *livrets* and plays of the Théâtre Italien after the censor had done so; if they happened to like a scene, they would take it for themselves, truncating the original so that it could not play well for the Italians.

Naturally, the campaign for liberty in the theatre was consistent with the powerful ideological, social, and political changes of the Revolution. Traditional laws of censorship went hand in hand with the seemingly irrational, cruel, and capricious rules for the theatre. The thought content of a script, or *livret*, was thus open to government supervision. *Le Mariage de Figaro* in 1784, with the travails it bore in order to be performed, is a typical example of what happened to a literary work that made fun of or criticized the church or royalty or the establishment. What occurred onstage was an affair of state, and the censor took his job very seriously. In January 1787, Marie-Antoinette mounted an Italian opera, *Il Re Téodoro* by Paisiello, at Versailles, and "in a scene where the king and his valet are out of money, they look at one another and wonder how they can get out of this fix. 'Call the Notables into session,' cries a voice from the parterre."[1] No censor monitored this performance; one month later the Notables were called into session.

The censorship was relaxed after the fall of the Bastille. Marie-Joseph de Chénier had succeeded in getting his *Charles IX* to be played, and other dramas, which had previously been refused permission to play, went on the boards: *Le Mariage de Figaro, Le Réveil d'Epiménide, Pierre le Grand, Louis XII*. The public demanded to be given what it wanted to see, and in most cases slowly got its wish: "The Censors, the administrators of the Police Bureau, the Assembly of the Commune, overflowing in each area, acquiesced before the powerful will of the Public and left them free passage."[2] The chief censor, Suard (formerly the position of censor was held by Crébillon), gave way to so-called public opinion. During January 6–19, 1791, the famous decree freeing the theatres, which was drafted by La Harpe, was discussed and passed in the National Assembly. The reporter, Chapelier,

Theatres in Paris

with the aid of Mirabeau's splendid oratory, announced the very important new decrees:

1. Any citizen can establish a public theatre and present in it plays of any kind by making a declaration to the municipality before its opening.
2. The works of authors dead more than five years are public property and can, former privilèges notwithstanding, now be presented in all theatres indiscriminately.
3. The works of living authors cannot be presented in any public theatres without the formal consent in writing of the authors, under penalty of confiscation of the total receipts for the benefit of the author.
4. The directors or members of the different theatres will be, by reason of their position, subject to the inspection of the municipality. They will receive orders only from the municipality which cannot stop or forbid any play except at the request of author or actor, and which can require nothing except that which conforms to the laws and to the police regulations.[3]

New houses opened (by 1792, more than two hundred theatres sprang up in Paris), and anticlerical plays were performed despite the censor. Though no drama or ballet was allowed to display clerics on the stage, "a ballet pantomime at the Ambigu-Comique, *Dorothée* by Arnould-Mussot, was the first that put prelates and monks onstage."[4] Also, "in 1782, at the Ambigu-Comique in the Foire Saint-Laurent, *Dorothée* was presented to an overflowing crowd; the heroine was imprisoned in a Gothic tower. This 'beautiful pantomime,' as Grimm calls it, would have more than 12 years of popularity; in 1790, a cortege of priests and archbishops, a tasty spectacle at the time, would be added."[5] Many changes took place rapidly within a few years, pro-Royalist sentiment gave way to patriotic sentiment, and the "passion play of the Revolution" the *sans-culottide*, was soon born.

But the freedoms were brief. During the Reign of Terror, new decrees, piled on top of the old ones, quickly abrogated the temporary period of liberty. On August 2, 1793, a law required that patriotic

Prologue

8. *Free performance at the Ambigu-Comique of the* Machabées. *Bibliothèque de l'Opéra.*

plays had to be performed three times a week. Ballets, operas, and dramas celebrating the glorious events of the Revolution were *de rigueur*. Censorship became a political problem, not a moral question, and actors again began to go to jail. The police took over *la censure* in September 1793, and though decrees relaxed after the execution of Robespierre in 1794, the Directory retained strong rules over the theatre. The will of the Five Hundred and the Directory, which was installed in November 1795, was firm. Many of the same questions that caused controversy before the Revolution came up once again: the questions of genres, of too much bloodshed onstage, of outrageous plots, and of too much spectacle. Chénier complained about the fact that there were too many theatres and that they were ruining the Parisian taste for excellence onstage.[6] Once again (in 1798), the Commune of Paris asked that all theatres submit their repertoire and their *livrets*, including those for ballet and pantomime, for scrutiny at least

9. The people forcing the closure of the Opéra on July 12, 1789. Note the exit of the two aristocrats near the center. Bibliothèque de l'Opéra.

one week before the showing. Patriotic plays had to be performed every decadi (tenth day of a ten-day week in the republican calendar) with patriotic music.

The tendency to censorship did not abate with the Consulate. In 1800, the minister of the interior, Lucien Bonaparte, was appointed guardian of the censor. Napoleon's interest in the power of the stage grew with his own power. Social behavior loosened, and people sought amusement after the strains of the revolutionary years. Napoleon wanted the theatre to present an image of role models society could adulate and imitate. In an extremely important message to the actors of the Théâtre de la République, he gave the first hint of what was to become one of the toughest theatrical censorship laws in 1807. Napoleon asked Jean-Baptiste Champagny, the minister of the interior, to tell the actors that myths and heroic tragedies had to continue to be performed. He wanted *petites pièces* thrown out, as well as useless *vaudevilles*. In

Prologue

10. *View of the Gaîté and the Ambigu-Comique theatres. Bibliothèque de l'Opéra.*

1807, the strictures became codified into a repressive system that virtually set the theatre back to where it was before the January 1791 decree that freed all theatres. This explains why the Opéra continued to produce myth ballets even though they were not really geared to the popular audiences. In 1807, only seventeen theatres were left—and Napoleon reduced these to eight.

This, then, was the atmosphere in which ballets continued to be created and performed. Now, we turn to a closer examination of the three major types of ballets during the period—ballets of myth, of revolutionary spirit, and of the bourgeois commonplace. Each of these, in turn, dominated the ballet, reflecting the shifting mood of the time as France moved from the Age of Reason through the Revolution to the Romantic period of the nineteenth century.

Part II
MYTHOLOGY SURVIVES THE CENTURY

4
BALLET'S LOVE AFFAIR WITH ANTIQUITY

Ballets based on Greek and Roman mythology were common to the world of dance long before the French Revolution. Literary and artistic currents affected the ballet, and myth—perhaps more than any other source—informed the realm of dance. Irritating Cupids, indignant Venuses, and diffident Psychés abounded on the stages of eighteenth-century Paris. Everyone knew these stories, which tell of human vices with a certain doleful tolerance. Love is their theme, and the threatened love affairs almost always end happily.

Since the sixteenth century, mythology had been taught methodically in school; manuals detailed who the gods and goddesses were and listed their accoutrements. Handbooks describing the adventures of Olympian gods provided pretexts for French opera, which became popular at the same time as ballet. Mythical metaphors absorbed courtiers from their school days on, and in the hands of court poets, Greco-Roman mythology was a veritable mine of ideas for *livrets*. French theatre (in imitation of the Florentines) was enticed by tales of pagan gods, as this exciting visual world took hold of people's imaginations. Père Menestrier understood the value of such theatrical magic when he exclaimed, "The machines of Gods and their enchantments are the most exquisite because they presuppose magic and supernatural events: here is the apotheosis of machine marvels."[1]

11. *Great Theatre of the Arts, or the Temple of Apollo, with a triumphal column in the middle of the principal plaza erected to commerce, the sciences, the arts, and republican virtues* (1795). *Cabinet des Estampes.*

Reality was transformed by remarkable feats of scenic engineering, both in ballet and in opera. These were learned from the Italians Jacomo Torelli and Carlo Vigarini, and under the veil of illusion, princely flattery was perpetuated. One might wonder why French politicians of the Revolution seated themselves so comfortably before the altar of these gods who had been used as aristocratic playthings. The answer may lie partially in their rejection of Christian allegory and their detestation of the clergy. Both Alfred Cobban and Harold Parker, historians of the French Revolution, insist that the interest in antiquity had profound roots in France:

> If we want to understand the revolutionaries, we must remember above all that they had been nurtured on a classical education. Robespierre, when asked what constitution he wanted replied, "that of Lycurgus." They wore Phrygian caps, built triumphal arches, and erected statues to all the classical virtues, crowned

12. *Costume d'une Bacchante* (1796). Cabinet des Estampes.

Mythology Survives the Century

their heroes with laurel wreaths, converted the appropriately classical church of Ste. Geneviève into a Pantheon to hold mortal relics of their prophets.[2]

A resurgence of interest in antiquity and especially the Roman world (a realm cultivated since the Renaissance) enhanced and gave meaning to revolutionary ideals and principles in Paris. The use of myths also reaffirmed the tradition of Renaissance humanism, with its accent on individual freedom. Thus, the old gods, with new vitality, still spoke to the spectator of the late eighteenth century in all the arts. Ballets and pantomimes based on myth presented a half-human, half-magical adventure in which Jupiter flew supreme. Marie-Françoise Christout, the French dance historian, makes the interesting point that when the public was democratized soon after the Revolution, the gods, no longer being worshiped as gods, lost some of their magical qualities, their miraculous powers, as well as their wonderment which had been produced by pyrotechnics, wires, and staged "supernatural" events. Nevertheless, myths remained popular. Amidst the awesome space of the mythic world, with water sprites, sylvan dales, and green paradises, Cupid played his antics and nasty schemes. Almost every obstacle gave way before his wily, dominating desires. But no matter how much trouble he or any other deity caused, "Happy endings reigned in these idyllic abodes where human vices corrected by god-like stratagems, were laughed at and tolerated with the relief of a glad finish."[3]

During the regency of Catherine de Medici in the sixteenth century, when ballet had just been brought over from Italy and was developing in the court, Catherine compelled the court ballet masters to stay away from tragic or sad endings.[4] Consequently, the *ballet comique* (the ballet with a happy ending) became the most common genre from the late sixteenth century to the late eighteenth century. The bucolic pastoral myth, combining humans and deities, shepherds and Cupids, found tremendous popularity. People were familiar with the gods and adored the fantasy. Later on, during the Revolution, the audiences were able to use these tales in order to lose contact briefly with the horrors of violence and the terror of famine.

Ballet's Love Affair with Antiquity

The use of tragedy in which the gods insist that death is the only path for the hero is rarely seen in dance before Noverre, but he created thirty tragic endings out of his hundred ballet *livrets*. There were several choreographers of the eighteenth century who, like Noverre, preferred the depth of a tragic love story or myth to lighter tales. The power of ancient Greek and Roman theatre motivated this thinking, but so did the potential for exciting and dramatic movement ideas. Gaspare Angiolini, in his *Dissertation sur les Ballets-Pantomimes des Anciens* published in 1765, points out that *saltation* (dance) of the ancients was nothing other than true pantomimic dance, or the art of moving the feet, the arms, and the body in cadence to the sound of instruments, of making intelligible by gestures and expressions the myth one wished to represent. Angiolini adds that he had read a description of the dance-in-pantomime called *Le Jugement de Paris* by Apuleius, a myth often reproduced in dance. The Roman pantomimes presented these works as if they were plays, and everything was completely acted out. Angiolini writes sadly that eighteenth-century dance is far from being able to move an audience to terror or compassion. His model, though essentially based on Greek and Roman literature, did not follow the dramatic unities, which were not in the best interests of a ballet. The new tendency, then, was for myths to be serious and touching; but it took time for the notion of the serious to penetrate the Paris Opéra ballet. Angiolini emphasizes this point: "But I cannot stop myself from exclaiming that there is nothing less sensible for the art of ballet-pantomime than plots of French operas; and especially if one would wish to follow them from start to finish. One finds oneself in the land of enchantments and there is nothing less interesting today. Too many unrelated episodes occur and worse are brought on by means of the wave of a wand."[5]

Angiolini is pleading for meaning and expression in the new dance with a plot, the *ballet d'action*, and somehow the perpetuation of the sweet Greco-Roman myth did not give dance its proper profundity. He exclaims, "The 'tragic pantomime' of dance therefore is equal to the 'tragedy of poetry'; as with the tragedies of Sophocles, Euripides, Corneille, Racine and Voltaire, its dancers are themselves the great actors of tragedy."[6]

Mythology Survives the Century

But the longing for a return to nature and hearkening back to idyllic simplicity continued as a force for the production of comic bucolic myths. Combining the best of the two worlds, with memories of Bacchanalian rites, Cupid threatened shepherds and their loves in a kind of hide-and-seek game of innocence trapped. An alchemical change of both the marvelous and the natural intertwined and reminded the audience that an essential mystery of illusion controlled their lives. Everything was moving and becoming and nothing was what it seemed, especially when Cupid manipulated the action. Danger and violent threats challenged the heroes, often as nature's thunderstorms or in the underworld of Hades. There, the mythic figures overcame their enemies, so the setting returned to its former repose and the balance was reestablished. The following chapter will consider these ballets in some detail, in chronological order.

5
BALLETS FROM OLYMPUS
1787–1801

*Maximilien Gardel, Le Premier Navigateur, ou
Le Pouvoir de l'Amour, Ballet d'Action,
Revived February 1, 1787, at the Opéra*

The first ballet in our discussion was performed as a popular revival on February 1, 1787. It was originally choreographed for the Opéra (at that time called l'Académie Royale de Musique) on July 16, 1785, by Maximilien Gardel.[1] *Le Premier Navigateur* is a passionate love story that has little to do with the first navigator and everything to do with the power of love. According to Karl Engel, an eighteenth-century writer on pantomime, the elder Gardel based this ballet on a highly sentimental poem by Salomon Gessner. In the poem, the young protagonist has a miraculous dream that haunts him and has left him with a violent desire for the lovely Mélide. As Engel says, "With that enchanting dream that strikes him, the image of the charming Mélide remains constantly in his thoughts and imagination, however without the possibility of ever reaching the isle in which she lives."[2]

The setting for this mythological story is an enchanting village near the sea. Mélide is the center of attention, with many suitors, young and old, bringing gifts in the hopes that she will agree to marry. Though she is showered with flowers and lovely things, her mind is set on Daphnis as her future husband. All the old men of the village, as well as the young

13. Mlle Guimard in *Le Premier Navigateur. Bibliothèque de l'Arsenal.*

shepherds, parade before her in an interesting reversal of the beauty contest. The men then perform games and acts of strength as she and her mother, Sémire, watch Daphnis pull far ahead of his rivals in the struggle for Mélide. Athletic grace remains the significant attribute, and he defeats all other contenders. A village feast celebrates both his conquest and their marriage, and dances are performed in honor of the god Hymen. In the midst of the joyful gathering, a tremendous storm, with thunder and lightning, shakes the Temple of Love, while Cupid's statue teeters in the earthquaking tempest. Since the lovers must endure terrible trials, perhaps at Cupid's instigation, before their eternal union, the land shifts and divides into two separate continents, leaving Daphnis and Mélide on either side of the sea. Roaring waves, howling winds, and blinding rain stop the exhausted Daphnis from reaching his promised bride. Like Paul and Virginie at the moment before the shipwreck, the lovers collapse and fall in a faint. Morpheus, the god of sleep, descends in a chariot and generously brings quiet to their terror. This frightening scene is witnessed by Cupid, who is moved to disperse the clouds over the sea. At the same time, he places a raft filled with small Cupids in the water not far from where Mélide is seen begging the gods to reunite her with her lover.

The dream sequence from Gessner's poem appears at this point, and Daphnis imagines that he is holding Mélide only to discover that he is alone. He hears Cupid's voice directing him to be courageous, to fight the elements, and to listen to Cupid. Filled with the dream and Cupid's reassuring words, Daphnis jumps into the boat to brave the power of the sea. When he reaches the savage island where Mélide is languishing and wishing for death, he runs to her—she, upon seeing him, faints once again. The island of Cythère then changes to a large temple dedicated to Venus. Cupid and his court reside in this lavish site given over to the luxuries of love. Mélide's mother observes the young lovers as they vow eternal devotion to Venus, who typically descends in a chariot, while fauns and bacchantes dance for the love of love.

The denouement reestablished calm and hope in a tumultuous world. Though nature, in the form of a storm (controlled by Cupid), was responsible for separating the lovers, nature also responded, but gently, when birds sang in constant harmony in an attempt to rouse Mélide from her despair. An interchange between the elements and people makes the urgency of the love between Daphnis and Mélide all the more pressing. As we can see, the *Idyllen* by Gessner has served minimally as a source for the ballet; however, the atmosphere of strong passions reveals early urgings common to Romantic poetry—which is often said to be inspired, in part, by Gessner's verses. Also apparent is the need for good acting and expressive gesturing in order to bring across this intense story.

Le Premier Navigateur was not exactly a box-office smash, for it earned only 4,554 livres on February 1, 1787. Usually, ballets at the Opéra made more money that the operas themselves.[3] This was apparently due, in part, to the fine dancing of Opéra stars La Guimard, Gaetan Vestris, and Marie and Pierre Gardel. When Maximilien Gardel died on March 11, 1787, his brother, Pierre Gardel, assumed control of ballet at the Opéra, not venturing to produce one of his own full-length ballets until 1790.[4] Rather, he restaged several of the more critically successful pieces by his brother, Maximilen, such as *Le Premier Navigateur*.

Pierre Gardel, Télémaque dans l'Isle de Calypso,
Ballet Héroïque, Music by Ernest Miller,
February 23, 1790, at the Opéra

The premiere of *Telemachus on the Island of Calypso* took place at the Opéra on February 23, 1790.[5] Like the contemporary English paintings of Constable and Turner in which sudden winds and tumultuous seas disturbed a once peaceful environment, the setting for this ballet contains some early signs of Romantic ballet. The music often suggests changes in both physical and emotive circumstances, and the portrayal of an almost-doomed passionate relationship ensured the success of Gardel's work. The story of Telemachus, the child of the powerful wanderer Ulysses, returns us to Calypso's island, where enchanting and intoxicating events restore us to antique domains as Telemachus learns the ways of the world.

The beginning of *Télémaque*'s *livret* asks that the composer Ernest Miller, "the drunken father" of Marie Gardel, Pierre's wife, produce sounds of music descriptive of thunder and swirling seas.[6] When the music subsides, the curtain rises on a battered landscape, where debris

14. *Profile of Pierre Gardel (1809). Gardel was a member of the Société Philotechnique, thus attempting to be a follower of enlightened ideas of philosophy and science. Bibliothèque de l'Opéra.*

15. *Costume for youthful Pierre Gardel by Louis-René Boquet. Bibliothèque de l'Opéra.*

Ballets from Olympus

from a ship fills the seascape. Sailors are struggling to hold on to the rocks, and Télémaque grasps Mentor's hand. In the myth, Mentor, the cold, rational guardian of the young boy's whims, is really Athena in disguise. Thanks to Mentor's strong arm, they land at the shore of Calypso, well known to Mentor as the place where Calypso's enchantments cause men bitter experiences. When Calypso catches a first view of the boy, she recognizes him immediately as Ulysses' son. Just as she enticed the father, she proceeds to lure the boy by promising him immortality.

But Télémaque has already seen and fallen in love with the beautiful and innocent nymph Eucharis, and though Calypso is clever and startlingly attractive, she cannot touch Télémaque's heart. Venus and her son, Cupid, are thus called in to assist Calypso in their standard roles as capricious matchmakers. When Mentor sees the harm about to befall Télémaque, he tries to take him off the island. But instead, a voluptuous *pas de deux* takes place between Télémaque and Eucharis, tying him even closer to the innocent nymph. Calypso enters in a fury and turns herself into Diana, the huntress, aiming her lethal lance at Eucharis. Télémaque saves his lover and they perform another dance, throwing care to the winds in a manner that brings to mind the sensual paintings of Fragonard. With the power of their love, even Calypso, who is planning a horrible scheme to burn Eucharis in the boat that will take them away, cannot overwhelm them. They jump into the raging sea but are saved from Venus and Calypso. A fascinating scene occurs, just before the ending, in which Calypso goes mad and behaves like an animal. Hell hath no fury like a woman scorned! Télémaque wishes to take Eucharis with them, a desire that angers the sober old guide, Mentor. The boat is burned by Cupid, who heads a troop of mad bacchantes dancing and jumping with flaming torches and wild hair. Eucharis is duped by Calypso and is caught in the middle of the flames burning the ship. Flying to her aid at the last moment, Cupid swoops down and carries her up into the clouds to be reunited with Télémaque and Mentor.

Calypso has been foiled, the lovers joined, and Cupid has become a hero who has saved the reputation of Mentor. Exaggerated romance abounds in this ballet—the storm as an initial introduction to nature's anger; the shipwreck close to the dangerous island; the pure and perfect

16. *Mlle Clothilde as Calypso. She was one of the most beautiful women dancers of the late eighteenth-century ballet at the Opéra. Bibliothèque de l'Opéra.*

Ballets from Olympus

love threatened by an evil princess with magical powers—all these factors whetted the appetite of Parisian audiences for more of Gardel's ballets, though the receipts of the first performances were not high, 3,829 livres, (one month later, on March 20, 1790, it brought in the huge sum of 10,960 livres). Even Noverre praised the choreographer of this marvelous ballet: "Since his appointment to the position of *maître de ballet* of the Opéra, Gardel has presented in 1790, *Télémaque*; his first attempt in a difficult art was a *'coup de maître.'* This ballet has obtained a most brilliant success."[7]

The ballet was well received by the critics generally, and brought Gardel some mentions in The *Correspondance Littéraire*:

perhaps the best work we've seen of its kind since Noverre. The story of the ballet is too familiar to recount; we are satisfied to observe that this new composition, without disturbing our interest, or the rapidity of action the choreographer knew how to vary the character scenes and the scenes of passion which could only be in pure pantomime and the fêtes with other episodes; they were happily connected to the plot and gave to their advantage the most beautiful developments in the art of dance itself.[8]

Not only is Gardel's marvelous ability as a choreographer touted in this ballet, but according to Baron Grimm, his unique talent in choosing dancers and in teaching dance is also obvious: "The role of Calypso was so beautifully performed by Mlle Victoire Saulnier, that of Eucharis, with an infinity of interest and grace, by Mlle Miller. It was Monsieurs Gardel and Huart who played the roles of Télémaque and Mentor.[9]

One of the major reasons for the triumph of *Télémaque* was that the dancing, with its intense feelings, appears to have been appreciated far more than in the past. Cupid, a role usually played by a man, was danced by Mlle Clothilde Chameroy "with much finesse," and the important character of Calypso, played by Mlle Saulnier, "with all the exterior qualities of the goddess Calypso; she created an admirable interpretation of her anger and her despair."[10] The ballet remained in the repertoire for thirty-six years and played 408 times.[11]

In the spring following the production of *Télémaque*, larger audiences for the Opéra brought more complex obligations to the city of

17. Pierre Gardel in the role of Telemachus. Bibliothèque de l'Opéra.

Paris. This was also due in part to a change of administration. From April 8, 1790, the Opéra was no longer under the aegis of the king but rather under the direction of the Municipality of Paris. Its commitee of administration were Pierre Gaspard Chaumette, François Henriot, Georges Jacques Danton, and Jean-Jacques le Roux. Once again, interesting notes occur in the *Journal de l'Opéra*, indicating some of the more pressing problems that faced the company. On March 30, 1790, a discussion in the Assemblée de la Commune ensued concerning a "project d'une nouvelle salle de l'Opéra." On August 28, 1790, a "decision of the Departement de Paris fixed the fee of the *maîtres de ballets* for their *ballets d'action*," strong evidence that the new *maître*, M. Gardel, had succeeded in gaining great popularity for his dramatic myth ballets. On September 19, 1790, the receipts were donated to the survivors of the terrible fires in Limoges. Often as an honor and bonus, the proceeds of the night were given as an homage to a particular dancer or composer; on November 6, 1790, Alexandre Piccini was celebrated.[12] He was a well-known composer of operas and ballets of the period and the foremost rival of Gluck.

Ballets continued in the magic spaces of never-never myth land and the Paris Opéra. Pierre Gardel sought his next theme from Jean-Georges Noverre, his teacher, and Dauberval, his colleague, both of whom created successful ballets based on the myth of Psyché. This tried and true love story returns the mercurial Cupid and the jealous Venus to center stage, with the beauteous Psyché as the character who provokes conflict.[13] Before discussing Gardel's 1790 production, it would be interesting, for the sake of comparison, to give a brief description of the earlier *Psyché* by Noverre and Dauberval.

Jean-Georges Noverre, Psyché et l'Amour, *Ballet Héroï-Pantomime, London, January 29, 1788, King's Theatre, Music by Massinghi, Originally Performed in Stuttgart to Music by Johann Joseph Rodolphe in 1762, Revised Again 1797*

In the short and concise *livret* for Noverre's 1788 revival of *Psyché*, we notice that he calls his work a *ballet héroï-pantomime* rather than the traditional ballet-pantomime. The description is but eight pages and is divided into *parties* rather than acts—perhaps in order to differentiate it from a literary work. Noverre begins with Venus' temple looming large in the setting and then cuts immediately to Cupid's sumptuous palace, where it is evident that Psyché has been seduced by Cupid, the god of love in the guise of a mortal man. There are few scene changes, giving the action a pronounced clarity. Though Cupid turns into a monster, as commanded by the furious and scorned Venus, he is still adored by the innocent Psyché. A symbolic spark from his lamp burns Cupid and again he changes and becomes Tisiphone, the god of the underworld. This is the moment of transformation that introduces the terrifying Infernal scene.[14] But it should be noted that Noverre emphasizes human encounters, rather than spectacular scene changes. Cupid resembles a traditional young hero, especially in the long Hades scene in which he fights off the demons and the fates before they murder the pure Psyché.

A fascinating last *partie*, where we meet the stunning future mother-in-law Venus, is devoted to an Oedipal confrontation between Cupid and his mother. Cupid manages to convince Venus that she must accept Psyché as her daughter or he will leave forever. In this act, Venus is accompanied by Adonis, her *amant chéri*. If Venus already has a devoted and gorgeous lover, Noverre suggests, then why in heaven should she exploit her son as a dutiful worshiper? Indeed, her consistent, arrogant selfishness is made all the more apparent when Psyché embraces Venus' feet and begs feverishly that Venus pardon her "involuntary hubris." The impact of these singularly intense moments brings a certain lucidity and simplicity to Noverre's story line. The last scene in Noverre's *Psyché* finishes cheerfully with dances and the marriage of Cupid and Psyché. We are left with the sentiment that each one of Noverre's characters has learned something significant that justifies the proverbial happy ending to this myth.

Jean Dauberval, Psyché, Ballet-Pantomime, Music by Franz Joseph Hayden, Alexandre Piccini, February 16, 1788, at the Grand Théâtre in Bordeaux

Dauberval's February 16, 1788, *Psyché livret* also sounds a different note and tone from the usual myth. Like Noverre, Dauberval writes

18. Marie Miller Gardel in the role of Psyché. Bibliothèque de l'Opéra.

19. *Profile of Jean Bercher Dauberval. Cabinet des Estampes.*

economically (eight pages) and with few literary flourishes, although he divides his ballet-pantomime into acts and claims that he has depended on great French writers for his inspiration. He commences his ballet by depicting the rage of passion that Cupid feels for Psyché, ripping off his own wings, a symbol of fickleness, as a gesture of complete fidelity to the beauteous Psyché. When Cupid sees Psyché, he repeats one hundred times that he adores her. It is curious how melodramatic Dauberval's descriptions tend to be. But then, melodrama as a genre, as well as an exaggerated style of presenting drama, became important at the time of the Revolution.

If this Cupid strikes the reader as more emotional than the Cupid of Noverre, then his Psyché really fulfills our notion of the typical passionate Romantic heroine. She borders on the ridiculous in her daring competitiveness, gambling away her future in a series of impertinent actions. She sits on Venus' throne and clasps on the symbol, a waistband, that endows her with Venus' sensational beauty. When Psyché sees her image in a pool of water, she dares to compare herself to Venus, while the mooning Cupid looks on. Venus startles them, thundering in on her chariot; her anger and exasperation mount with each glimpse of Psyché. Once again, Psyché flaunts her girlish powers by announcing that nothing matters to her but Cupid's love. At that statement she is swallowed up.

The ballet scenario continues in Hell, with Psyché's hideous tortures and her subsequent begging for pity. One unusual quality (not apparent in the other *livret*) motivates Psyché; her every step is guided by a profound hatred for Venus. And Venus' despicable actions confirm Psyché's dislike. For example, Venus informs Psyché that Cupid will always be an unfaithful lover. This is the nature of his being. No matter, Psyché carelessly remarks, "I shall always love Cupid, even at the risk of being abandoned." This "Psychian" courage in love is also unique to Dauberval's *livret*. The image of evil and infernal meanness, Tisiphone, is Venus' agent in Hell. He drags Psyché away and throws her into a stormy sea. In Hades, where demons are delighted to find a new victim, Cupid bravely enlists his grandfather Jupiter's assistance (in the other *livret*, Venus requests his help). The great king of the gods works his wonders and benevolently awards Cupid his heart's desire. Venus is magically appeased; this conversion seems all the more remarkable in light of her Medea-like rage throughout the ballet.

Pierre Gardel, Psyché, *Ballet Pantomime, Music by Ernest Miller, December 14, 1790, at the Opéra*

Pierre Gardel sensed that the wonder woman Psyché would be a winning subject for his talents. Indeed, he was correct. The erudite spectator of the period, Baron Grimm, gave *Psyché*'s first performance a rave review: "It is perhaps the most magical spectacle that has ever been performed on any stage."[15] He goes on to explain that this tale of Psyché was inherited from Apuleius and reworked by La Fontaine[16]

Mythology Survives the Century

and Moliere before Gardel choreographed it. Actually, there were several ballets based on this myth produced in Paris as early as the seventeenth century.[17] Grimm lauds Gardel's use of scenes that develop dramatically and rapidly, keeping the spectator on the edge of his seat. The visual rewards were immense: "The spectacle of this charming ballet leaves nothing to be desired; the execution of the scenic machinery for which we are grateful to M. Boulai, appeared so marvelously that illusion could not have been carried further."[18] No less than the *livret* and spectacle, the ballet dancing proved impressive. Gardel used the whole corps de ballet, with clever designs and strong movements; his wife, Mlle Miller, who became one of Gardel's best interpreters, played Psyché notably, with Auguste Vestris as Cupid, Lombard Laborie as Zephyr, Mlle Saulnier as Venus, and Mlle Rose as Terpsichore. The technique and acting ability of these dancers kept them in the public eye for years, each one having established a reputation for a particular kind of role or dance. However, this association of stars with certain genres (*héroïque, comique,* etc.) began to diminish and disappear in the early years of the nineteenth century.[19]

At the beginning of the Psyché *livret*, in Gardel's "brief reflections of the author," he advises his public that he has no intention of trying to compete with the excellent Psychés by Noverre and Dauberval.[20] Though he admires them (and probably fears their extraordinary artistry), he is encouraged to realize that his own ideas for *Psyché* are quite different from theirs and could not be compared. Admitting that perhaps he has not achieved all his aims, he also foresees that some people will say that *Psyché* was plagiarized, as they accused him in the case of *Télémaque*; but the charge, of course, was not true. Gardel need not have worried about his adversaries, as the receipts of *Psyché* grew from 5,590 livres on opening night to 9,332.50 livres per night in the next month. This was remarkable in a time of such inflationary economic strain.

Gardel's ballet begins in a vast countryside dominated by the Temple of Venus, which flanks the superb palace belonging to Psyché's father. In the background is a painted sea scene with a high rock. These design elements will all play a part in the course of Gardel's ballet. Cupid, or "l'Amour," the Don Juan of Olympus, confesses to Zephyr his determination to marry Psyché, the most exquisite mortal in the land; Zephyr naturally wonders at this admission. At this moment, Psyché enters, accompanying her newly wed sisters and her parents. She moves away from them to give an offering to Venus' statue. Zephyr cunningly displays his authority over nature, rocking the scene with thunder and lightning, and, as Psyché kneels to pray to Venus, the statue miraculously disappears. This is where the trouble begins. Psyché climbs on to Venus statue altar and assumes the same majestic position. Innocent and frolicsome, Psyché runs to find her parents to show them her likeness to Venus. People begin to admire Psyché and bring her offerings. More thunder and lightning indicate rumblings from the gods and give witness to Venus' fury. At Psyché's daring usurpation of Venus' role, in a *coup de théâtre*, the Temple of Venus disintegrates and Psyché faints. An inscription appears that explains to some degree the visual change: "To Psyché, the guilty person, who must be led away with death's shadow to this horrible rock, a monster will unite with you in your destiny." In a gesture of desperation, Psyché's father offers himself and his wife in lieu of his daughter, but another scroll replaces the first and warns: "Parents, friends, in vain do you all offer yourselves to expiate her crime; Venus in her justifiable fury wants Psyché alone as a victim." Thus, Psyché must suffer her torment alone. To compound this punishment, Venus insists that her son, Cupid, contribute to Psyché's destruction, and the first act is over.

In the next act, lavish eighteenth-century painted backdrops, worthy of François Boucher, appear, depicting cherubs and cupids who flaunt their conquests and voluptuous delights. This is Cupid's palace, where Zephyr has carried our heroine, Psyché. Here Cupid, forced by his jealous mother disguises himself as a monster and lustfully courts Psyché. Though he will later return to his human form, the darkness will prevent Psyché from recognizing him. In this act, not only Cupid is in disguise, but so is Venus, who shrewdly dupes the unknowing Psyché by pretending to be Psyché's loving and trusting mother. Venus lures Psyché into believing that the beast with whom she danced and loved must be killed. Dressed as the mother, Venus hands Psyché a dagger and a lamp and cautions her to hide until the monster enters. Sleep-inducing poppy seeds had been sprinkled on the bed by Venus before she left. The spectator, by now on the edge of his seat, is nevertheless slightly bemused by the number of visual props and the magic of the spectacle.

Cupid, still disguised as a monster, creeps into the bedroom, breathes in the aroma of the poppy seeds and, of course, becomes sleepy. As he dozes, Psyché lifts the lamp to glance at this creature. Suddenly, another transformation takes place; he becomes the most handsome Adonis. Psyché thanks the gods for this remarkable alteration and leans over to kiss him. But her luck runs out, and the lamp tilts, releasing a spark that burns and shocks her paramour. He becomes brutally angry, uttering nasty insults.

Without reason, the palace disappears and Psyché is found lying in the desert, where Venus swoops down like an antique vulture and carries off Psyché to Hell. The stage is split in two, and a deep chasm forms in the center. In Gardel's words, "A thousand tortures are invented to overcome the miserable Psyché." She begs for grace and release from her struggle. Figures that represent the cardinal sins harass her; venomous serpents slither, aiming deathly bites at her heart. She is chained and beaten and watches her nuptial dress, a last vestige of her love for Cupid, thrown into the depths of Hell. Then, pursued by young women with flaming swords, she is chased to the top of a volcano where she faints before Cerberus' piercing screeches. The horrible Furies rejoice with "danses infernales," while Venus gloatingly demands more punishments. She has Psyché tied to a huge rock, like Prometheus, where her agony will intensify. Psyché awakens and in a painful gesture of submission asks Venus to forgive her. But even in this harrowing condition, Venus cannot bear Psyché's beauty, and she becomes all the more outraged.

At this moment, just as Psyché's lifeline is severed by the Fates, Cupid belatedly rushes to help her. He sets himself upon the women of Hell and throws them into oblivion. He seizes Venus' bow and arrow, symbols of her Olympian power, crushes them, and hurls them at her feet. Crying bitterly at the sign of Psyché's crumpled body, he unchains her hands and drops down to embrace her. Surprisingly, when Venus observes this pathetic passionate scene, she relents. Despite her jealousy and exaggerated vanity, she forgives her rival and awards Psyché immortality, calling upon the supreme power of her father, Jupiter. Thunder resounds, Hell covers over with velvety soft and luxuriant clouds, and a breath of life returns to Psyché. The heavens open to reveal Mount Olympus, and a joyous dance of celebration leads to the final tableau on Olympus, where Jupiter presides over an idyllic and peaceful dominion. How the Paris audiences must have longed for such a salvation in 1790! Gardel's *Psyché* played to good houses. Perhaps the spectacle of Psyché's suffering mirrored the violence in the streets of Paris, where people were becoming accustomed to bloody tortures.

Thus, we have seen three versions of the same myth and three rather different interpretations. Pierre Gardel tells a longer, more complicated story, with numerous scene changes that tend to emphasize dazzling visual transformations. There are many indications of magical events—at one moment, we see Venus' statue, at the next, we see Psyché in Venus' place. And extravagant disguises are often used, hinting that things and people are not what they seem to be. The courting of Psyché in a long, voluptuous boudoir scene stresses the open sensuality of the drama and helps to underline Cupid's distress at having to choose between his mother and the tempting Psyché. Paralleling Cupid and Venus as a family is Psyché's family, who are not mentioned by Noverre or Dauberval. Interestingly, Gardel's *Psyché* was presented again and again all through the 1790s, at the same time that the French populace anxiously and very closely followed the activities of the royal family, from the time of the storming of the Bastille through their escape to Varennes in 1791 to their imprisonment and finally to their beheading in 1793. Gardel must have seen the importance of the family as a character, both on and off the stage, during the Revolution. Psyché's helplessness and childlike qualities are exaggerated, as we observe her desperate dependence on her parents and sisters at the beginning of the story.

But it is Dauberval who creates the more real, passionate, and interesting Psyché character. She is both imperious and impetuous, tremulous and innocent. At one point, she is even taught to dance by Terpsichore. She tends to taunt the Fates and tempt her own demise with her arrogant behavior. Noverre's statement, on the other hand, lies in the humanization of Cupid and the wonderfully tense and intimate confrontations that focus so clearly on the emotions that motivate human relationships. I have no figures to substantiate the

Mythology Survives the Century

popularity of Dauberval's or Noverre's *Psyché*. But Gardel's has the honor of being the second most-performed ballet (564 times) at the Paris Opéra (the first is *Coppélia*). The enduring attraction of the Psyché theme lasted until the 1850s when August Bournonville produced his version.[21]

As we have seen, Psyché is an important symbol of the times; she must endure demons, curses, physical harm, and even death in order to reach her lover Cupid and freedom; perhaps she symbolized France in her effort as an adventurer to brave impossible feats and survive. Through her essential courage, she, like the French women of the Revolution, no longer succumbs as a victim, she wins. Meanwhile, events in the Assembly and on the streets began more and more to impinge on the routine of the dancers and singers at the Académie. An interesting number of benefit performances and *capitations*, or head taxes, were given over to the poor and the bereaved. On June 24, 1791, the Académie Royale de Musique officially became l'Opéra, but there were months without any performance of new ballets.

Jean-Baptiste Hus, Les Muses, ou le Triomphe d'Apollon, Ballet Anacréontique, Music by Louis-Charles Ragué, Décors and Costumes by Fontaine and Porfillion, December 12, 1793, at the Opéra

Glitter and the rays of Apollo's sun are warming, and, "as if to seek refuge from revolutionary strife,"[22] this Anacreontic ballet satisfied a need for escape. The ancient Greek poetry of Anacreon (sixth century B.C.) extolled a life in which wine and love were the only treasures worth seeking. This Bacchanalian pursuit of happiness usually occurred in dreamy meadows or sylvan dales. Noverre laid down certain artistic standards for this genre: "Anacreontic ballet demands varied scenes, agreeable situations and tableaux. Sentiment and love must be sketched; ingenuous grace must be painted; all must be light in these ballets and bear the delicate character of artless love."[23] In contrast to Bacchus, Apollo signified the reasonable, the harmonious, and the rational. Equated with the sun and the gift of light, Apollo kept a close friendship with Terpsichore, the goddess of dance, though Bacchus probably inspired her more.

Ballets from Olympus

Jean-Baptiste Hus saw this moment during the Reign of Terror (the close of 1793) as a unique opportunity to create a safe dreamworld, while his comrade choreographers at the boulevard theatres were forced to reel out patriotic pageant themes. Interestingly, Hus did not last long at the Paris Opera; but neither did any of Gardel's ambitious rivals or colleagues.[24] Not without a certain guilt about this flight to fanciful places, Hus speaks in his dedication of the *livret*, *Les Muses*, to his "brave brothers in arms, *les sans-culottes*." He calls them defenders of liberty and incorruptible supporters of the Republic. "Is it not for the arts [Hus says] that all your work aims? The god of the arts, Apollo, will not be indifferent to your civic efforts." Hus continues by mentioning the "Muses who were debased by the dishonest adulation of despots for centuries. They will soon celebrate the true light of reason and the ardent love of country." Thanking his composer, M. Ragué, and the decor and costume designers, Fontaine and Portfillion, he extols Apollo as the god of revivifying light and best friend of the dance.

The ballet *The Muses, or The Triumph of Apollo*[25] begins in a cheerful countryside spotted with shepherds and shepherdesses. They bow before the dazzling Apollo (played by the dancer Auguste Vestris) as they are preparing a feast for him; his impressive temple dominates the scene. Gifts are offered by everyone; a young couple places several doves at his altar and then joins in an ensemble dance. Pan plays his pipe and leads a procession to Mount Olympus, where the Muses reside. There Apollo stands, again surrounded by herdsmen, shepherds, and dryads. He asks each Muse to come before him in turn. Not a jarring moment disturbs the ballet except when Melpomène, the goddess of song and tragedy, arrives carrying a crown in one hand and a symbolic dagger in the other. Apollo recoils when he sees the dagger and makes her throw it down—interesting, in light of the guillotine. The nonthreatening mood and constant parading and processioning in this ballet were also common in the gigantic patriotic choral works performed contemporaneously which were organized at the instigation of the Committee of Public Safety.

The lack of a strong and convincing story in this ballet in no way detracted from the reviews, which were very favorable. A contemporary critic observed ecstatically, "The ballet was executed by dancers whose

Mythology Survives the Century

talent approached perfection. It is not surprising that we add to the list of names already mentioned those of Citizen ladies Duchemin and Colomb, and Citizen men Nivelon, Goyon, Huard, Deshayes, Jr., and especially Vestris whom artists have appropriately named the god of the dance as he represents here Apollo, the god of the arts."[26]

Bubbling brooks, velvety green countrysides, and golden goddesses guiding bejeweled chariots through the heavens evoked the proper awe from the spectator at the Opéra, but unluckily they cost the directors of the Opéra far more than they were able to earn. Louis Joseph Francoeur and Jacques Cellerier, after sixteen months of administration, were arrested on September 16, 1793, for promoting proaristocratic operas and ballet themes and counterrevolutionary politics. The Commune turned the direction of the theatre over to the actors themselves. The *Journal de l'Opéra* does not mention this important fact, however, at one point in September, a decree was passed (noted in the *Journal*) calling for the procuration by the Commune of the proper commissioning of operas. The Commune asserted itself in every phase of the Parisian's existence, and playwrights were forced to laud revolutionary ideals; anything spoken or sung had to relate to the cause. Luckily for ballet and pantomime, they were silent arts. In October 1793, the Opéra was renamed "Opéra National" and received a warning that box-office receipts from performances be better organized and the money go to *le peuple*. Interestingly enough, no receipts are indicated in the *Journal de l'Opéra* from September of 1793 to July of 1794. Perhaps the administration was trying to hide its profits.

In 1794, the Opéra moved from the Porte Saint-Martin Théâtre to a sumptuous new building on the rue de la Loi, as ordered by the Committee of Public Safety. Formerly directed by Marguerite Montansier, the new theatre had made important changes before the Opéra moved in. Marvin Carlson noted that the most significant difference was that the *parterre* patrons, who paid the least for their tickets because they stood, were for the first time seated on permanent stepped benches on an inclined plane that ran from the orchestra to the first boxes.[27] Thus the *sans-culottes, le peuple*, were able to relax and enjoy their evenings without shifting from one exhausted leg to another. The move to the rue de la Loi took place, the *Journal de l'Opéra* indicated, on the very day that the infamous Robespierre, *l'Incorruptible*, fell (July 27, 1794).

Several months before the move, the *Journal* states that more free performances were required by the Committee of Public Safety, and somewhat later, the artists of the Opéra were watched for disciplinary problems. In January 1795, a special performance was given for and by the young people of France, as homage to the defenders of liberty, their parents. The *Journal* mentions that "homage to children's piety, the orphans' defenders of liberty and '*la patrie*' united under the title of the Society of Young Frenchmen, gave for the profit of their mothers, a performance of the old and new regimes followed by a fête in honor of Jean-Jacques Rousseau, a *sans-culottide* in 3 acts, with songs, dances and gymnastic exercises."[28]

After the Reign of Terror, plays, ballets, and operas with patriotic themes no longer had to be played. On February 14, 1795, a decree ended the rule that *pièces républicaines* must be performed. Given the complex politics of the day, however, Gardel did not produce an expensive new myth ballet until 1799. Rather, he revised his brother's myth and comedy ballets and kept on playing his own very popular *Psyché, Télémaque,* and *Jugement*. In 1797, in a moment of weakness, or perhaps it was his strength, he revised Noverre's *Annette et Lubin*, a pastoral; then, in 1798, he mounted Noverre's *Les Caprices de Galathée* as a benefit performance for the aging and poor Noverre. In order not to be upstaged by the old man, Gardel created a showy new divertissement to conclude the program, so that the evening became a triumph for Gardel.[29]

Louis-Jacques Milon, Héro et Léandre, Pantomime, Music by Xavier Lefebvre, December 4, 1799, at the Opéra

Héro et Leandre, a ballet-pantomime in one act, was danced at the Opéra with rousing success.[30] Paris audiences liked ballet (as proven by ticket sales), and operas with large ballet divertissements always did better in their receipts than those without any dance. This one was Louis Milon's first full-length ballet at the Opéra. Chosen by Pierre Gardel to be his assistant ballet master, a position he held from 1799 to 1826, Milon created excellent ballets, and some critics believed he

20. Portrait of Louis-Jacques Milon. Cabinet des Estampes.

Ballets from Olympus

was superior to Gardel as a choreographer.[31] Noverre mentions him in his *Lettres* with great respect: "M. Milon has created four ballet-pantomimes; these productions have been well received and have made a name for the choreographer; he should be content with his success. To succeed next to his neighbor, Gardel, is to obtain the acclaim of his public without intrigue or lies, and is to demonstrate, all at the same time delicacy, modesty and merit."[32]

"More than competent and extremely conscientious," Milon had also proven his ability at the Ambigu-Comique with his *Pygmalion*.[33] He seemed to have worked in perfect harmony with Gardel, probably because of his affable personality.[34] In an interesting *avertissement* to the public in the *livret Héro et Léandre*, Milon writes that beautiful poetry, whether read or performed onstage, may create an "uncertain effect," and he expresses a fear that the eyes of the audience are accustomed to hearing what they see, and that they may not appreciate the charms of the movement alone. Milon goes on to explain that he inserted scenes with Cupid and Venus to heighten the dramatic tension. He hopes the public will not accuse him of plagiarism, since he also used an incident from the *Judgment of Paris* story, though only the names of the characters are the same.[35]

The ballet begins on a sad note, with Léandre agitated and dejected because Héro, the priestess, has refused his love; "he falls to the ground overwhelmed by chagrin."[36] His response strikes one as overdone, too melodramatic; but this seems to be the new tone as we move into the nineteenth century. Then Cupid appears, shooting arrows hither and yon for fun. This inimitable superlover of myth has taken on more youthful qualities and by the end of the century is generally danced by a woman. Léandre begs Cupid to inspire Héro to respond to his lovemaking. At first, Cupid playfully refuses to aid him; but, intrigued by the challenge, the god of love decides to create a ruse to catch Héro off guard.

The scheme involves a charade, a play within a play, and Cupid, the theatrical manipulator, asks Héro to be his heroine in a pantomime of the *Judgment of Paris*. Naturally, Léandre plays Paris. Héro-Venus works to seduce Léandre-Paris with "the beautiful contours of her slim waist, her voluptuous movements, her nobility, her lightness, her

21. *Mlle Clothilde in 1798 in the ballet* Judgment of Paris, *originally choreographed by Pierre Gardel in 1793. Bibliothèque de l'Opéra.*

perfection."³⁷ None of these details escape Léandre-Paris, and the two young people are profoundly attracted to each other. As Paris is offering her the golden apple, a remarkable event occurs: a dove flies down from the clouds, scoops up the apple, and returns to the skies. Cupid kisses Héro, thereby awakening in Héro a deep ardor for Léandre that she cannot hide. An amorous *pas de deux* seals their affection, though Héro's shy innocence is also dramatized. When Léandre must leave her for the night, he starts to swim to an opposite shore; Héro watches with trepidation as a storm begins to brew: "The winds unleashed, the bellowing of the waves, the whistling of the air, a terrible and general disorder causes Héro deep anguish." Begging the gods for help, she falls to her knees. Unheeded by any divinity, all her hope is destroyed; a lightning bolt, the "flame of death," sends a shaft of light to the waters, where she sees Léandre's weak and struggling body swallowed up by a cavern in the waters, and "black thoughts take hold of her imagination, and sink her slowly into despair. Constant loud thunder from the skies mirror the sobs and oppression in her heart. She kneels and throws her head down, then gets up, furious with the gods for seeming to take a barbaric pleasure in prolonging her torment. She begins to walk quickly not knowing where and collapses."³⁸ Such are the passionate, dramatic scenes in this *livret*. The descriptions are more vivid and overdrawn than those found in the past—a fact that tells us something about the taste of the time.

Though Cupid has observed this entire scene and appears to have compassion for Héro's suffering, he does nothing. Rather, it is Héro, reassured by a mysterious dream, who runs into the treacherous waters, resolved to share her lover's fate. But Neptune intervenes to save the lovers. Héro is perched on a raft of roses resting on a cloud, groups of Cupids lifting her from the sea. At the same time, reanimated Léandre appears, carried by two fish, and Venus descends from the skies. In Milon's words, "Cupids, Plaisirs, graces, and the splendor of Olympus beguile the lovers; they demonstrate respect and eternal recognition of the gods for their happiness."

Héro's tribulations bring Psyché to mind, as well as Mélide in *Le Premier Navigateur*, though the expression of Mélide's misery is far less extended and not as touching. In *Héro et Léandre*, Héro becomes a sentimental heroine, tortured and desperate, willing to risk everything for her lover. The stormy seas and angry nature strike the reader as more terrifying than similar elements in the earlier ballet myths, and Milon's characters emerge from their mythic past as heroically real and believable people.

6
AN END TO SUFFERING PSYCHÉS AND DEVILISH CUPIDS

Perhaps more important than any other innovation during the late eighteenth century was the new attempt to be accurate with the costume and decor of the historical period portrayed in the drama. Voltaire, among other dramatists, also required this in his own historical plays. As already pointed out, ballets traditionally were costumed in the same restrictive manner as the operas in which they were presented as divertissements. Generally, the characters were clothed in the dress of the time, making no attempt to wear togas or Greek drapes if they were antique. Gradually, this tradition changed as a result of theatrical experiments by François Talma, the actor, and Jacques-Louis David, the painter. At an early age, Talma wished to look the part, even in minor roles such as Proculus in *Brutus* in 1789, and he appealed to his friend David to sketch an authentic costume in the style of one he had seen in London worn by the actor Charles Macklin. In *Charles IX*, his attention to costume led him to wear black hair, unpowdered, and to dress simply but strikingly in a black velvet coat decorated in gold—a great success, although very controversial.[1]

But something strange happened in the late 1790s. Classical drapes moved from the theatre to the salon. The fad for Grecian tunics and Roman togas went to extremes. Ostentation and display were the mode for snobs outside the theatre. Such women were called *merveilleuses*.

Mythology Survives the Century

The result on the stage was a fantastic mixture of costume styles. According to historian Marvin Carlson, "At the Opéra, in *Anacréon* the princesses wore costumes out of paintings by Gainsborough or Lawrence while their confidantes wore Greek tunics and the soldiers wore Arlequin costumes, with pigtailed wigs under their helmets."[2] The ballerina and the male dancer enjoyed the freedom of a Grecian sandal or a glove-fitting slipper. This might also have been influenced by circus riders and ropedancers, who commonly wore these slippers.[3]

Studying the mythic *livrets* common to the period between 1787 and 1801, one discovers that old traditions die slowly; they are familiar and therefore comforting in a world filled with bloodshed and pain. The themes of Héro and Léandre, Venus and Adonis, Psyché and Cupid, continue to be of interest even in modern times. Only the way in which these myths are treated and interpreted at different periods changes.

During the revolutionary period, the significance of traditional myth in ballet was gradually altered. Though it is true that Gardel made at least twelve more myth ballets at the Opéra and that the great nineteenth-century choreographers Charles Didelot, Salvatore Vigano, and Carlo Blasis continued to seek characters from Olympus, their essential symbolic value for both the popular and the more affluent audience waned. But even when the subjects remained the same, during the Revolution the classical myths were infused with more realism and more heightened emotions. Significantly, the chief figure in these mythic love tales is Cupid, who through the 1790s becomes increasingly devilish in his pranks. In his guise as an antihero, a bad guy who turns to "do good" at the end, he loses both his cherubic and his playful qualities. The heroines, Psyché, Mélide, and the female ingenues, threatened with the horrors of Hades and the stormy seas of Olympus, were becoming the beleaguered ladies of the later melodramas and Romantic ballets. Perhaps these heroines in sheer innocence and purity—and new daring?—represented the longed-for innocence and beauty in a female which the noble savage signified in a male counterpart.

A truly significant development in mythic themes is the fact that the *ballet d'action* realized its full possibilities as a vehicle for great and passionate dancing. The principles set down by Noverre, Hil-

An End to Psychés and Cupids

verding, and Angiolini for stories that are cohesive and, at the same time, portray people in touching situations found fruition in Paris during this period. The characters of Psyché, Télémaque, and Mélide all move through their suffering parts with grace, grandeur, and humanity. A realism associated with comic pantomimes at the fair, with the Italian actors, and with David Garrick's English theatre began to surface in these ballet dramas. The difficulties that the characters endure needed portrayal in a movement vocabulary that projected pain. Therefore, the choreographer of the Revolution was called upon to seek a language that effectively depicted the new emotional aspects in the myths. Imagine the theatrical spectacle with Antoine Watteau, François Boucher, and Jean-Honoré Fragonard as the visual guides: Venus, gorgeous and vengeful, appearing magically from the rafters; Cupid flitting and darting through exquisite climes where the clouds and the sky are as accessible as the grassy ground beneath. Flight through these ups and downs, with the help of highly sophisticated machinery, kept the spectators' eyes busy and full. But though the moving gods of antique mythology were dressed differently, they reflected the real world in their various forms. Their struggle with and for one another was a human one, fought out in the larger-than-life terms of the myth. In this timeless visual and literary framework, man sought to identify good and evil.

Despite the bitterness, hunger, and violence of the Revolution, the traditional conventions hung on; myth ballets, with their happy endings, secured the fragile hopes of a distraught population. Even if Cupid and Psyché had their wings clipped, they returned in new shapes in Romantic ballet as sylphs and swans ready to take off once again into the heavens. Thus, despite the Revolution with its terror, hunger and inflation, regicide and war, the theatres presenting these myths in dance were filled, because as we have seen, they offered a spectacle that suspended the realities of the moment and that, increasingly, depicted exaggerated human emotions as well.

Part III
REVOLUTIONARY SPIRIT

7
BALLET AS THE SERVANT OF POLITICS

Dancing played a surprisingly large role in the French Revolution. Ballets continued to appear as part of opera, as entr'actes of plays, and as productions in their own right even in the times of most social disruption. Dance could also be seen more casually in the marketplace and at fairs. Especially during the Terror, the dancing of people, called "La Carmagnole," occurred with a fervor that expressed the pulsing, jubilance, and anger of the revolutionary mob.

Across the Channel half a century later, Charles Dickens described the wild dancing of "La Carmagnole" in the streets during the Revolution so vividly that it is worth quoting at length:

> Presently she heard a troubled movement and shouting coming along, which filled her with fear. A moment afterwards, a throng of people came pouring round the corner by the prison wall, in the midst of whom was the wood-sawyer hand in hand with La Vengeance. There could be no fewer than five hundred people, and they were dancing like five thousand demons. There was no other music than their own singing. They danced to the popular Revolution song, keeping a ferocious time that was like a gnashing of teeth in unison. Men and women danced together, women danced together, men danced together, as hazard had

Revolutionary Spirit

brought them together. At first they were a mere storm of red caps and coarse woolen rags; but, as they filled the place, and stopped to dance about Lucie, some ghastly apparition of a dance-figure gone raving mad arose among them. They advanced, retreated, struck one another's hands, clutched at one another's heads, spun around alone, caught one another and spun round in pairs, until many of them dropped. While those were down, the rest linked hand in hand, and all spun round together; then the ring broke, and in separate rings of two and four they turned and turned until they all stopped at once, began again, struck, clutched, and tore, and then reversed the spin, all spun round another way. Suddenly they stopped again, paused, struck out the time afresh, formed into lines the width of the public way, and with the heads low down, and their hands high up, swooped screaming off. No fight could have been half so terrible as this dance. It was so emphatically a fallen sport—a something once innocent, delivered over to all devilry—a healthful pastime changed into a means of angering the blood, bewildering the sense, and stealing the heart. Such grace was visible in it made it the uglier, showing how warped and perverted all things good by nature were become. The maidenly bosom bared to this, the pretty almost-child's head thus distracted, the delicate foot mincing in this slough of blood and dirt, were types of the disjointed time. This was the Carmagnole.[1]

Dickens wrote in fear and loathing, his sympathies fully engaged by the Romantic view of the *ancien régime*, yet his description of the revolutionary spirit expressed so freely and demonically in the streets of Paris powerfully conveys the capabilities of the dance to sway emotions. Little wonder that even to this day, any crowd worries the Paris authorities. Thus, Honoré de Balzac, in his study of Stendhal, quotes a minister of his time in the nineteenth century: "Absolute Power has this advantage, that it justifies everything. Every year we shall be afraid of a 1793, and everything that can reduce that fear will be supremely moral."[2] Dance and politics are strange bedfellows; still, during the French Revolution, bedfellows they often were. Dances could be presented when plays could not, since words are often extremely dan-

22. Figure of a revolutionary—"Let's Dance the 'Carmagnole,' Hooray for the sound of the cannon." Cabinet des Estampes.

gerous for playwrights and performers in times of political repression or violent change. They are too easily understood by both the popular audience and the police. Dance, on the other hand, can be mere spectacle, or when, as in some ballet *livrets*, it is endowed with a fervent revolutionary message, dance is saved from some dangers by the ambiguity of its expression.

Lamentably, although *la liberté* was one of the great catchwords of the Revolution, artistic liberty was not achieved. Though what was deemed sacred and what heretical had been transposed by the destruction of the monarchy, government control over all artistic productions was only briefly relaxed and then ferociously tightened again. The new leaders, whose hold on power was not blessed by the dignity of custom, were as aware as the old that the arts could best serve the state as purveyors of propaganda. Formal licensing and censorship of all theatrical productions was and is a fact of life in France, whether in the eighteenth, nineteenth, or twentieth century. Underlying that policy is the clear realization that the arts can be, and often are, a subversive influence. Along with that perception comes the attractive idea of harnessing the theatre's ability to influence sympathies and disseminate information, of using it to produce and maintain popular support for the status quo.

As early as 1573, Catherine de Medici, then in control of the monarchy, used dance as an instrument of statecraft when she entertained a group of Polish ambassadors and the court with an evening of ballet. *Le Ballet des Polonais* in which the sixteen provinces of France were represented in regional costumes flaunted the power and wealth of the country. Le Père Menestrier, in *Des Ballets Anciens et Modernes* (1682), recalls that in 1641, in the ballet called *La Prospérité des Armes de France*, poetry and song adulated the monarchy, immortality, and French power. Young Louis XIV played a role in this entertainment prophesying France's conquest of the world—the sun itself asked Louis to climb up to meet him. The image of the king, likened to the sun that brings forth the day and calls forth the night, was again used in the *Ballet de la Nuit* in 1653, when Louis danced as Apollo. Could there be any metaphor more potent? It was in the *Ballet de la Nuit* that the sobriquet "Le Roi Soleil" was born.

23. *Figure of a woman dancing to a famous revolutionary song, "Ah we'll win, we'll win" (1791). Cabinet des Estampes.*

Revolutionary Spirit

Louis de Cahusac, in his *Traité de La Danse Ancienne*,[3] quotes Père Menestrier in order to propose themes that will bring honor to ballets during his time. Cahusac accentuates the idea that dance can be a virtuous means of exploiting the political ideas of a government. He notes that it was especially Cardinal Richelieu who forced people to admire a particular ballet, because it enhanced his concept of power.[4] Père Menestrier identifies the happiness of the nation with the dances that give the spectator a sense of pride in his or her country: "We celebrate with public spectacles and offer ingenious allegories, events represented for the good of the State, in order to give people a taste of sweetness, in the guise of pleasure and amusement, which makes them more sensitive to national pride."[5]

During the French Revolution, the people did discover their national pride and consequently demanded those "public spectacles" and "ingenious allegories." Dance, hitherto used as an instrument of royal power, had become a vehicle for republican propaganda. It is interesting to note the many references in the *Journal de l'Opéra*, to the organization and governance of the Opéra during the Reign of Terror (March 1793–July 1794). Obviously, what happened onstage in Paris had to be controlled. The young leaders of the new Revolution had unleashed the power of the mob; this fury could be manipulated against them unless strict measures were taken. The Commune, made up of passionate idealogues, established the Committee of Public Safety: its power, under the baton of Danton and Robespierre, tyrannized all aspects of French life. It was, essentially, a dictatorship imposed on a nation at war on many fronts. By 1794, France had over 850,000 men in its armies (because of national conscription). The young general under the Committee of Public Safety developed the principle that might, brilliance, and courage could fashion greater leadership, a concept that eventually paved the way for Napoleon.

So it was that the Committee of Public Safety protected the political climate by insisting on prorepublican, anticlergy and antiroyalty presentations. In March 1793, a decree of the Commune authorized that the performers at the Opéra had to augment the number of their appearances and to alternate them with free or benefit shows for needy groups such as the poor and the widowed. In August, the official proclamation stated that there would be no more of the "infinity of plays full of injurious allusions to Liberty, whose only aim is to deprive the spirit and public morals." Still, republican tragedies had to be shown three times a week. Dramatic works such as *Brutus, Caiius Gracchus,* and *Guillaume Tell* were proper for the education of the people in republican principles of equality and liberty. Furthermore, once a week the receipts of the theatre and Opéra were to go to the government. That must have been a bitter blow to the artists. Naturally, any theatre that presented material contrary to the spirit of the Revolution would be closed.[6]

In September, the Commune issued a statement that in the future they would decide what operas and ballets would be shown as well. One year later, on June 30, 1794, the decree was followed by a rule that applied specifically to publishers. The ballet and pantomime *livrets* had to conform, along with the tragedies and comedies. There would be no more lords or ladies on the stage, only citizens (*citoyens* or *citoyennes*). Every aspect of publishing was to be under the immediate authority and surveillance of the Committee of Public Safety. All authors and editors must supply three copies of their work to the Committee before it was published, sold, or used. All directors and editors of newspapers, periodicals, and pamphlets were required to submit to the same obligation. Peddlers of books were equally under the watchful eye of the Committee.[7]

During the Reign of Terror, no receipts are recorded in the *Journal de l'Opéra*. One can speculate that this omission might have protected the management from the Committee of Public Safety's insatiable appetite for control over all funds. Also, there was a note indicating that official discipline would be instituted for artists who hindered the interior functioning of the Opéra. Here too, one wonders whether this refers to politics, improper behavior, missing rehearsals, or drunkenness. Certainly it was taken for granted ten years earlier that artists would be sent to prison or reported to the police if they did not comply with the rules. This mention in the books gives official power to outside governmental forces previously thought unnecessary.

Police and soldiers became common spectators in the theatres of Paris, which often had unruly and excitable audiences. According to Jacques Hérissay, "In 1789, the Académie de Musique had sixty men from the regimental guard, commanded by two sergeant majors, four corporals; and, on the evening where there would be ballroom dances, forty more soldiers would be assigned."[8] During the Revolution, the police were so constantly present that much of our information about opening nights at theatres and the frequent accompanying riots comes from police records (kept now in the National Archives in Paris). The police were there not only to spy on the artists but to keep order. The public became an unreasonable force in the theatres and had to be regulated and controlled. Even the Opéra, which traditionally catered mainly to the well-to-do, had a republican audience by 1793. A police report on the opening of *La Siège de Thionville* (June 14, 1793) gives us a picture of the new patrons. Overwhelming applause greeted the lines, "We have a king no more; we are republicans. The sceptre is broken forever." The report goes on:

> When the inhabitants at the garrison of Thionville gathered about the altar to Liberty decided to sustain the siege, and Commander Wimpfen began the "Marseillaise," its stirring words turned all the audience into actors and their voices spontaneously supported those on stage. It was pleasing to hear the women in the audience join in the singing of the hymn, but it was noble and glorious to hear the men do the same. . . . D'Autrechamp was generally hissed and applauded only by a few spectators who resisted the illusion; at such plays the Frenchman is a citizen first, a spectator after.[9]

Many of the important measures of theatre reform adopted by La Harpe and Mirabeau in the liberalizing proclamation of January 1791 were dropped. Even the rights of authors were curbed as a result of political pressure, since the authors dared not appear selfish or unpatriotic. Plays, ballets, and operas were monitored by police agents or fickle, angry, or hungry audiences rather than by the spirit of creativity or the process of open competition.

Naturally, anyone with an ounce of political acumen spoke of his love of liberty and fidelity to the Republic. Choreographers such as Pierre Gardel and Sebastien Gallet came up with ballets and pantomimes that either stayed completely away from Revolution themes or,

Ballet, Servant of Politics

that in some way, delicately (or fulsomely?) praised the love of freedom. Producing boring pseudo Greek and Roman triumphal processions with immense numbers of people and no real story must have seemed harmless enough payment for the privilege of continuing one's profession—or life—in a time of surprising bestiality.

These years were difficult for all artists. For dancers, there was the special problem that ballet had been patronized by the privileged class, the court and the monarchy itself. "Guilt by association" was a reality. Some performers found it sensible to depart for London or the theatres established at the regional fairs. During the period of 1787 to 1801, London's King's Theatre saw the Frenchmen Coindé, Gallet, Dauberval, Noverre, Didelot, and Gaetan and his son, Auguste Vestris. In short, almost every producer and choreographer of note found it advantageous to leave the country at least for some time. Perhaps that dispersion was not entirely due to a morbid fear of the guillotine, however. If someone of Didelot's stature were offered a place in Russia, he might well take it, dancers then (as now) were attracted by big audiences, money, and the pleasures of working with other well-trained artists.

Dancers, though not much given to writing, occasionally recorded horrific stories about their experiences during the Terror. A ropedancer called Mme Saqui, who had a theatre named after her in early nineteenth-century Paris, describes her memory of an afternoon of her youth on September 3, 1792:

> My family once again began its trip as an adventure. At noon, a modest carriage was traveling down the rue Saint-Antoine when it was stopped by a huge crowd. A group of crazy-looking men poured out of the rue des Ballets in a wild frenzy. One of them was carrying at the tip of his pick axe a bloody head whose hair was hanging down in clotted plaits; another, a coal man, exhibited another trophy at the top of a stick with some shreds of a blouse. Several moments before, the person who had been the charming Princesse de Lamballe had just been massacred in front of the Prison de la Force. [Mme Saqui was asked in her old age to recount this horrible memory from her childhood.][10]

Revolutionary Spirit

Little wonder that in such an atmosphere, artists who seemed intimately associated with the aristocracy and who did not leave for foreign countries were sometimes imprisoned. Such was the case of Mlle Dervieux, a famous dancer at the Opéra. Penalized for her lands and associations with wealth before the Revolution, Dervieux was detained in the prison of Plessis and accused of conspiratorial acts in July 1794. Put in a tiny cell,

> where one could not see the light of the day but for a window slit almost entirely obstructed and where certain of the women remained who were suffering, sometimes dying and whom no one cared about. Children who were lacking in nourishment and hygiene became pitifully thin and quarrelsome and cried incessantly. This miserable humanity, who were once the fine flowers of society, agonized in vermin-ridden cells. They knew the anguish of sleepless nights, obsessed by the fear of receiving the death penalty.[11]

Lucky not to have met up with *la lanterne*, (to be hanged from a lamp post), Dervieux managed to survive into the nineteenth century, as did her colleague in hiding, La Guimard.[12]

Interestingly, La Guimard, a ballerina of amazing capability and talent, had been in charge of a committee of the Opéra made up of politically active artists at the Opéra. A rebellious spirit is not unusual among dancers, although generally it does not manifest itself politically. As early as 1783, a group of dancers, including La Guimard, formed a committee to wrest power from the director of the Opéra, Papillon de La Ferté. La Guimard's letters to La Ferté and the minister to the king, Amelot, remain marvelous examples of La Guimard's personal convictions and her lack of fear of the Opéra directors. In an unequivocal request for more money and authority, she notes her dissatisfaction: "I repeat it once again, I cannot believe it. I have always known you to be frank and honest, as much as possible. And now you are capable of such a great injustice towards honest people who have sacrificed everything in order to better serve and please the public."[13] Note that though it is eight years before the establishment of the

Republic, the audience La Guimard wishes to please is the "public," not the king.[14]

Although La Guimard used whatever political powers she could against her enemies, even arranging a *lettre de cachet* (a letter under seal of the sovereign ordering imprisonment) against her rivals, I have no evidence that any dancer denounced another dancer to the Commune after it took supreme power over theatrical events in 1793. This does not mean that dancers were not imprisoned. As we have seen in the case of La Dervieux and La Guimard, they spent time in prison both before and during the Revolution. Dauberval himself was briefly imprisoned for his participation in a coup against the Opéra administration of M. de Vismes. Dauberval was sent to Fort l'Evêque, "where recalcitrant artists were locked up. . . . But there was nothing particularly dramatic there because everyone knows that this prison is very welcoming to rebellious performers and that it was good form to have the opportunity to be incarcerated there."[15]

This particular insurrection against the Opéra administration had the support of Les Vestris as well as La Guimard. On one occasion, Vestris and Dauberval were supposed to dance dressed in bourgeois costume instead of their usual shepherd or Grecian outfits; they refused and were again imprisoned. On another occasion they refused to dance in "Armide" and were sent straight away to Fort l'Evêque.[16] These fights between dancers and administration, which resulted in a few evenings spent in a not terribly unpleasant place where one's servants were permitted, were quite different from the jailings during the Revolution. Depending on the charges, a person taken to prison after 1789 and before 1795 might suffer real deprivation.

Despite the dangers, dancers did defend their interests and friends in the theatre during those troubled years, though any strong position against the Revolutionary Tribunal could affect their careers.[17] In 1793, the directors of the Théâtre de la Nation, Mlle Montansier and M. Noeuville, were denounced by the radical newspaper *Père Duchesne*.[18] They were falsely accused of planning to set fire to the Bibliothèque Nationale and were sent by Robespierre to the prison, La Petite-Force, on November 14. This occurred even though Mlle Montansier had given large sums for the war effort, frequent presentations of patriotic plays, and lavish pageants enacted in honor of the immortal Jean-Paul

Revolutionary Spirit

Marat. But her former ties to Marie-Antoinette and her quick success caused her misfortune. Noeuville was also judged guilty and went to jail. Especially interesting is the response of the dancers, who signed a petition asking for their director's release—though without avail in this case. Montansier directed the activities of her theatre while she was in jail, however, and was released in 1795.

In 1793, the actors and dancers of the Théâtre de la Nation were told to move to the Egalité in the Faubourg Saint-Germain, the former home of the Comédie-Française, whose actors were in jail. The dancers of the new theatre, called l'Egalité, formed a special committee with cooperative rules and expressed serious grievances against their new, inadequate, and small facilities. In a letter to Bertrand Barère, an important member of the Committee of Public Safety, the dancers Gallet, Didelot, Laborie, and Mme Rose complained. Though they wished to comply with the Committee of Public Safety, they found it impossible to perform large pantomimes on such a small stage—notably *Le Siège de Granville* and *Les Horreurs du fanatisme au Pérou* by Gallet.[19] They went on to speak of their considerable expenses for daily ballet exercises, "which are essential in order to acquire and conserve one's talent." Also, it cost money for shoes and dance clothes. The letter ends with a plea to Barère, a "friend of the arts," that he not lower their *appointements* or salary, and that he realize the precious differences in the art they profess. Indeed, these dancers, émigrés from the Opéra, received fine salaries by comparison with other artists, especially when they were at the Théâtre de la Nation.[20]

As any student of the Revolution knows, there was more dramatic rhetoric in the streets of Paris and in the Assembly than might be heard on the stage. The influence of politics on ballet was different from its effect on the theatre. Plays, *faits historiques*, *pièces patriotiques*, and verbal demonstrations of political propaganda were all common to the theatre of the 1790s. The ballet usually did not create political pieces per se, although *Le Déserteur*, a very popular ballet during the Revolution, had a lightly comic, political theme about an accidental desertion by a love-sick French soldier. Ballets tended to be divertissements added on like postscripts rather than anticlerical or antimonarchical incantations to the Revolution. There was also a famous comic play, *Le Réveil d'Epiménide* (January 1, 1790), containing an important

24. *Illustration of "Heroic Deeds," theatrical presentations that recorded the struggles of the republican army. Here, the War of the Vendée (May 3, 1793). Cabinet des Estampes.*

ballet by Jacques-François Des Hayes. The comedy had a great success at the Théâtre de la Nation and was one of the first to make an allusion to the Revolution. Of course, it was followed by many more.

Not many dancers are mentioned as having fought in the wars against the frontier countries. Though outspoken about their physical needs and philosophical inspirations, most dancers do not find politics or the war of words particularly fruitful, once these have little to do with gesture and movement. But, a certain Muller, trained as a dancer, fought as a general in the army at Vendée, an extremely important trouble spot of the Revolution where insurrections against the Republic were constant.[21] Muller could not pursue his career as a dancer, as he was later drafted into the Volunteers of the Butte de Moullins.

8
BALLETS OF POLITICAL PASSION, 1790–1796

Politics, ideology, and dance do combine, however, in the *Fêtes Révolutionnaires*.[1] Though not normally conceived of as either ballet or opera, these grand processions were often choreographed by Gardel and movements with symbolic gestures filled these massive festivals. The *Journal des Théâtres* declared in 1794 that "of all the institutions that constituted revolutionary genius, the *fête nationale* is without question one of the most important to call attention to Republicans."[2] Such was the thinking of revolutionary patriots in the years after the taking of the Bastille. In the tradition of antiquity, the French politicians set up large outdoor celebrations that encouraged popular participation. They reflected the very nature of democracy, so it was thought, and encouraged people to enjoy themselves in a natural setting inspired by feelings of fraternity.

The role of producing these spectacles was taken by Jacques-Louis David, who was appointed by the Committee of Public Safety to orchestrate the gigantic *tableaux vivants* of which he became the unchallenged leader. David attended the French Academy in Rome and won the Prix de Rome in 1774. He painted with a rigorous attention to classical detail and brought the "cult of antiquity" to new heights of popularity. The Jacobin Club, of which he had become a member, commissioned him to immortalize the Tennis Court Oath. This event

Ballets of Political Passion

25. "Here we dance"—view of the decoration and illumination of the site of the Bastille in honor of the storming of the Bastille on July 14, 1790. Bibliothèque de l'Arsenal.

celebrated those people who wanted to create a revolutionary government or confederation of the monarchy. The painting (1791) was destined never to be finished, as David became a member of the Convention.

In his costuming and direction, David insisted that the Greek and Roman characters in the theatre have a new veracity. He also consecrated those days or dates the new leaders thought appropriate. France was to be ruled by the people, and therefore everyone had to act, sing, and dance in these mass fêtes, just as they did on religious feast days: "The element of mass participation, especially from the lower classes, was David's most important contribution to the Fêtes révolutionnaires. Almost all the arts—architecture, painting, sculpture, poetry, oratory, music, drama, and the dance—were combined to form a flexible propaganda weapon, a skillful technique of social control, and a truly 'revolutionary' art."[3]

Marie-Joseph de Chénier (Lyrics), La Fête de la Fédération, pour Célébrer le 14 Juillet, Sets and Costumes by Jacques-Louis David, July 14, 1790, Champ de Mars
On the first anniversary of the taking of the Bastille, July 14, 1790, the city of Paris celebrated a holy day, La Fête de la Fédération. The National Assembly had voted huge sums of money for the spectacle. Chénier wrote the words and David directed the production.[4] The National Guard and an army corps also took part. The place chosen for the ceremony was the Champ de Mars, a vast parade ground that was transformed into an amphitheatre. It was said the twelve thousand workers were employed to work day and night to remove earth from the center area and heap it on the sides. Since there were not enough laborers for the project, an appeal was made to the citizens of Paris to help: "Soldiers, priests, beggars and women of high rank worked side by side. Different sections rallied to the sound of drums and marched to work together, banners flying."[5] Parisian theatres also committed themselves to the undertaking. Each actor chose a partner to whom he offered a delicate spade, decorated with ribbons and bouquets. All wore gray muslin dust-resistant costumes; the actresses also wore gray boots and silk stockings, a tricolor scarf, and a large straw hat. Orchestras accompanied the actors, but despite their spirit, they were soon asked to leave the project as they were inefficient earthmovers.

The festival was launched at Notre-Dame. Actors, musicians, and dancers from the Comédie-Française, Comédie-Italienne, and many other theatres were brought together for an introduction to the rite. Opéra singers sang a song, "The Fall of the Bastille," and mixed in parts of biblical text with the songs. One wonders how Notre-Dame survived such a musical show. Early the next morning, a huge procession of federal deputies from the provinces and federal troops left from the Bastille and marched to the Tuileries. The National Assembly met them, as did the Paris municipal officers. They went through the streets into the amphitheatre to cheering throngs. At the Champ de Mars, there were four hundred thousand spectators, the king included,

Ballets of Political Passion

26. *Night view of the* Fête de la Confédération *(July 14, 1790). Note the dancers in the foreground. Bibliothèque de l'Arsenal.*

despite a torrential rain. Three hundred priests in white surplices and tricolored scarves opened the ceremony with a mass. The king swore to uphold the Constitution. All over France, oaths of obedience to the laws and loyalty to the king were recited.

The procession returned and the people danced at the Bastille, which had been converted into a huge dance pavilion. The celebration went on for some time, with the grand hope that reforms would continue in "this best of all possible worlds." The experience proved a success, and *Fêtes de Fédération* were planned for several years.[6] Impressed by the prodigious emotion thus aroused and haunted by classical reminiscences, legislators, journalists, and pamphleteers— men like Honoré-Gabriel Mirabeau, Charles-Maurice de Talleyrand, Vienot-Vaublanc—soon were consciously wishing to imitate the policy of classical governments.[7] They had learned that the fluid crowd was a phenomenon that could be given form and organization and could be enlightened.

In December 1792, Jean Paul Rabaut faced the Convention and asked how it would be possible to communicate to all Frenchmen an enthusiasm for liberty, equality, and fraternity. He suggested that the Cretan and Spartan means of public education might succeed and proposed that each canton build a national temple to be used as a school building and an assembly hall, where, on Sundays, citizens would gather, listen to a lesson in ethics, and sing in honor of liberty, equality, and fraternity. In fair weather, they should engage in public games, gymnastics, and military exercises. The aim was to make Spartans (or Romans) out of Frenchmen—a seeming impossibility given the average Frenchman's love of good food, wine, and love. In this Utopian dream, all Frenchmen would live in health, dress alike, and be active in natural exercises. To excite their love of country, they would be required to read Plutarch; while they were reading, they would listen to warlike marches so that the institutions of Lycurgus might be better engraved on their hearts. One wonders how many people actually believed in this possibility. Some of the French were surely bemused by such extravagant ideals.

The Committee of Public Instruction cited Rousseau as its prophet, since he had recommended that one's time be filled with physical exercises, gymnastics, and warlike dances set to music. "And since, as in Sparta, girls as well as boys were to be educated, the boys with female contemporaries would go through the evolutions of a Pyrrhic dance while the girls would respond with a virginal dance which would recall the ancient festivals of Diana."[8] Other large processional outdoor spectacles such as this were staged for public enlightenment and amusement in all the cities of France.

Jacques-Louis David, La Fête de l'Achèvement de la Constitution, September 18, 1791

As in *La Fête de la Fédération*, military processions were prominent in *La Fête de l'Achèvement de la Constitution*, "where the National Guard, on foot and on horse play large roles. The celebration ends with the ascension of a hot-air balloon covered with allegorical and god-like symbols dating from the theatre machine days of Servandoni."[9]

We may recall that during the summer of 1792 a so-called second revolution was initiated by the revolutionary Commune, which met all night on August 9 near the Hôtel de Ville. *La Reúnion du 10 Août* tried to invest more power in the people; they stormed the Tuileries and killed eight hundred nobles and Swiss Guards. Danton, Marat, and Robespierre were the victors.[10] The action of August 10 succeeded in destroying the authority of the Legislative Assembly and overthrowing the monarchical constitution. War on the frontiers and fear of a Prussian invasion had given rise to fearful riots and violence in Paris. All aristocrats were suspected of collusion with the enemy. When the news of Verdun reached Paris on September 2, the Commune issued a panic-stricken proclamation: "To Arms! The Enemy is at the Gates!" Indeed, these words became the litany of the next several years of theatrical chorales and dramas. The Parisians sporadically invaded prisons to massacre the nobility and the clergy from September 2 to September 7. As late as September 10, a party of 53 prisoners sent from Orléans to be tried at Paris was set upon at Versailles by a mob and slaughtered. Of some 2,600 prisoners in Paris, it is estimated that between 1,100 and 1,400 were killed. Between 67 and 72 percent of the total ironically were ordinary criminals, not nobility or clergy.

Pierre Gardel, La Contre-Révolution, *Ballet d'Action, 1790s (?) at the Jacobin Club*[11]

For a small but vociferous portion of the French population, the nobility and the clergy still held tremendous value and power. The counterrevolutionaries fought valiantly against the new and radical republican ideology. Their belief was that the king and the Catholic church might still hold sway, though without the injustices of the *ancien régime*. Consequently, monies and weapons were poured into France from foreign countries in order to promote the cause of the counterrevolutionaries. Indeed, there was even a ballet that reflected these concerns, called *The Counter-Revolution*, though the tone was far less serious than reality. It is a fascinating example of an enthusiastic and satirical approach to both politics and ballet, poking fun in a manner usually unseen during deadly serious periods of history. Many names and events are alluded to in its *livret*, helping to convey the mood of the time. Also, it is the only real ballet that depicts political experience. For these reasons, a discussion of some length seems necessary for its understanding.

Rather than a typical *livret, The Counter-Revolution* exists in the form of a letter from Pierre Gardel to his publisher. The Library of Congress' National Union Catalogue lists this ballet under Pierre Gardel's name, but it is not described or mentioned in ballet histories or any of the literature with which I am familiar. I found it bound in a collection of plays and ballet *livrets* from the Revolution.

Most revolutions are followed by counterrevolutions that seek to stem the tide of radicalism. One of the more dramatic events of the French Revolution was the flight to Varennes from Paris of King Louis XVI and Marie-Antoinette in June 1791. Their betrayal of the Revolution and their fear for the monarchy highlighted what already seemed the major counterrevolutionary question of the time: Should France construct a constitutional monarchy based upon democratic principles, or should France become a Republic? The execution of the king would be the radical's solution to this problem, resulting in one of the most tragic events in French history. Prior to King Louis XVI and his family's attempted escape, this issue was hotly debated in all sectors of Parisian life, and naturally in the theatre and ballet of the time.

The Counter-Revolution amusingly depicts the political controversies of the early Revolution (before 1793). At the time, there was a great deal of discussion about what constituted nationalism and revolution. Below the title of the ballet on the front page is a statement that the ballet should be played at the beginning of spring. The mention of spring suggests the celebrations of nature that were being revived in order to replace Christian saints' days, perhaps a satirical dart thrown at the anticlerics by the conservative Gardel. But the letter states that the performance of this ballet had to be put off because of the indisposition of the principal dancer, General Bender. This, of course, is a joke, as General Bender was a seventy-nine-year-old Austrian field marshal who had bragged that if he fought the French, he would not stop until he left his boots in Paris. In 1792, when war was declared on Austria, a popular tune of the Revolution sang of General Bender's boots. Also appearing on the title page is a short extract from a poem by Boileau, a seventeenth-century French writer, that predicts the plot

Ballets of Political Passion

of the ballet rather gently but explicity: "Louis, you need no longer fear any insane audacity; you will see your crown replaced in its proper position. But there will be some battles, such is the decree of fate."[12] Indeed, the ballet concerns the threat of counterrevolutionary war. I suspect that the whole affair seemed a "plaisanterie" until the king actually lost his head. Curiously, the printer of Vienne, so it says, has its address as the "Printery of Fugitives." Is the Vienne in Austria, is it the Vienne in France near Lyon, or is it simply a cunning fabulation to lull the censors?

Though no list of dancers is presented on the frontispiece of this ballet, the second page begins with the letter from Monsieur Gardel, *maître des ballets* de l'Opéra to the publisher. The Académie Royale de Musique changed its name to the Opéra National between June 1791 and August 1792. An editorial footnote tells us that Gardel is an excellent citizen, who has measured up admirably during the course of the glorious Revolution and has kept up a good correspondance with the publisher. Known for his vanity, Gardel angrily comments on the public's lack of appreciation for his recently performed and most famous ballet, *Psyché*. We know from his other prologues to ballets that Gardel had an egotistical manner of writing and an exaggerated concern for his reputation. He mentions, however, that there are few people whose burning passion for the Revolution has not consumed their taste for the arts. Gardel found the "patriotic ladies of affected elegance" contemptible and points out that their acceptance of his ballet *Psyché* only stemmed from the lubricious scene in which Cupid makes love to Psyché center stage on a couch. He notes that these ladies compared the charismatic revolutionary leader Mirabeau,[13] a true ladies' man, to the Cupid of his *Psyché* ballet. Gardel suggests that this erotic scene might best explain the "success of its receipts." Gardel then gossips about the artistocratic members of his audience, "Le Jeune Montmorency et sa douce amie Laval," who lustfully gape at the ravishment of Psyché on a special sofa.[14]

No fool of the political moment (after all he survived as ballet master of the Opéra during the Revolution, the Reign of Terror, the Consulate, the empire, and the restored monarchy), Gardel speaks of making a patriotic statement in the manner of his colleagues at the Academy of Music, "for it is time to show off the symbols of liberty on the ballet stage." In the old days, he says, the Opéra stage used to encourage the portrayal of the idols of despotism cultivated by Louis XIV and worshiped by such composers as Philippe Quinault. But he says, "today the Opéra will resound with the sacred words of liberty, equality, patriotism and revolution. The dancers and singers formerly plump during the old regime, and currently lean since the coming of Revolution, will demonstrate their hatred of the aristocracy." Is Gardel serious, or is he really writing sarcastically of the new leaders' devotion to liberty and to democratic principles so tyrannically demanded both on and off the stage? Cautiously, Gardel asks the editor to let him know what he thinks about this piece, and whether it would be too risky to put on. This seems to be a straightforward question by Gardel, anxiously expressing his fear of the censor and the danger of offending the revolutionary authorities.

The letter becomes more interesting when it refers to those politicians who had starring roles during the Revolution and the orators and politicians who drafted the most significant social and political reforms. Still, Gardel's tone has a haughty, condescending quality and a slightly contemptuous tinge. In speaking about the title of his ballet, he says that the new National Assembly owes its great good deeds to its title, which used to be the Estates-General. He cites the Abbé Sieyès, who wrote the famous *What Is the Third Estate?* Gardel facetiously notes that without Sieyès, the Estates-General would only have worked in accord with the king to reform abuses, reestablish finances, consolidate the monarchy, and make the people happy. In other words, the paradise on earth could have worked if Barnave, Lameth, Péthion, Robespierre,[15] and that "bunch of grand legislators" had not intruded themselves into the political picture.[16] This clearly identifies Gardel as a Royalist rather than a republican.

Gardel then goes on to say that the bourgeois reforms were too expensive for Robespierre and his crowd to afford. At this point, he begins a more profound diatribe against the group and the present government. For example, he jibes at the fact that "heavy" silver has been replaced by "lighter" paper money, saying that it is similar in weight to the light ideas these men perpetrated upon the public. Instead of a state police force, Gardel says, "they are weak-bellied types who indiscriminately allow the practice of the right of man." (Is Gardel

Ballets of Political Passion

describing the eighteenth-century equivalent of the bleeding heart? Is he anti- democratic? It seems so.) "Instead of the prison of the Bastille," he says, "we have committees of inquiry; instead of Parlement," we have national supreme courts, and "what do we not have? Everything except peace, happiness and opulence." In this manner Gardel argues for the principle and the title of his ballet, *The Counter-Revolution*, an idea to which he seems quite partial. And what, indeed, did this title signify? In essence, it represented an opposition not of the monarch but of the aristocrats, the leaders who had taken flight and were preparing to instigate a counterrevolution from abroad. This implied a new siege of power, a desperate call from the outside, as any successful resistance could no longer come from within.

The interesting title apparently caused the board of inquiry to be frightened at the publishers, and Gardel admits that a M. Voidel[17] trembled at the thought that the demagogic General Bender would attack Gardel for his political ballet. According to Gardel, despite the fears of others, he set to work and the ballet was composed in less than fifteen days. At the point of handing out the roles, Gardel frankly confesses that he needed the "secours," or sure help, of the men who had created the new Constitution, despite his suspicions of their ideals. Without them, he would run the risk of not seeing it performed. The august Academy of Music (Opéra), though filled with talented people, would not be able to provide his ballet with the "National Perfection" demanded in the decrees by the Senate. Gardel is referring here to the new censorship decrees that asked theatre managers, including those of the Opéra, for subjects that reflected the events or political principles of the Revolution. Gardel importuned various of the patriotic clubs for their assistance, and indeed, it was the infamous Jacobins who agreed to give space for rehearsals and the final performance. I was astounded to find that this ballet seems to have been performed only within the Jacobin Club in Paris. "I would find it difficult," Gardel assures us, "to describe the gracious welcome I received from all the members of these patriotic clubs; some embraced me, others gave me honorable mention, while couching my name in their police reports, still others paid me the honor of filling the roles that I might alot to them." Is Gardel mocking the reader? Did Gardel write this *livret*? The prologue to this letter ends with self-acclamatory pats on

Revolutionary Spirit

the back saying that Gardel's ballet will be a success in the city of Paris, as well as in the eighty-three departments, subsidiaries of the emergent club of tyranny, the Jacobins.

Revolutionary clubs played a leading role in both politics and art during these times. The old authorities had collapsed and new ones had hardly begun to function. Consequently, clubs became major meeting places for discussion and the real centers of power. By 1793, there were between five and eight thousand such clubs. The political Jacobin Club, formerly called the Breton Club, which had assembled at Versailles, followed the Assembly to Paris, a metaphorical as well as physical move to the central power structure in France. They hired a hall from the Jacobin Convent on the rue Saint-Honoré. In October 1791, they threw open the doors to the public and built galleries to accommodate the new masses. I assume that this added space made the club more attractive for a ballet performance, though I know of no record of an actual performance. Dramatic moments were not uncommon to the young orators, and the clubs became rallying points for patriots and the Third Estate. A high subscription fee of thirty-six livres, not to mention twelve for entering, was a sufficient safeguard against the Jacobins' being called "Vauriens." Jacobins were middle-class landowners or wealthy, liberal aristocrats. "They held together with the development of an odd ritual, tests of orthodoxy, purges and public confessions."[18]

It is interesting to note that up to the eve of the Republic, that is, September 1792, the Jacobin Club supported the monarchy and took no part in the petition of July 17, 1790, for the king's dethronement. Nor did the club participate in the insurrection of August 10, 1792. Long before it emerged as the principal focus of the Terror, however, its character had been changed by the secession of the moderates, such as Joseph Barnave, Alexandre Lameth, and Adrien Duport, in 1791. Thus, the suggestion by Gardel that his ballet, controversially called *La Contre-Révolution*, be played with the blessing of the Jacobins leads us to believe that it had to be played, if ever, before the proclamation of the Republic on September 21, 1792. In the letter, Gardel commences his scenario by acknowledging the local importance of the national song, "Ça Ira," which was obligatory before and during the ballet. He orchestrates this air with various instruments, indicating another song, "The ditty of the Hung People," which Mirabeau, Lameth, Barnave, and le Duc d'Orléans would consent to sing. Gardel terminates this overture with a tidbit of the large and vigorous "Dies Irae, Dies Illa." What a mishmash of religion and patriotism! In addition to this eclectic prelude, Gardel decides to add a "Lamentation of Jeremiah," perhaps an indelicate reference to the destruction of Paris via Jerusalem—all this with vivid sound effects of bombs, mortars, and cannons.

Gardel's parody begins, he tells us, with the unsubtle intention of describing the good deeds of the Revolution (we have already heard his real thoughts on the matter), its innocent games (what irony), and its accompanying pleasantries. In the first scene there is a combat between metal money, or *numéraires*, portrayed by M. de la Borde, and paper money, or *assignats*, played by the Marquis de Montesquieu, no doubt a descendant of the great political philosopher. The allegorical struggle between the hard money, or *ancien régime*, and the *assignats*, or revolutionary government, is played to the hilt. The *ancien régime* is dressed in eighteenth-century velvets, silks, and wigs with a decidedly well nourished demeanor. The *assignats* on the other hand, skinny and weak looking, are thinly cloaked in paper.[19] The *assignats* are attacked but, suffocating from the stranglehold of their enemies, manage to squeak out a last rallying tune, "Mirabeau, Onward with the People."[20] The power of the *ancien régime* is briefly deflected by a siege of National Brigands who try to defend the *assignats*. (These are the mob patriots who behaved more like sadistic thieves in the night than upright citizens of the "Revolution.") The paper money vainly invokes the name of Mirabeau, however, and the hard money overwhelms its paper enemies, tearing off bits of costume, demonstrating its flimsy value. In a mock act of condescension, the hard-money people hand out coins to their prisoners who are begging for help. They then dance a *pas de deux* to the words, "There is only one evil, there is only one virtue, and that's to have everything or nothing at all."

So far, we see that the scenario bites away at contemporary economic events with facetious motives. When the *Domaines Nationaux*, or National Treasury, enter doing ropedance tricks and acrobatics, Gardel has them climb eighty-three steps, one step for each Jacobin Subsidiary, then do a backbend, after which they jump into a basket of paper. These movements are accompanied by the song, "The clerics are very honest men, we must drink to their health, drink to their health." Mention of the clergy brings out an effigy of King Louis XVI, the nemesis companion of the church during the Revolution and the star of this show. He rises out of the basket of papers. Everyone fills his pockets with National Treasury money and sings, "Vive la nation." The next arrow is aimed at a M. Roederer, who enters as a tobacco trader. He meets an unlikely choir of dancing Alsatians who offer him another big basket filled with gold coins. A well-known and long-lived politician, M. Roederer made a good deal of money on tobacco at the time. Like the court jester, Mirabeau finally shows up dancing to the words, "Ah, what are you saying, what are you saying, you greedy man." This inspires Roederer to hop around doing *brisés*, and *un coulé*.[21] They finish with the *pas de deux*, danced to the song of the two miser's who chant "At least we will always be together."

The next scene conjures up images of Roman history at its most bloody, tyrannical, and arbitrary moments. Barnave enters as the demented Nero, Lameth as Diocletian, and Martineau as crazy Caligula. Without reason, the character playing the Civic Sermon points his knife toward the heart of a French clergyman who, undaunted, sings, "knocked down but still heard." Civic Sermon responds by jumping upon the clergyman and tearing out his teeth. The act concludes with a song and dance entitled, "When one has no more teeth, one must no longer eat." Gardel informs us that this first act, episodic and diffuse, will be followed by a more cohesive plot in the second half. He adds that the first half of his ballet attempts only to paint the unselfish interest and honesty of our great and revered statesmen. No teeth, but tongue in cheek.

The second act features the character of "La France," a pale, skeletal woman who first appears addressing the heavens with her prayers. She hears thunder and lightning, climactic events that often occur in myth ballets. A voice from the heavens, like God speaking to Moses, booms out the following fateful words: "There will be no antique splendor in France until a famous warrior, crossing the Rhine with a valiant army, overcomes all the kings of an unhappy rule." Could this be a northern Napoleon? The phlegmatic and starving La France barely understands these pronouncements. But suddenly, in the distance, she hears the voice of Louis XVI, who is imprisoned in a tower. He intones, "Oh sweet hope of liberty." France replies, singing, "Poor Louis, when I was near you, I did not sense my misery. But today, now that we are without you, and without law, I am no longer anything on this earth." The haughty and powerful figure of the counterrevolution enters now, played by General Bender. This is amusingly footnoted: "General Bender could not make the rehearsal at the Jacobin Club, but he has solemnly promised to arrive for the performance at the beginning of spring." In the meantime, a certain M. Suleau[22] will fill his famous boots. *The Counter-Revolution* dance is a warrior march performed by some Croatians and some Pandours, or Hungarian infantry solders. They sing out, "Get up, you beautiful sleepy one, O Louis, O good King, this universe abandons you; only I, on this earth, am interested in your fate." Immediately some Jacobins arrive, alarmed by the apparition of the counterrevolution and armed with picks, hatchets, and daggers. Now the true combat begins. Terror grips the Jacobins, who are ready to run away when the assassin of the king, played by a M. d'Or, tries to reorganize them for a better fight. Since the Jacobin king killer sees his imminent defeat, he charges an emissary, Barnave, with the job of entering the tower and stabbing Louis. Barnave is ready to plunge the knife when Marie-Antoinette grabs the weapon and kills the killer by running it through Barnave's heart. Courageous and passionate, Marie-Antoinette has single-handedly defeated the Jacobins. The king's chains are removed, a crown is placed on his head, and he returns to his throne. A ballet of different "characters," that is, Croatian and Hungarian Hussards, ends this act with enthusiam. Once again, Parisian dancers finish their *bourrées* on a happy note, perhaps not immortalized on Olympus but nevertheless returned to a beatific normalcy where the "antique splendor" of France radiates from the gleaming crown of the Capet King Louis XVI.

Gardel's script is a parody, often puerile in tone. He refers to profound economic and political problems of the day by focusing upon two spicy battles: the first between paper and metal money, the second among Louis, La France, and Marie-Antoinette and the Jacobins; they epitomize the serious conflicts of opinion. Gardel's lighthearted style skirts the urgency and terror of the times by using allegorical metaphors and by diminishing the importance of certain political characters with inappropriate behavior. Somehow, we cannot imagine French General Jacques Menou climbing a ladder of eighty-three steps, doing a backbend, and flip-flopping into a paper basket. Nor can we accept the irony of a skeletal La France sitting stupified and unresponsive when she is asked to fight for her former magnificence. Unlikely comrades illustrate a certain confusion of beliefs in Paris at the time, as, for example, when Civic Sermon enters with Caligula and Nero, two criminals from the unglorious Roman past. As mentioned before, political orators of the Revolution tried valiantly to resurrect Roman history and mythology. The ultimate twist of the scenario comes when the moderate Barnave is asked to kill Louis XVI; we know that Barnave left the Jacobins in order to fight for the king and a counterrevolution. He was guillotined in 1793 after being denounced and judged guilty by the Legislative Assembly. Mirabeau, the famous Casanova, died in 1791; in another twist of fate, he interests the dance historian because two female ballerinas were accused of poisoning him. Fortunately, Mlles Hilligsberg and Coulon protested their innocence in the newspaper *La Feuille du Jour*, and the charges were dropped.[23] The king was executed on January 21, 1793, and Marie-Antoinette, the ballet's heroine, waited until October for the same fate.

As the Revolution continued, news events became a steady source of political and intellectual content for the stage, and artists wishing to maintain their positions sought direction from the new forces that were changing institutions. Gardel, for example, held sway over the Opéra and wished to prove his ability to keep abreast of political events. The composer Gossec came into his own in part because of the Revolution. Gluck, the leader and reformer of music at the Opéra, had fallen into disfavor as a result of his association with Marie-Antoinette. Prior to the Revolution, Gossec had also been eclipsed by Grétry, who did much of the opera and ballet music, and even more so by Hayden, whose symphonies were praised everywhere. Thus, Gossec was suddenly rejuvenated in 1789, at the age of fifty-five, by responding to France's need for a patriotic composer. A story is told that one evening in 1792 he and Gardel went to a café *guinguette* at the Porte Maillot: "During dessert, they sang patriotic tunes. 'La Marseillaise' was blasted out with great energy. François Lays and Augustin-Athanase Chéron

Ballets of Political Passion

27. *Commemoration of the storming of the Bastille, with the destruction of various symbols of the aristocracy—flags, swords, armor (1792). Cabinet des Estampes.*

(Opéra actors), climbed upon some barrels and thundered 'allons enfants.' When they hit the couplet, 'amour sacré de la patrie,' all the people watching, moved by the same sentiment, got down on their knees and repeated in a chorus that refrain with a solemn gravity."[24] Moved by the grandeur of such a spectacle, Gardel turned to Gossec and said, "Now that's an idea to explore!" There was born the scenario for *L'Offrande à la Liberté*.

Pierre Gardel, L'Offrande à la Liberté, Divertissement Lyrique, Music by François-Joseph Gossec, September 30, 1792, at the Opéra

Gardel's scenario for *L'Offrande à la Liberté*[25] was a triumph. The song called "La Marseillaise" was sung onstage: "A true drama unfolds before one's eyes harmoniously mimed as the verses are sung by Lays, taken up and repeated in the chorus by the figurants (women, children and warriors) who come running in from all directions to the Temple of Liberty to invoke the Goddess, dance in her honour and then take up arms to defend her."[26] According to the Almanach des Spectacles, "*The Offrande* was the "War Song for the Army of the Rhine" (composed at an earlier time by Rouget de l'Isle) and "Let Us Watch over the Salvation of the Empire." "It is majestic, commanding, and worthy of the subject it treats."[27] The love of country assured the success of this opera ballet. When Paris learned of the battle of Valmy and the proclamation of the Republic on September 21, 1792, it had come out of the black depression that the massacre in the first days of September had caused.

L'Offrande opened with a hymn sung to the goddess Liberty who, onstage, stood on a summit while a great crowd around her, some on horseback, paid tribute with dances and gestures. Children, dressed in white, burned incense. The last stanza of "La Marseillaise" was repeated "in a whisper," organs, bells, and cannons bursting. The couplet "Sooner death than slavery, this is the slogan of the French" and the strains of "Aux armes citoyens, formez vos bataillons" resounded in the opera halls and on the battlefields. Charles Dumouriez, who commanded the armies of the Republic, estimated that the proliferation of revolutionary chants in the conquered provinces constituted excellent diplomatic strategy. Consequently, *L'Offrande* was sent on tour to stimulate patriotic fervor after the victory of Jemmapes that united Belgium to France. According to the historian Louis Du Franc, "Of all the political plays of the Revolution, *L'Offrande* is the one which had the greatest impact on the Public."[28] It was replayed in 1848 for exactly the same purpose as in 1792.

Pierre Gardel, La Fête pour l'Inauguration des Bustes de Marat et Lepeletier, *Music by Christophe Willibald Gluck, François-Joseph Gossec, and François-André Philidor, October 17, 1792, on the Boulevard in Front of the Opéra*
This is all the information the *livret* for *La Fête* provides.

Mlle Montansier brought volunteers from Paris to perform for the troops at the front. They created quite a flurry upon their arrival, as they rode in garlanded triumphal chariots. Montansier wanted to

28. *Le Triomphe de la Montagne (May 31, 1793)*. Note the dancers around the tree and the clergyman expiring in the foreground. Cabinet des Estampes.

do a victory pageant in which dancers took part, celebrating Dumouriez's defeat of the Belgians at Jemmapes. A huge outdoor theatre was set up on November 12, 1792, in the face of the enemy. There were performances of *The French Republic*—a cantata sung by MM. Elleviou, Gavaudian, and Lartique of the Favart in Paris and *The Austrian Dance, or the Mill of Jemmapes*, a ballet staged by M. Sebastien Gallet. This ballet was concluded by a *sauteuse* (a jumping dance) executed by French dancers dressed as Austrians. Montansier achieved great success, and when they returned to Paris, the Parisian audiences came in droves to her theatre and showered the stage with flowers.

Pierre Gardel, Le Triomphe de la République, ou Le Camp de Grand Pré, *Divertissement Lyrics by Marie-Joseph de Chénier, Music by François-Joseph Gossec, January 27, 1793, at the Opéra*

On January 27, 1793, six days after the execution of Louis XVI, this chorale dance drama was presented at the Opéra.[29] Its title glorifies the triumph of the Republic in more ways than one. Once again the team of Gardel and Gossec collaborated, using words by Marie-Joseph de Chénier. The *Journal de Paris National* heartily praised the opening of this "fait historique" on January 29, 1793: "*The Triumph of the Republic* completely succeeded in satisfying everyone's expectations. The success of our armies is the guarantee of our victory song when the poet is worthy of his subject and when the listeners are French."[30] "However [the review continued], Gardel's ballet that crowned the entire production appeared to be too long and exhausting for the plot, if we may say so."[31] In another judgment, the *Mercure Français* on February 3, 1793, calls it "a simple divertissment, a kind of celebration where one would not expect a dramatic intrigue. It is a framework meant to assemble odes, chants, patriotic songs from national celebrations that the public would want to hear again. At the end of the piece, Liberty, evoked in the tradition of older gods, descends from the skies in a 'fort beau ballet' witnessed by different peoples."[32]

The *avertissement* to this *livret* states clearly that "inspired by the marvelous talent of Gossec, this divertissement brings to the heart a

Ballets of Political Passion

29. Hommage à la Liberté *(July 30, 1792)*—"*Sacred love for our country, let our enemies die while witnessing your triumph, and our glory.*" Cabinet des Estampes.

love, a passion and a need for the liberty of citizens who are not degenerate. This is the purpose stated by the author in his writings." The writer Chénier professes a love for liberty, which he attempts to display in this divertissement, and which he had shown in other works several years before the Revolution. The setting is a French army camp near the Prussian border. "La Patrie en danger,"[33] the leitmotiv that threads its way through the 1790s, is heard once again. It should be mentioned that though soldiers are the source of national victory, each Frenchman in his provincial town played a crucial role in the Revolution and in the fight against the monarchies of other countries. At Valmy, the Prussian invasion was checked. Kellerman, general of the French army, was victorious and was consequently named the Duc de Valmy. There were other battlefield successes: Dumouriez defeated the Austrians at Jemmapes, and Custine had conquered at Spire and Worms on September 30 and at Mayence on October 21, 1792.[34] France also declared war on Great Britain on February 1, 1793, and

30. Mlle Maillard, the quintessential Miss Liberty (1790). Bibliothèque de l'Opéra.

on Spain in March 1793. These military decisions were economically draining. Chénier brought this news of battle into the performance: "In the Camp of our warrior-enemy on the Aisne, liberty will be achieved. And from the generous decrees of our legislators, to William and to Brunswick they will carry their alarm. The soldiers of other nations will put down their weapons and will wish to become Frenchmen."

The opening scene of *Le Triomphe* calls upon all Frenchmen to celebrate their victory. Over them is God or "le Dieu du Peuple, des Rois, des Cités, des Campagnes, de Luther, de Calvin, et des enfants d'Israel." The same grandiose homage given in *L'Offrande à la Liberté* may be heard here. In the classic tradition, symbolic images of Liberty, Peace, and Reason are evoked. A duet between the choir and the mayor sings that France's defeat at the frontiers will become victories in the future. The peasant fighter is praised as much for his courage in battle as for his working the land. Men and women sing and dance around the Tree of Liberty: "For the state drink a full cup, Be a soldier and a citizen." The propagandistic values, outrageously evident, become even more pronounced. When the trumpet sounds, all run for their arms, and the old people exhort the young to come home triumphant. They sing of former battles lost because they were fighting for a monarch and not for themselves. When the soldiers of Chateauvieux arrive onstage victorious, the general calls everyone to dance and then to listen to his story: "Explosives burst and fly, blood flows in streams over our paths." At this point, Liberty (played by the ever-in-demand Miss Liberty, La Citoyenne Maillard) descends from the skies on a cloud, accompanied by the genies of the arts and of abundance. She tells her worshipers, "Do not envy ancient Greece any longer, the French nation has better known her freedom; banishing her kings, she knew how to proclaim the unity of a Republic." The allegory is played out further when Liberty enters the military camp with her entourage and sits on trophies, weapons, and flags taken from the enemy. Many nations of the world, depicted by different costumes, enter singing "Vive à Jamais, vive la Liberté." All proclaim the glory of France and her victorious battles at Namur, Spire, Mayence, and Chambéry. "All peoples" they say, "will break the bounds of the triple tyranny of priests, aristocrats and kings at the same time." In a resounding finale, the call to fight on other battlegrounds is pronounced: "The Brabant calls us, and Liège implores our warriors to come. Let us run through the walls of Brussels, and conquer with new laurels. If Austria continues to resist, we will attack Vienna and we will also plant our tricolored flag in the Palace of the Caesars."

The dance technique in this work is negligible, but the choreographed parades, processions, and huge crowds that mill around and make gestures or uniform movements have importance. Previously, the emphasis in dance was on the small, elegant, attitudinizing; now the accent is on mass movement. Thus, the Opéra became a serious organ of propaganda for the government; and even if one did believe in revolutionary principles, it must have been obvious that fine talents were being wasted on such repetitious and empty exercises. The Parisians were rapidly becoming a popular audience for their ballet and opera, and attended these partiotic spectacles with enthusiasm: "By 1793 even the aristocratic Opéra had become republican, not only in repertoire, but in audience."[35] The average Frenchman, knowing himself a citizen of an extraordinary nation, became a leading actor in a great epic drama called the French Revolution. He seized the moment in his lifetime to make a mark by participating in the events that summoned every man, woman, and child. In his desire to take center stage, the Parisian citizen was driven by pride, fear, fury, hunger, and even madness. Leaders such as Marat were able to capture imaginations and encourage bloody deeds. For example, in Jean Paul Marat's *Ami du Peuple* of February 25, 1793, "He pushed the patriots to break into shops and stores."[36] Crowds ran amok in the Paris streets, looting and stealing at their pleasure. From the earliest moments of the Revolution, the crowd reflected the desire for change and social upheaval.

Contrary to the Declaration of the Rights of Man, however, members of the Committee of Public Safety were able to meet in secret and to pronounce their sentences without due process of law. Marat called it a despotism of liberty; it was undeniable that all aspects of Parisian life were severely disturbed. On March 20, 1793, Beaumarchais' *Le Mariage de Figaro* had been revived. Now, however, the public and government were more prepared to understand the sharp satire and enjoy the accepted implications for reform that the Revolution had brought about.

Ballets of Political Passion

31. Tragic end of Louis XVI (January 21, 1793): "I die innocent of the crimes for which I am accused. I have never wanted anything, but the happiness of my people, and my last wish is that God will pardon my death." Cabinet des Estampes.

Pierre Gardel, Le Siège de Thionville, *Drame Lyrique, Lyrics by Saulnier and Dutilh, Music by Louis Jadin, avec Partie de Ballet, June 2, 1793, at the Opéra*

As I mentioned earlier, overwhelming applause greeted the lines, "We have a king no more; we are republicans. The scepter is broken forever."[37] When the inhabitants of the garrison of Thionville gathered about the altar of Liberty, they decided to sustain the siege and Commander Wimpfen intoned "La Marseillaise." Its stirring words turned all the audience into actors, and their voices spontaneously supported

Revolutionary Spirit

those on stage. "It was pleasing to hear the women in the audience join in the singing of the Hymn, but it was noble and glorious to hear the men do the same . . . at such plays the Frenchman is a citizen first and a spectator after."[38] The Commune passed a decree insisting that free performances of *Le Siège* be given for the *sans-culottes*. The end of June saw the passage of the Constitution of 1793 and July, the death of Marat. On August 28, the English took Toulon, but the uprising of anti-republicans were suppressed. The fêtes continued to be performed ritually, as if by some magic they would bring victory and peace to the French nation.[39]

In 1793, Gardel was entrusted with the staging of two "solemn spectacles." The first production took place in July 1793. Jacques-Louis David made his report to the Assembly on *La Fête Héroïque pour les Honneurs du Panthéon à Décerner aux Jeunes Barra et Viala*. Here is an excerpt from the scenario:

> Forming six groups, artists from the different theatres will march in the following order: the first group will be composed of musicians, the second of a male chorus, the third of male dancers, the fourth of a women's chorus, the fifth of female dancers, and the sixth of poets who will recite the verses they have composed in honor of the young heroes. When the urns have been placed on the altar, the young danseuses will perform funeral dances of the most intense sorrow around it, and lay branches of cypresses on the urns; at the same moment, musicians and singers will deplore the ravages of fanaticism which have taken these young lives from us.[40]

Pierre Gardel, La Fête de l'Unité et de l'Indivisibilité de la République, *Jacques-Louis David, August 10, 1793*

On August 20, 1793, *La Fête de l'Unité et de la République*, also staged by David, was enacted. According to Frantz Funck-Brentano, "On top of the ruins of the Bastille was a statue of Nature pressing her breasts from which sprayed streams of milk."[41] De Seychelles held a cup that caught the milk spray; he drank from it and then passed a

32. La Fontaine de la Regénération
(*August* 10, 1793). *Cabinet des Estampes.*

cup to others. The importance of August 10, 1792—the seizing of the Tuileries and the arrest of the king—is celebrated in opera and ballet as well as civic festivals *à la mode américaine* throughout the Revolution:

> Apart from the official press, the greatest and perhaps the most successful propaganda effort took the form of grandiose processional pageants that were organized by David. To celebrate the anniversary of the revolution of the tenth of August, 1792, and the promulgation of the Constitution, the Convention voted the sum of 1,200,000 livres for the Fête of August 10, 1793. Delegates of the primary assemblies from all over France, members of the Convention, of the Clubs and a miscellaneous collection of the sovereign people, gathered at the Place de la Bastille, and after speeches, songs and dances, formed in procession with chariots and floats symbolizing the republican virtues, moving

down the boulevards, with halts at triumphal arches or colossal plaster figures, till they reached the altar of the "Patrie" or the "Champ de Mars." Huge crowds watched or participated in the celebrations which lasted from seven in the morning to eleven at night.[42]

Joseph Lavallée (Songs and Dances), La Constitution à Constantinople, Pièce Patriotique, avec Franconi et Sa Troupe Equestre, August 15, 1793, Théâtre National, La Fête Civique, Divertissement, Ballet by Sebastien Gallet, August 29, 1793, at the Théâtre National
In August, the boulevard theatres also participated in the passion for patriotism ordered by the committees. *La Constitution à Constantinople*,[43] with dances by Joseph Lavallée, opened at the Théâtre National on August 15, 1793, with innumerable choruses of "La Marseillaise." On August 29, Sebastien Gallet, the *maître de ballets* of the theatre, created *La Fête Civique*, a divertissement in one act. According to Henry Lecomte, "No criticism has spoken of the work; it was thought to be, as in all the fêtes of this epoch, composed of dances and songs where patriots replace, to advantage, the seigneurs, and the shepherdesses of old times. It was often given as a prologue or a conclusion to other spectacles."[44]

Coindé (Ballet), La Liberté des Nègres ou Sélico, Opéra, Music by Bernard Mengozzi (Ballet Shown Separately from the Opéra), October 5, 1793, at the Théâtre National
The ballet in this opera, which was used separately as a patriotic interlude, received acclaim from critics. It professed the importance of freeing all enslaved peoples but specifically concerns the blacks of the West Coast of Muslim Africa. Once again, the team of Didelot, Laborie, and Rose were praised for their suppleness and grace.[45] Several months later, Didelot, Rose, and Laborie, as well as Coindé and M. and Mme Rochefort, reset the ballet successfully. Their ballet was then performed separately from the main work that introduced it.

33. Fête Civique, *Civic Festival* (August 10, 1793). This document shows the order of the procession for this festival, including a group of children carrying the Rights of Man and the Constitution. Bibliothèque de l'Arsenal.

34. "Liberated as you are, in accord with nature, the French Republic has deemed it necessary; am I not your sister?" Cabinet des Estampes.

Ballets of Political Passion

Planterre (Lyrics), La Fête de l'Egalité, *Mélodrame Pantomime-Lyrique*, Music by Desvignes, November 14, 1793, at the Théâtre de la Cité

The last months of 1793 marked the end of a critical year in the annals of the Revolution. On October 16, Marie-Antoinette was guillotined and the republican calendar was adopted retroactively from the Constitution of September 21, 1792. A one-act verse *pantomime-lyrique* melodrama, *La Fête de l'Egalité*, by Planterre, was shown at the Cité-Variétés on November 14 to music by Desvignes.[46]

This danced drama was created in honor of the soldiers fighting on the frontiers. The *livret* offers the following description: In the plaza of a village, Mayor Matthew preaches heroism to the volunteers, among whom figures his son Justin. They sing and dance and share a barrel of wine, and each takes a sip. Then the vessel breaks and out jumps Diogenes with a lantern, singing: "O you who rename me, you who guide my steps for so many nations, Extinguish forever your rays, For some time I have been searching for one man and here I find millions!" At the sound of a symphony, Equality then emerges from a trapdoor. Standing on a four-and-one-half-foot altar, Equality leans on a collection of weapons; a cortege begins to form with old people, children, and the young. The goddess accepts presents, singing, "Come and walk, follow my steps; French people, for you what a day of glory. If you carry me into combat, I shall bring you Victory." The drama was a success, especially as it honored the soldiers leaving for the frontier.

But the strength of the central government and the nation was dependent on the machinations of a fanatic whose political acumen allowed disagreement only at the altar of the guillotine. Robespierre, for some time disturbed by the unfavorable politics of Hébert and Danton, decided to eliminate all threats to his power in the spring of 1794. The Hébertists were an ultraradical *sans-culottes* organization professing atheism and true communism. Hébert was executed on March 24, 1794. At the same time, the political views of the moderates, expressed by Danton, had gathered momentum in the Convention. Danton asked Desmoulins to write an article denouncing Robespierre's violent response to any criticism. "Where is this system of terror to

Revolutionary Spirit

lead?" he wrote in the *Vieux Cordelier*. On April 15, 1794, Danton and Desmoulins were killed. Robespierre, without sanction or order, commanded 1,285 deaths between June 12, 1794, and July 28, 1794. The bloodbath did not leave him free of opposition. An assassination attempt was made on his life by a young girl, Cécile Renault. The dance historian Mary Grace Swift has discovered a flattering and obsequious message from several dancers relieved that Robespierre had survived.[47] Flattery was a sign of fear on the part of these dancers and choreographers, a fear that assured their safety, as it persuaded Robespierre that they were too frightened to be dangerous. The young girl who attempted to kill him was executed on June 17, 1794.

If we look at some of the titles of the operas from 1794 to 1799, they indicate that tyranny, as opposed to republican sentiments, continued to occupy the minds of Frenchmen, especially with the memories of recent wars: *Denys le Tyran, La Nouvelle Camp, ou Le Cri de Vengeance, La Pompe Funèbre du Général Hoche, Le Chant des Vengeances, Les Français en Angleterre*. Though the Opéra, now called Le Théâtre de la République, was no longer required to play as many prorevolutionary works, an interest in them was still very strong.

Pierre Gardel, La Réunion du Dix Août, *Performed Outdoors March 13, 1794, Then Indoors, Sans-Culottide, Lyrics by Philippe Moline and Gabriel Bouquier, Music by Bernardo Porta, Costumes and Sets by Jacques-Louis David, April 5, 1794, at the Opéra*

It was also performed at the Opéra-Comique, Théâtre de la Cité, and Théâtre Molière. The outdoor festivals went indoors the very day of the execution of Desmoulins and Danton. That day, April 5, 1794, also saw the opening of *La Réunion du 10 Août*. Two politicos— Gabriel Bouquier, member of the National Convention and of the Committee of Public Instruction, and Philippe Moline secretary-reporter to the Convention, collaborated on the verses. The music was by Porta, but he preferred not to have his name on the program. The receipts were to go to the Republic by decree of the Convention of November 24, 1793. In the *Bibliothèque Musicale de l'Opéra*, Lajarte says: "This inane piece was performed 24 times!!!"[48] the *Journal de Paris National* reports, however, that

> the ensemble of ballets by Gardel were worthy of what would have been expected from such an estimable artist. Its execution was beyond all praise. It was necessary that the ingenuity of Gardel created with grace and nobility the "Pas de Militaires Cannoniers," The "Rondes de Citoyens Travailleurs," "Le Ballet des Héroïnes des 5 et 6 Octobre," "des Villageois des Artisans," and, just for the most pure souls of the spectators, with the "Pas des forts de la Halle."[49]

La Réunion du Dix Août, a choral dance drama, attempts to reunite the same spirit and scenery the huge outdoor festival had previously brought together on August 10, 1793. There are some interesting facets to the *livret* of this large piece, and they shed light on the mentality of the artists working at the Opéra. For example, the massive statue of Nature at the Opéra poured water from her breasts rather than the milk originally used at the *Fête de l'Unité et de l'Indivisibilité*. The emphasis on work and workers is as apparent here as it was outdoors, as is that on Liberty, which "destroys pride, cupidity, cheating, impudence, and ignorance! The dead are soldiers and patriots, heroes in the cause for liberty and against tyranny." The Bastille is the first locale of this scenario, which speaks of incarcerated men whose hope and will were totally broken. Words left on the cell walls are revealed: "I have been dying in this cell for thirty years," and "My dear children, what has become of you?" Then choral cries demand praise for the courage of the Frenchmen who fought on the frontier in order to win liberty at home. The play goes on, daylight appears, and each act separately takes the spectator to the most important places sanctified by struggles during the Revolution.

As we have seen, women take on an increasingly important role in politics, and their participation is noted in the second act at an *arc de triomphe*. Women are seated on the cannon carriages as they were on the road to Versailles. On the arch is written, "Like a vile prey, the women have chased the tyrant before them." A heroine mounts this triumphal arch, singing that this monument will overcome the odious memory of ferocious and perverted tyrants. Like a war cry, they sing of conquering all the tyrants of Europe and freeing the enslaved peoples. References to the god Mars give him an importance he did not have in earlier *livrets*. The heroines then do a ballet that, as we might imagine, is ferocious and triumphant.[50] Before the second act ends, a group of blind people, orphans, nurses, and artisans sing out: "Do not worry, children, your parents are the nation, the Republic is your mother, you will bless the day of the Revolution." In mawkishly sentimental scenes that include the embracing of children and the honoring of parents, the action then moves on to the Place de la Révolution. A pyre is made of crowns, scepters, and coats of arms. The symbols of royalty are piled high, a fire is lit, and these evil emblems disappear. A crowd of doves flies high out of the flames; two of them settle on Liberty's skirt! A chorus sings, "A million birds have broken their chains and taken flight; again a ballet of liberty is performed."

Threats abound in these resounding choruses: "The clock of liberty sounds your last hour, tyrants, one day you will no longer exist!" Orphans parade at the Invalides shaking swords and singing. They are hopeful: "With our talents and our values, let us astonish future races." The whole choir booms out the words, "Yes, we consecrate our lives to the salvation of the state, we all swear to conquer or perish." In the last act, at the Champ de Mars, there are urns filled with the ashes of fallen soldiers, two tricolored ribbons are held, and sounds of artillery and cannon fire burst out. All eyes are fastened upon the ashes of the soldiers as "Vive la Constitution" and "Vive la République" are sung. Tremendous crowds appear onstage and dance in honor of the courageous dead and the future great deeds of the young French people: "Happy children of Mars, your blood, your life have cemented our Liberty." Cannons burst and laurel leaves fly. The famous Mlle Maillard played the heroine in the second act.

35. The Freedom of French Women (August 1791). The arrow tip reads "Freedom or Death," and her belt buckle reads "Liberty hastens Victory." Cabinet des Estampes.

Pierre Gardel, La Fête de l'Etre Suprême, *Scènes Patriotiques, Outdoors on June 8, 1794, the Same Night at the Théâtre de la Cité, Lyrics by J. G. A. Cuvelier, Music by Othon Vandenbrock, the Opéra Performed This Work on August 20, 1794*

One of the largest outdoor festivals was *La Fête de l'Etre Suprême*, which took place on June 8, 1794. The chorus of the Opéra had already begun rehearsal of a great new anthem by Chénier and Gossec when word came that the public would sing the "Hymn to the Supreme Being" and that Gossec should write new music for the verses by Desorgues. Robespierre had ordered this change, and Chénier realized that his past symphathies would not be forgiven him, even though he had burned his play *Timoléon* at the Jacobin Club. He left his home and went into hiding. The fête proved exhausting to the participants; the actors and artists of Paris, 115 in number plus 600 apprentices, had not eaten (nor had anyone else) since early morning, and they complained of the heat and hunger. "But Robespierre believed that the smell of incense was sufficient nourishment on this memorable day, and Talma and David were forced to distribute food to their companions surreptitiously to avoid attracting the attention of the Jacobins."[51] Public spirit was so fired by this event that several Parisian theatres risked the danger of anticlimax to re-create the festival in song and dance that evening, even though the actors were exhausted. According to Alfred Cobban, "At this celebration in the Jardin des Tuileries, Robespierre set fire with a torch handed to him by David to a huge cardboard figure of Atheism, which went up in flames, exposing to view a rather smoky statue of Wisdom, after which the whole of the Convention, and delegates to Sections, ascended an artificial mountain where appropriate ceremonies were performed."[52]

After Robespierre was elected president of the Convention, his supremacy, both political and ideological, was assured. On the previous May 7, he had succeeded in persuading the Convention to recognize the new religion of the Supreme Being. At the *Fête de l'Etre Suprême* on June 8, 1794, he walked at the head of the Convention. The symbols signified the accoutrements that were touted as sacerdotal in the new religion. Henri Welschinger notes that Robespierre sets

36. Fête Célébrée en l'Honneur de l'Etre Suprême (1794), *showing the tablets of the Rights of Man, the red bonnet, the republican flag, and children. "The true priest of the Supreme Being is Nature, her temple is the Universe, her cult is truth." Cabinet des Estampes.*

37. Fête de la Raison, or Festival of Reason in Honor of Philosophy *(November 10, 1793)*. *Bibliothèque de l'Arsenal.*

fire not only to "Atheism" but to all the emblems representing "les vices et les passions."[53]

The opening performance of *La Fête de l'Etre Suprême*, a celebration of a deistic god, written and performed by the Cité troupe, was to be enacted the evening of the day that was entirely devoted to the outdoor dances and ceremonies of the same *Fête de l'Etre Suprême*.[54] Lajarte lists it as a "ballet ambulatoire," featuring Robespierre and his comrades. The script was conceived by Cuvelier de Trye, the "Crébillon des Boulevards," with music by Othon Vandenbrock. In a florid dedication to his father, Cuvelier says, "Your lessons have taught me to know and to love the 'Supreme Being': your example, to serve my country well, and your virtues to flee from vice."

The chorus of the Opéra and the Institut National appeared with a mayor, a commander, a wounded soldier, a *sans-culotte*, a peasant, an old man, two women peasants, and children "des deux sexes." The tone and narrative expression of this spectacle seem different from that

Ballets of Political Passion

of the outdoor experience. The focus of the opera, like that of the outdoor festival, is directed toward a citizen's work and his love of country and the Eternal One, the new god whose worship lies in the perpetuation of revolutionary principles. An altar of grass, a Tree of Liberty, tricolor ribbons, tumbrils, urns full of wine and bread, the Constitution, the red bonnet, trousers instead of knickers, old men, and children—these are symbols for the century to come.

Peasant women sing about the "book of nature," and the mayor sings of "vile priests who are friends of kings and liars painting more lies." Children are picked up and taken to the altar of Liberty as sacrificial lambs, as "Only this god can break our chains, only Nature is the Priest, who loves virtue and a pure soul." Kings of other countries are told to beware of the French soldier—"Let George shiver," the children of France will keep their liberty. A peasant lady sings in a dialect of the village cure who used to speak of immortality in order to frighten his flock with Hell, a notion that could not have been fabricated by a just God. The dancing, mostly by children, continues throughout the piece. Once again priests are reviled for their corruption, for getting fat from their victims—a true God would not enjoy goods taken from the poor and innocent.

The end of the pageant contains a short drama to grip the attention of the spectator. A peasant girl, Adèle, and a *sans-culotte*, Tristan, are lovers who must separate so that he can fight: "to go far from one's lover is to die, but to fight and die for one's country is to be consoled." Adèle's lover Tristan goes off to war, but ironically, during the attack, it is Adèle who is hit by a bullet. As Tristan holds her, she sings that it is sweet to die in the arms of one's lover. Tristan, in a second attack, fights valiantly and becomes a hero. Adèle does not die but lives to marry Tristan and to bring a future soldier-son to the Republic. The obvious message is easy to grasp. Similar slogans had been used during the American Revolution.

Robespierre's time was up; he was unable to gather enough support for his own politics. On 9 Thermidor, he was condemned to death. On 10 Thermidor—July 28, 1794—he was executed. On July 27, 1794, the receipts from the Opéra (which had not been recorded from September 1793) are once again shown in the *Journal*. The patriotic operas, ballets, and plays were continued for awhile and attracted large audiences. In fact, *La Réunion du 10 Août*, the choral dance drama, opened the new opera house.[55]

Robespierre's death did not necessarily free the theatres of the requirement of patriotic subjects. In fact, a backlash against Jacobin power became the matter of new political themes that were explored in order to attract the public. During the closing months of 1794, the groups opposed to the Jacobins became steadily bolder and more cohesive. The young men from persecuted families formed the nucleus of this new group, but soon women, former aristocrats, and all the enemies of the "Revolutionary Canaille" joined them. This party began to adopt distinguishing colors, manners, meeting places, phrases, and dress. The gaiety and the ostentation of the old days returned with more pronounced brilliance than ever. David, who was *the* costume designer for the Revolution, inspired the women to wear pseudoclassic tunics and sandals, often with one breast exposed. The men wore large cravats, black collars, and, for those who had lost someone, black armbands. Called *muscadins* (fops) by their enemies, the so-called gilded youth demonstrated for, and cajoled, the spectators at public events and especially at the theatre.

Chevalier Peicam de Bressoles, La Fête Américaine, August 24, 1794, *at the Opéra-Comique*

Business continued as usual on the stage, and so did the proliferation of prorepublican plays. On August 24, 1794, *La Fête Américaine* was played at the Opéra-Comique. In the opening scene, a magnificent alley of trees was displayed. In their midst stood a coconut palm hung with garlands of oak leaves and tricolored ribbons, the latter fastened to the points of pikes carried by two rows of volunteers who were gathered about an altar to the *patrie*. In the foreground stood a representative of the American people carrying a scale with two children, one black and one white, balanced on it, indicating that no racial distinctions existed in that happy land.[56] The *Journal des Théâtres* speaks of this as a "patriotic dream ballet" in which a black man and a white man together hold hands around the Tree of Liberty. The scene is a forest of symbols common to Jacobin thought of this time:

Ballets of Political Passion

a black baby, a white baby, busts of Marat, Le Peletier, Barra, and Viala, a Tree of Liberty, and a goddess Liberty. In America, so suggests the Rousseauistic tradition, all distinctions are abolished; the blacks have broken their chains, which they throw away with indignation. When they hear "Death before Slavery," the whites and the blacks embrace. The ballet succeeded. There was "La Carmagnole" and some difficult variations by Mathieu-Fréderic Blasius. The critic mentions that the ballets were not well danced at the Opéra-Comique National, but that Peicam was a good choreographer.[57] Although he had a wounded arm, Peicam danced in his own ballet with grace and agility. M. Walter composed the music.[58]

Themes that dealt with events of the French Revolution were frequently performed at the theatre called the Cité-Variétés, which therefore suffered less from retaliation by any parties during the Revolution. Their company behaved as it was told and satisfied the authorities of the moment. The very night of Robespierre's fall, anti-Jacobin plays were performed there. The audience, with sighs of relief and great rejoicing, stayed in the theatre until one in the morning.[59] The morning after the fall of Robespierre, the Committee of Public Safety accepted petitions for the release of political suspects. Soon after, many of the ten thousand in this category were freed.[60]

On September 2, a premiere of the opera with dance, *La Rosière Républicaine*, opened. It had been postponed from August 31 because of an explosion of the "poudrerie de Grenelle." The proceeds of this series of revolutionary tableaux went to children and widows who had lost their men in this disaster. The dances were notable for a curé and a vicar who ripped off their habits in the course of the drama; they both appeared in *sans-culottes*, or pants, and, instead of their skull caps, put on the red bonnet of liberty. According to Valentine Gross Hugo, "The festival begins: they dance, young girls ask the vicar to dance with them, and a young shepherd engages two nuns . . . to dance the 'Carmagnole.' "[61] *La Rosière Républicaine* featured the superb Vestris, who, costumed as a *sans-culotte*, danced with two women dressed in religious habit and taught them to enjoy the pleasure of movement. "The other ballet combinations composed by Gardel," Hugo says, "were danced with the well-known talents of Citizens Goyon, Huard, Deshayes fils, etc."[62]

38. "March of the Marseillaise," sung at various theatres during intermission (1792). Cabinet des Estampes.

Ballets of Political Passion

Songs and dances of the Revolution retain the distant cadence and rumble of a meaningful revolt for us to this day. *Les Fêtes et les Chants de la Révolution Française*[63] by Julien Tiersot attempts to give the genesis of famous revolutionary songs and dances such as "La Marseillaise," "La Carmagnole," and "Ca Ira." In order to understand these songs, one must comprehend *l'esprit public*; Tiersot emphasizes the importance of *foi* and *spectacle* to the soul and the senses. Certain passwords and symbols came to denote revolutioinary faith, such as the cocarde, the tricolored ribbon, the red bonnet, and pant legs. A school of national music, largely the work of Gossec, was formed and was influential at the time. This situation is reminiscent of Russia in the early twentieth century.

Historian Julien Tiersot mentions Jacques-Louis David's designs for a funeral cortege as being of great importance. The funeral took place on the death of Viala and Barra, temporary heroes of the Revolution, on the ninth and tenth of Thermidor. On having arrived at the Place du Panthéon in a procession, singers sang regrets with plaintive accents, while dancers danced in sad or lugubrious pantomimes, using military gestures. "What a curious idea to celebrate a funeral rite with pyrrhic dances performed by Vestris and ballerinas trained in the tradition of la Camargo," Tiersot comments.[64] The singers sang of their horror of fanatics and federalists. The dancers continued their "évolutions funèbres." The monument, decorated with mourning veils, remained closed. Drums beat and cannons sounded, then the choir exclaimed that the revolutionaries were immortal. The dancers, in a gay divertissement, threw flowers on the urns, and with martial movements and positions that accompanied the music, they celebrated the glory of the two heroes. This fête united poetry, dance, and music—which, of course, was an ideal of classical antiquity. One wonders how such obviously inferior productions could induce patriotism and rally victories on the battlefronts—but they did!

In January 1795, important battles were won at Amsterdam. In April, the provinces on the west bank of the Rhine were declared French; in October, Coblenz and Cologne were secured. Nine new departments were ceded to France by Belgium and Holland. The Opéra also continued to play the republican fare. The audiences were tumultuous because of the *muscadins*, or *jeunesse dorée*, who inces-

39. Vue de la Montagne Elevée au Champ de la Réunion, *or* View of the Mountain Built on the Champ de la Réunion (June 8, 1794). Cabinet des Estampes.

santly interrupted performances and entr'actes. On July 14, 1795, when the "Hymne des Marseillais" was played, the elegant young ruffians insisted that the "Réveil du Peuple" be sung (music by Pierre Gaveaux, words by J. M. Souriguière). The "Réveil du Peuple" symbolized furious Royalist sentiments, a mixture of the mourning and angry emotions of rich children who had lost their right to rule. The summer before the Directory assumed power in October 1795, a new Constitution had been adopted, and the Directory's rule established some important services for the arts, notably a conservatory and school for professions in the arts.

Because daily expenses mounted as a result of inflation in 1795, the Opéra renewed old ballets, including *Mirza* (January 22), *Télémaque*, *La Rosière*, *Psyché*, *Le Premier Navigateur*, and *Le Déserteur* (April 1), and *La Chercheuse* (July 6). Most of the patriotic chorals ceased after the playing of *L'Offrande à la Liberté* on February 16. Dancers performed at least eighteen times a month, and no doubt

Ballets of Political Passion

they suffered as much as most Parisians during this period of economic privation. No new ballets were presented at the Opéra until 1800, when Gardel created *La Dansomanie*. The pleasure-seeking crowds and "gilded youth" of the Directory relished the adventures of anti-Jacobin Arlequin plays and pantomimes common to the boulevard theatres. Dissatisfied with politics, the audiences continued to upset the action onstage. Agitation increased rapidly until October 5, when a major insurrection broke out—the first since those inspired by patriots in April and May. According to Marvin Carlson, "Napoleon, attending a production at the Théâtre Feydeau, learned of the disturbance and went to the Convention to volunteer his services. The young Napoleon was placed second in command to Barras to put down the revolt."[65] After this event a decree of the Convention suppressed the gatherings of the *jeunesse dorée*.

Anger was also directed toward those who found themselves abetting a fruitless cause. David was thought to be a traitor and had to go to jail for four months during the Thermidorian reaction, in part because he was director of the outdoor pageants for the Committee of Public Safety.[66] David wrote a letter on May 30, 1795, denying any participation in the Terror. He says that "I devoted myself with enthusiasm to the defence of freedom. Several of my companions strayed from the path of justice, polluting the spring of pure patriotism . . . committing criminal excesses."[67] David designed uniforms for republican functionaries and created the costumes and scenery for the fêtes; he says, "I was indeed a member of the Comité de Sûreté général, but everyone knows that I rarely went to meetings, that I never submitted a report. It is also known that I was, at the same time, a member of the 'Comité d'Instruction publique' and that I was responsible for the supervision of the work done in the Jardin National and for the organization of fêtes decreed at various seasons by the Convention."[68]

The fêtes continued to be produced under the Directory, though less frequently. Scenic innovations, such as the mountain in the *Fête de l'Etre Suprême* (which was worthy of the Cirque-Olympique), were transposed to the Opéra stage, where improvements were made in the technical features of design. The crowds loved to march in the processions. When the president of the Convention spoke, they would echo his key words in a soaring, liturgical manner.

Chevalier Peicam de Bressoles, La Fête de l'Agriculture, June 18, 1796

One of the last outdoor patriotic processions, *La Fête de l'Agriculture* (June 28, 1796), was organized by another director, Antoine-Marie Pèyre. It was so grandiose that the so-called *fêtes villageoises* of the nineteenth century could be said to have been patterned on it. Included were statues, chariots, children, and young girls, all decorated with flowers, leaves, baskets of fruit—anything that symbolized farm life or agricultural crops. At the end of this festival, the president of the Convention traced a furrow around the statue of Liberty and of Agriculture, while a ballet and a chorale were performed to the music of Jean-Jacques Rousseau. Horses, in the style of Franconi's group, performed evolutions and fancy stepping (which later inspired the Cirque-Olympique). Winter notes that David must be credited with "important innovations that were gradually incorporated into the theatre: the development of *praticables* or lifelike movable stage sets, altars, temples, which he knew how to imbue with a fine authenticity, the designs of combat and battles, as well as ballets, or parades that were slow symbolic processions."[69] The nineteenth-century ballet would know how to utilize these remarkable devices.

9
THE TREE OF LIBERTY

Outside France, during the government of the Directory, Bonaparte was busy achieving military victories and creating his image as a hero at a time when France was seeking a new leader. In November 1796, Napoleon defeated the Austrians at Arcola, and routed them again in January 1797 at Rivoli. In May 1797, Bonaparte occupied Venice, and his name became important in the French capital. In May 1798, he departed on the famous Egyptian expedition, and in July he was victorious in the Battle of Pyramids. Unfortunately, his navy could not compete with Nelson's, and Bonaparte returned defeated and without his fleet in August 1798. In spite of the embarrassment, he brought extravagant booty home to Paris, which pleased the French. Heavy convoys of bullion and works of art arrived in Paris as the first fruits of the Italian victory. After Bonaparte was defeated in Egypt, another coalition against France was formed in 1799 by Russia, Britain, Turkey, and Austria. Once again, France feared invasion and further humiliations and defeats.

Under the Directory, the Opéra, whose business affairs were disastrous and disorderly, was run by a committee formed to oversee the administration and accounting. A decree was passed by the Directory on February 2, 1797, asking that closer ties be established between the government and the Opéra. It was renamed Théâtre de la République et des Arts. Francoeur, who had been jailed during the Terror, returned to head the new administration. Interested in appeasing the government, Francoeur mounted Rouget de Lisle's *Chant des Vengeances*,[1] in May 1798, but the public was not interested in a new "Marseillaise," and the work failed.

The main concern of the ballets and fêtes of this time was to instill national pride or patriotism in the public and to teach the audience lessons in civic duties at a time when France was beleaguered. The scenarios may not have been finely tailored to please the artistic taste of the literate, but that was not the principal purpose of the arts as far as the government was concerned. To maintain the ardent fervor for France among the Parisians, great spectacles, processions, and parades had to be provided.

In the theatre, the emphasis of the stories was upon large crowds who demonstrated their passion for the principles and ideals of the Revolution—"Liberté," "Egalité," and "Fraternité." These ideals, which were plastered on governmental buildings and revealed in the Declaration of the Rights of Man, were seen as universal, applying to the downtrodden everywhere. The *livrets* were ready to uphold the victims of tyranny: slaves, Indian natives, peasants, and blacks in particular. The church was pictured as corrupt. Thus, the new leaders called upon Roman history to become the tie to an acceptable past. Outdoors, in large spaces, there is room enough for everyone to play a role. Songs of victory and military heroism replaced saints' days. There was no shame in attacking the clergy as well as the aristocracy—peasants could now be free of the threat of court and church that had traditionally been imposed on them.

Another common trait of these scenarios was the exaltation of family ties. Woman was the symbol of motherhood and nature; she created and affirmed the cycles of life. Significantly, she also represented courage and defiance; she was often the heroine of the narrative, the valiant defender of men. It is not surprising, therefore, that France and Liberty were pictured during the Revolution as strong and daring women. Children, France's future, also played large roles in the *livrets*, saving their parents from danger and thereby implying a renaissance of revolutionary courage.

The Tree of Liberty

Accompanying these major characters were the new symbols of the Revolution that prepared the viewer for a changed value system and a semiotic imagery of the Revolution. People danced and held hands around trees of liberty, black man and white man together. There they danced ritualistically in a latter-day paganism, with altars, flags, cocardes, red bonnets, urns, weapons of the aristocracy, branches of cypresses, and figures of Nature, Reason, and Liberty—these were the props of a new religion invented by the young radicals. Evil insignias of the *ancien régime*, such as coats of arms, crowns, and the accoutrements of the clergy, disappeared from the stage. As has been said, costumes reflected the mode of pseudo-Roman society, even in its decadence, both on and off the stage. With the demise of Robespierre, the wronged upper classes and aristocrats heaved a sigh of relief at finding themselves alive and not in prison and dressed in Roman tunics, often with one breast exposed, or in outlandish silks and brocades with feathers and colors meant to shock the passerby. They dressed to kill, these *muscadins*. Even more shocking, they attended evening celebrations called *bals à la victime* to which only blood relatives of guillotine victims were invited. The women wore red ribbons around their throats as an all-too-obvious reminder of the blade. During the dance, one shook one's head back and forth as if it were about to roll off."[2] Although a tiny minority, they were a visible sign of the blacklash in sentiment as people recoiled from the excesses of terror.

The *livrets* were carefully designed to say nothing against the prevailing government. Censorship, the bane of artists at all times, was particularly harsh at this period. Still, ballet and pantomime were at a distinct advantage, since there were no spoken words. As we have seen, the creators of ballet and pantomime, in order to survive, were tuned into the events that shaped the political climate. The heart of the political *livrets*, thin story lines based upon historical events or allegorical themes, suggested that there would be spontaneous rewards for the worship of revolutionary principles. They did not contribute to the expressiveness in ballet that Noverre and his disciples demanded. Rather, they represented ephemeral impositions by the political authorities and were not rooted in the artistic currents of the time. The

Revolutionary Spirit

livret for *La Contre-Révolution*, a ballet that was perhaps never played, indicates the extraordinary importance of the moments, of the names and events of actuality. Generals falling off ladders, and moderate politicians killing kings—these episodes represented material not destined to live beyond the moment.

The pageants did have an important effect, however. The Revolution, a popular revolt, brought the public to participate actively with the actors onstage. The rapport between audience and performers became closer and more rousing. Work and worker were extolled. The individual at home, on the farm, became an essential cog in the wheel of government. These people, too, fought for freedom, though not on the battlefield. Choruses of women sang of overcoming tyrants and the freeing of slaves. They chanted and danced songs that struck their sense of pride, such as "La Marseillaise," "La Carmagnole," and "Ca Ira."[3] To this day, the Frenchman is moved by the strains of these popular songs that recall the difficult class struggle of a people.

Part IV
REDISCOVERY OF THE COMMONPLACE

10
THEATRE AESTHETICS AND THE BALLET

The ballets in part IV deal with stories close to everyday life, reflecting an innovative trend in ballet that was inspired to a large extent by theatrical reforms. Popular ideas in the theatre were far ahead of those in ballet choreography, despite the cries for change by Noverre, Angiolini, and Cahusac. The eighteenth-century audience was attracted to theatre and to the new dramatics of Denis Diderot (1713–84) and Pierre Augustin de Beaumarchais (1732–99). These two dissimilar geniuses created a public taste for character study and authenticity that had been previously disavowed by the court. Naturally, these playwrights inherited Molière's appetite for satire, especially of the middle classes and their aggressive interest in fashion. The aesthetics of the *drame bourgeois*, or *drame sérieux*, were predicated upon a clear analysis of social struggle. Diderot's *Le Fils Ingrat*, or *The Ungrateful Son* (1757), told of domestic situations filled with pathos and moralistic messages rather than of the violent deaths of heroic tragedy. Beaumarchais' plays *The Barber of Seville* (1775) and *The Marriage of Figaro* (1784) also appealed to middle-class audiences, as they ridiculed class structure and comically defended bourgeois and peasant virtues such as patriotism, religion, love, and the acquisition of hard-earned money. Figaro epitomizes the French self-conscious defiance of a powerful

Rediscovery of the Commonplace

ruling class built like a fortress around him—he is clearly a character worthy of the Revolution.

Both Diderot and Beaumarchais were influenced by the subject matter and technique of the Italian comedians who catered to popular audiences of the eighteenth century. Italian comedians toured regularly in France and were common performers at the fairs. Their tradition of farce and satire, improvised with the help of pantomime, brought vitality to plots. Several important French writers contributed their plays to the Italian repertoire: Pierre de Marivaux (1688–1763), Louis Sebastien Mercier (1740–1814), and Charles Favart (1710–92), director of the Opéra-Comique. Favart and his wife were responsible for three of the scenarios of the ballets in this chapter: *La Chercheuse d'Esprit* (1741), *Annette et Lubin* (1743), and *La Fille Mal Gardée* (?). It was due to the actress-dancer, Favart's wife, Mlle Chantilly, that lyric types of opera, adapted from Italian models, were instituted at the Opéra-Comique and later became French comic opera. Mlle Chantilly was also a bold reformer in matters of stage costume, playing the peasant with bare arms, in wooden shoes and linen dress, rather than in traditional court costume with enormous hoops, diamonds, and long white kid gloves.

The productions of the Opéra-Comique, which merged with the Comédie-Italienne in 1762, attracted innovative choreographers; Noverre often worked for them. Not surprisingly, like the dramatists Diderot and Beaumarchais, these choreographers sought fresh ideas outside the stuffy nationalized and subsidized theatres. The Opéra continued to play the stories of old mythic war-horses, such as *Oedipus at Colonus*, *Iphiginia at Taurus*, and *Phèdre*. At the Opéra-Comique, they performed funny, down-to-earth musical comedy and, during the Revolution, critical, political comic reviews. Catchy tunes, stories with popular appeal, and happy endings were the fare for *citoyens*. They found relaxation in dangerous times, as well as Gallic wit that exploited the traditions of farce and parody so beautifully done by the Italians. Also, the vices and foibles of everyday domestic life were burlesqued and caricatured. Such comedies differed from the grand opera done at the Académie Royale and the Opéra not only in subject matter but also in alternation of spoken dialogue with songs and music and in

Theatre Aesthetics and the Ballet

the frequent insertion of tableaux with pantomime to provide clarity and energy for a theatrical moment. The power that the Italian players wielded over dramatic and choreographic ideas cannot be underestimated; their physicality, spontaneous energy, honesty, and authenticity in stories about people close to eighteenth-century life all brought a greater sense and sensibility to the pre-Romantic stages.

Another important type of drama in the late eighteenth century was the "tragedy of the masses," a new genre that alternately frightened and charmed the observer. These *mélodrames* were tragic in their dealing with life-threatening situations or other serious themes, but they always had happy endings. Women in distress (usually peasants or bourgeoises), terrifying or sentimental plot lines that evoked exaggerated responses, and scenes of prisons and crowded battles typified this melodramatic theatre.

The word "melodrama" is said to have first been used in 1766 by Rousseau in a critique of an opera by Gluck in which music interrupted the dialogue. Later in the early nineteenth century, the term was not applied to opera but rather to plays with pantomime, music, and heavy scenery. When Rousseau used the term "melodrama" in reference to his own composition *Pygmalion* (1762), he was experimenting with the mixing of genres (pantomime, ballet, music, and drama) in order to discover a more touching and meaningful entertainment. Pantomimes were a popular dramatic form, not only because they used a broad, dynamic movement technique with obvious gesturing, but also because they were relatively unthreatened by the censorship rules that became increasingly stringent before and during the Revolution.

The theatre of pantomime before the Revolution tended to concern itself with the amusement of the popular audience, in a farcical style without a strong story line, as we have seen in the case of the Italian players. During the Revolution, pantomime—occasionally with spoken dialogue and melodrama—became associated and developed into a more challenging art form in which serious stories were told with striking action and sets. The coarse directness often seen in the pantomimes at the fair theatres was replaced by boulevard theatre performances in which moralism and sanguine optimism prevailed in a world of extreme horror or extreme joy. These elements, though more

Rediscovery of the Commonplace

muted in revolutionary ballet *livrets*, hint of the expression that would develop into the Gothic scenes of the Romantic nineteenth-century ballet.

Some of the ballets discussed in the next chapter show an inflated sense of expressive violence. There are also battles with more realistic drama that depict indoor and outdoor scenes worthy of painters such as Greuze and Chardin. In addition, there are love plots that take place in strange, faraway places, where familiar characters from France find themselves pitted against exotic settings. Discoveries of new worlds in the sixteenth century provoked theatre and ballet pieces that suggested alternate forms of existence. Were people in foreign places any less evil because they had not been corrupted by the political and social systems of Western Europe? If man in a civilized state, is less good and less happy than man in a savage state, as the eighteenth-century world view often suggested, then perhaps the only hope is love. The wish to fantasize true love may explain the interest of revolutionary audiences in these dramatic and sentimental ballet scenarios.

11
REALISTIC BALLETS, 1787–1801

In this chapter, we meet the farmer, the carpenter, the merchant, the cobbler, the shopkeeper, and the pastoral romantic lover and villain. These are the protagonists of revolutionary ballet as well as the unsung heroes of the Revolution. In the realistic ballets, there is a new focus on sentiment, the innocent soul at grips with the cruel, and comic, everyday struggles in which love wins and everyone dances for joy.

Maximilien Gardel, La Chercheuse d'Esprit, Ballet-Pantomime, Revived January 1787, at the Opéra.

La Chercheuse d'Esprit, or A Young Woman in Search of Her Wits, was created in 1777 and then revived in 1795.[1] With a provocative, but essentially comic, story, the ballet is light in tone though it is a bit ironic. As usual, all ends happily—in this case, when the ingenue, Nicette, triumphantly discovers her wits and an appropriate lover as well.

The subject of this ballet is taken from the comic opera of the same name by Favart, with its setting in a village home belonging to Madame Madré, a rich lady farmer and the mother of Nicette. The ballet begins with Nicette, a simple beauty, dancing a lovely caper. She is so involved in her movements that any disturbance upsets her. M. Subtil enters and tries to frighten her. When he begins to declare his love for her, she laughs in his face and starts to run off. But he holds her arm and continues to profess his love for her. Madame Madré enters, sees the man on his knees, and laughs, telling him that he cannot possibly adore such a backward girl. The old Subtil begs the mother for Nicette's hand in marriage; he assures her that he prefers a simple woman for a wife to a coquette who would torment him endlessly. The handsome Alain appears and warmly converses with Nicette; this disturbs the mother and she immediately decides to marry Nicette to the clever, if aging, M. Subtil. She arranges a meeting in order to write up the contracts: one for her own unlikely union with the young Alain, the other for Nicette with M. Subtil.

This plan sends Nicette into a desperate state; she paces here and there, trying to figure out a solution to the terrible problem. A savant, M. Narquois, ambles along reading a book, cursing what he seems to be reading. She bows with a grand curtsy and asks him how one can acquire some wits. She tells him that she is searching for a clever mind and is willing to pay for it. M. Narquois (whose name means cunning and sly) smiles at this request, which hurts the feelings of Nicette. He reassures her that if she reads some good books she might improve her mind and lends her the book he is reading. When she drops it by mistake, he becomes angry and leaves.

Like the lead character in Molière's *Les Fâcheux*, Nicette constantly encounters different types of people. The next person is L'Eveillé, who, when asked to help, takes advantage of her innocence and tries to embrace her. He receives his just desserts when he is caught in the act by Finette, his girl friend, who leads him off. Then Nicette spots Alain, who seems very pleased to see her. They decide to go to Paris to seek a clever mind (*esprit*), ready for their exciting adventure.

Unfortunately, the shrewd mother ruins these plans. She sends Nicette back to her home and retains Alain for her own purposes. Mistaking Alain's coldness for innocence in the art of paying court, Mme Madré sets about teaching Alain how to display his affection to his lover. Enchanted by this lesson, Alain thanks the older woman; showing her how well he has learned, he kneels and kisses her hand.

Nicette also finds a teacher. She observes how Finette, in a sweet love scene with Eveillé, gently attracts the young man. When Alain arrives, he demonstrates the lessons Mme Madré has skillfully taught him. He kneels, presents Nicette with a ribbon, and speaks of his passion for her. Mme Madré enters with M. Subtil, Eveillé, and Finette. They separate Alain and Nicette, but when Finette and Eveillé insist that the lovers belong together, everyone realizes how stupid it would be to prevent this union. The three couples, appropriately matched at last, are married, and a celebratory dance concludes the ballet.[2]

In a new twist on the theme of the education of an innocent young girl, the heroine of *La Chercheuse*, Nicette, gradually acquires the wiles and coquettish qualities befitting a French lady. Unfortunately, her mother, Mme Madré, seems an unattractive model to emulate. Mme Madré's abilities as a rich landowner, however, and her acuity in manipulating people perhaps appealed to a middle-class public and explains why audiences of the Revolution enjoyed this ballet. The lead roles demand interesting performances by the women. The ingenue must be a versatile actress, while the mother, both cunning and selfish, is part villain, part comic character. Inevitably, love—helped out by the necessary *esprit*, or wit—triumphs in the end.

In addition to the insular, salon world of French society, a rich source of exotic plots for ballets and pantomimes was the scientific exploration of far corners of the earth during the seventeenth and eighteenth centuries. The *livrets* borrowed material from novels and plays with exotic backgrounds, travel journals, missionary letters such as the *Lettres Edifiantes* of the Jesuits, and even scientific articles. Journals of exploration brought faraway lands such as Asia, America, and Africa closer to home. These countries, previously lost in space and time, became the setting for a new theatre.[3]

Maximilien Gardel, La Fête du Sérail, Ballet-Pantomime
March 9, 1788, Panthéon

One of the first revolutionary *livrets* with a truly exotic setting takes place in the land of seraglios, where veiled women in hothouse intrigues evoke passionate and strange loves. *La Fête du Sérail*, or *The Harem Party*, was performed March 9, 1788, at the Panthéon in Paris.[4] Though the name of the choreographer is not printed, Noverre's name is handwritten next to the title. It seems unlikely that Noverre was

40. *Perspective view of the Panthéon (1796). Bibliothèque de l'Opéra.*

responsible for this *livret*, however, because he composed a ballet on the same theme called *Les Jalousies, ou Les Fêtes du Sérail*, or *Jealousy, or The Harem Party*, with quite a different plot.[5] Tales of seraglios and Muslim manners were very popular in France since the publication of various travel books such as the journals of Tavernier (1676–79), who went to Turkey, Persia, and the Indies. Perhaps the most important inspiration for *livrets* with seraglios as a setting was *Les Lettres Persanes* by Montesquieu. It tells the tale of two Persians, Usbek and Rica, who visited Paris from 1712 to 1720. They exchanged letters, writing to different friends in order to share their impressions and receive news of Persia, particularly of Usbek's seraglio in Ispahan. Though Montesquieu's ideas are presented to point up the political problems existing in France at the time, the story of disorder in the Persian seraglio gripped the imaginations of the readers.

In *La Fête du Sérail*,[6] the intrigues of the harem are complicated by the presence of the sultan's child, who is used by the so-called Favorite in order to excite deeper feelings in the sultan for her. But the sultan takes no joy from life; even the distraction of dances by lovely harem women does not perk him up. Suddenly, the passionate entrance of Almaide, a facinating dancer, arouses his blood. La Favorite becomes incensed and jealous, lifting up the child to demonstrate the importance of their union, but he is deaf to *la voix de la nature* (the voice of nature).

After a time, vengeance is threatened when the eunuch brings in another stunning woman, Zulime, who, now that his appetite had been whetted, also interests the fickle sultan. The old wife, La Favorite, and the newly spurned mistress, Almaide, join forces to avenge the affronts they have both received. They plan to murder the new slave, Zulime. About to plunge a dagger into Zulime, La Favorite is discovered and put in prison. Finally, the child appeals to his father for his mother's life and informs the sultan that the new slave, Zulime, has a husband who is also imprisoned and that he, too, should be freed. The child succeeds in his mission. Both Athénor, Zulime's husband, and La Favorite rejoice in having their chains removed, and each family is reunited.

Dances of an Oriental nature were performed throughout the ballet, but even in this setting, the historic values of the Christian world were reaffirmed and demonstrated to be "the good": the enduring belief in family, the fear of sensuality as a guiding mode of life, the caution exercised when there is disorder or chaos in a domain, and the public's dislike for prisons and captivity.[7] Perhaps more importantly, the novel and significant presence of a child onstage brought a freshness and clarity to the new realism of eighteenth-century ballet. The theme of revolt in the seraglio was brought to the Paris Opéra stage again in 1833 by Filippo Taglioni in *La Révolte au Sérail*, which was danced by his daughter Marie. It had eighty-one performances in the seven years that it played in the repertoire.

Maximilien Gardel, Mirza, Ballet d'Action, Performed August 19, 1788, at the Opéra

From the wondrous decor of a "Scheherazade" seraglio, we travel to the more austere background of an American island at the time of the American Revolution for the setting of *Mirza*. This ballet was originally performed in 1779 at Versailles before the king. Revised and staged in London in 1782, it was again revived—this time by Pierre Gardel—at the Opéra in 1788. It continued to draw large crowds until the time of Robespierre, when it was dropped. It returned after his fall in January 1795. Middle-class French and American colonials, blacks, Creoles, and soldiers all figured in the case of this timely sentimental tale.[8] Not as innocent as Paul and Virginie nor as complex as Chactas and Atala, the heroine, Mirza, and the hero, Lindor, a colonel in the French army, are presented as young lovers whose destiny at the outset seems as dark as that of Romeo and Juliet.

The ballet opens as Mirza, a well-educated young French lady, is about to give a concert. Her parents, the Mondors, have betrothed her to a corsaire officer, a high-ranking privateer who may really be a pirate. But Mirza is attracted by the romantic personality of Lindor, which is demonstrated when he woos her during the concert and daringly sneaks her a billet-doux asking her to run away with him later in the evening. A meeting place near a bridge in the rural countryside is the scene for their secret encounter; he is late and begs her forgiveness. The noise of combat and fearful sounds can be heard in the distance. Black soldiers are about to attack a French officer who seems desperate and about to surrender. Lindor takes his sword and assaults the assassins, forcing them to retreat. The victimized French officer is none other than the corsaire, who, though deeply appreciative of Lindor's bravery, is shocked by the identity of his liberator. Realizing that Mirza must love Lindor, the corsaire becomes angry and jealous. They beg him to keep their meeting a secret, but he does not promise to do so.

Lindor then leaves to rejoin his regiment and Mirza returns home, clasping her miniature painting of Lindor to her heart, worried and distraught about their future. Suddenly, the corsaire intercepts her on the way home and speaks of his profound love for her. When she rejects his advances, he grabs her companion, a black woman, threatening to arrest her and to take away Mirza. Mirza escapes from him, screaming as he pursues her. Lindor, hearing her cries, rushes to the scene and leaps on the corsaire. In their struggle, Lindor kills the corsaire. Not seeing Mirza, Lindor goes in search of her. In a scene reminiscent of *Romeo and Juliet*, Mirza arrives to find the dead corsaire. She sees Lindor's hat, blood on the ground, and his sword. Believing him to be dead, she considers jumping into the sea. She collapses in tears, alternately sobbing and looking at his portrait. In despair, Mirza raises her hands to the skies, takes Lindor's sword and places the hilt on the ground, preparing to fall, in the Roman manner, on his blade. Lindor discovers her in time to stop her suicide, whereupon Mirza faints, overwhelmed by this excess of emotion. He carries her back, still unconscious, to her parents and asks their forgiveness for having harmed her. When she awakens, the Mondors have given their consent to the marriage of their daughter to Lindor. A large celebration in the garden exhibits a grand spectacle of feasting Americans, Creoles, and blacks, as Lindor's regiment, in colorful panoply, and a corps of Americans, march in. Drums, cannons, and military songs resound, as the piece ends in a lively *contredanse*.

Unlike love stories that take place near battlefields, another genre called the pastoral ballet reappeared on the Paris stages. The history of rustic stories or pastoral ballet in France parallels the development of Baroque theatre of the period, which imported the pastoral genre from Italy and Spain. Sannazaro's *Arcadia*, Tasso's *Aminta*, and Guarini's *Pastor Fido* were translated from the Italian and *Diana de Montemayor* from the Spanish between 1554 and the end of the sixteenth century. These pastorals consist largely of long tirades and laments, with a minor amount of dramatic action. Alexandre Hardy (1570?–?1631) introduced more action into his pastoral dramas such as *Marianne*. Honoré d'Urfé, famous for his sentimental romance, *L'Astrée*, influenced many writers in the early seventeenth century. Baroque pastoral plays such as *Les Vendangeurs de Suresne* (1635) by Pierre de Reyer introduced an element of threat and terror that we see recaptured in the eighteenth-century pastorals that bordered on melodrama.

Ballets (often borrowed from pastoral dramas) were numerous. For example, Molière produced *La Pastorale Comique* a comedy with music, songs and ballet (1666) for a royal festival. Later pastoral ballets were melodramatic, elements of the sinister and the frightening become increasingly apparent. These qualities, with the addition of supernatural elements, reemerged later in *La Sylphide* (1832) and *Giselle* (1841). The mood of mysterious, shadowy, and fearful destiny so characteristic of Romantic ballet may be said to have its roots in the Baroque ballet that pastoral ballet absorbed and changed. The pastorals juxtaposed the rustic idyllic world and an evil gloom, without the intervention of the gods; often, scenes of comic relief were added. Intense emotions, dramatic pantomime, threats to the very lives of peasant heroines by wealthy suitors—all changed the nature of late eighteenth-century pastoral ballets.

Jean Dauberval, Le Ballet de la Paille, ou Il n'est qu'un pas du Mal au Bien, Ballet-Comique-Pantomime, July 1, 1789, Bordeaux

On the eve of the storming of the Bastille, Dauberval mounted his work in Bordeaux at the Grand Théâtre. Now called *Le Fille Mal Gardée*, or *The Poorly Guarded Young Lady*, the ballet belongs to the long tradition of pastoral romance and drama, but its tone and focus are realistic and humorous rather than overly dramatic and sentimental.[9] The vogue of Mme Favart's comic operas was not lost upon Dauberval. Like the middle-class Mondors of the ballet *Mirza*, the

Realistic Ballets

wily farmer widow Ragotte of *La Fille* worries that her daughter will not marry successfully.

The theme of *La Fille Mal Gardée*, a *ballet comique*, clearly resembles a comic opera of the time. The setting for the ballet takes place on the widow Ragotte's farmland. The word "ragotte" means little horse, or short and stocky. Her name has since been refined to the widow Simone. The opening of the ballet immediately throws the spectator into the busy activities of a farm. Lison, the young daughter of Ragotte, is seen leaving her house and seems to be waiting for someone. She opens the stable door and brings a pot of cream to a family of chickens. Then, she takes a ribbon from her blouse, hangs it at the end of a tree branch near the barn, and tiptoes back to her house. Soon after, a farmer, Colas, who is followed by some workers, looks around and beckons his reapers to leave. He then sneaks back to Lison's house but notices Lison's ribbon and stops to hold it to his heart and kiss it rapturously. Attaching the ribbon to a baton that symbolizes his family's coat of arms, he rushes to sit under Lison's window. There he proceeds to display his adoration for this charming lady by sending her kisses. Unfortunately, the ever-vigilant Ragotte sees his pantomime and angrily throws her hat at him while preparing to plunge her salad basket on his head. Lison furtively makes signs urging him to run away. Colas manages to dodge Ragotte as well as the flying objects. But on his way, he steals a kiss from Lison's hand.

The love theme is briefly interrupted by a group of peasants who are looking for work. Ragotte agrees to hire them after a satisfactory price is reached, and she hands each of them a scythe. Returning to the question of the new boyfriend under Lison's window, Ragotte demands an explanation from Lison as to why she is encouraging this young farmer. Meanwhile, Colas is playing a hide-and-seek game behind the mother and daughter. Ragotte chastises Lison and slaps her hand. She thinks that by insisting Lison stay on the farm, she will avoid her new lover. But Lison is not really "grounded," as Colas never leaves the farm. They meet surreptitiously in a charming encounter in which they declare their tentative and incipient love for one another. Lison attaches her ribbon to Colas' coat, whereupon he attempts to seize a kiss from her, but "she is too clever to give her lover what only belongs to a husband." With this moralistic reminder, the scene is suspended, and a group of young farm workers arrive to coax Lison into helping with the harvest, as if this task were a delight and a privilege. She declines, and Ragotte criticizes Lison's lack of enthusiasm for her chores. These chidings quiet when two new characters of some importance appear on the farm. Thomas, a wealthy winegrower, and Alain, his son, have obviously been invited for the serious business of arranging a marriage between Lison and Alain. A large celebration lunch attended by all the reapers and friends seals the engagement. Dances, rounds, and clinking of glasses are sadly witnessed by Colas, who watches these glad tidings with immense distress.

In act 2, Ragotte and Lison occupy the stage in an indoor scene that shows them at work with the spinning wheel and distaff. Eventually, when Ragotte falls asleep, Lison tries to steal the key so that she can see Colas. The reapers have finished their work and arrive to collect their wages. Lison escapes to the attic, where Colas is hiding, and then "a painful battle between love and virtue troubles the young lady." She tries to do some spinning, but tears begin to flow from her eyes. Colas rushes to dry them with his scarf, and they embrace. They hear Ragotte and run behind some furniture. With her eagle eye, she sees the scarf and wonders to whom it belongs. In a typical denouement, all the characters enter the stage. A notary decides that "il n'est qu'un pas du mal au bien," i.e., "it is but a short step from the bad to the good," and the real lovers come forward to announce their undying love and their plans to marry. Thus, propriety is upheld. A general divertissement terminates this most happy ending.

Dauberval enjoyed putting characters with a certain wit and earthiness on stage:

> In the history of ballet, *La Fille Mal Gardée* holds a special importance. It may not have been the first ballet in which common people were depicted in a realistic fashion, but it was the most successful and has therefore survived to represent ballet's emancipation from the artificial style of the eighteenth century, with its preoccupations with gods and heroes of classical legend and its tendency to sentimentalize.[10]

Realistic Ballets

The ballet's success was due to its accurate portrait of peasants or farm people as well as its well-designed intrigue that kept the action flowing smoothly. Through the course of the ballet, the young protagonists, Lison and Colas, move jauntily through their amusing situations in order to meet one another, while the mother, Ragotte-Simone, does her best to arrange a marriage with Alain, the winegrower's son. The fairs brought characters and situations of this kind to the public, and some moments that remind us of a Chardin painting, such as Ragotte's throwing her skullcap at Colas' nose when she catches him trying to see her daughter, raising her fist at Colas, snarling at Lison, and scolding them both. Many scenes from everyday farm life occur, reminding us that these people are real: food baskets are carried here and there, butter churners do their vital work, pots of cream are put in their rightful places, laborers haul farm tools through vast fields, and spinning wheels and distaffs occupy important spaces in the home. All these indications of farm life bring us into closer contact with the real world of the French peasant, as opposed to the idealized world of perfect shepherdesses such as might be seen in Watteau's *Fêtes Galantes* or in Marie-Antoinette's dairy farm, where the ladies dressed in satins and brocades. Though Ragotte initially envisioned a good match in the wealthy Alain (often played as a simpleton), realism ultimately triumphed when she also understood that Lison loved Colas and that love, not money, should win out.

The ballet received its present title from the London production in 1791 at the Panthéon. It was presented in Paris in 1803 at the Porte Saint-Martin, and in 1828 at the Opéra, Jean Aumer revived *La Fille* with a different score by Hérold.[11] New choreography has brought a freshness and vitality to *La Fille*, which is kept in the repertoire of several contemporary ballet companies.

Citoyen Beaupré, Annette et Jacques, ou Les Semestriers, Alsaciens, Ballet-Pantomime, November 12, 1792 at the Théâtre de la Gaîté

In *Annette et Jacques*, or *The Alsacian Tenant Farmers*, war enters the bucolic farm setting, as it did in reality in most Frenchmen's lives. Citizen Beaupré situated his ballet in Alsace and included the presence of a lubricious *bourgmestre*, mayor of the canton, who wishes to steal Annette and make her his wife.[12] Beaupré dedicated his ballet to Pierre Gardel and asked for his help, patience, indulgence, and advice. A comic dancer at the Opéra until 1818, Beaupré also mounted this ballet at the popular boulevard theatre, Cité-Variétés.

As the ballet opens, two young peasant lovers, Annette and Jacques, vow eternal fidelity, as they have assumed, since their birth, that they will one day be married. Julien, the father of the boy, sends his son to train with his old regiment, while Moyer, the father of Annette, sees this event as a chance to marry Annette to a wealthy *bourgmestre* who is old and unattractive. The peaceful peasant village in Alsace witnesses Jacques' return with his corps of dragoons. When he learns of his fiancée's intended marriage, Jacques is shocked and dismayed, especially that a "little gold could be the reason for her infidelity." In the middle of the night, dressed as a dragoon, the absurd *bourgmestre* attempts to steal Annette from her thatched hut. Aware of this ruse, Jacques also puts on a disguise, as a lady with an enormous cape covering most of his body and head, and plants himself where Annette should be located. The *bourgmestre* carries off Jacques and, when he is uncovered, tries to fight, but Jacques charges at the old man with his sword. Not to be vanquished, the cowardly *bourgmestre* hides behind a tree, takes out his gun, and fires but misses Jacques. An ensuing fight shames the *bourgmestre*, and the dragoon uniform he has profaned is ripped off of him. Though he is permitted to live, his reputation is ruined. The lovers are united with their parents' approval.

The brave dragoon reminds us that, in 1792, vicious wars were being fought on several frontiers, and plays, pantomimes, and ballets were commonly set on the Rhine and the border. Audiences were delighted to participate in the war effort, even by watching a fairly lighthearted ballet, and the papers were positive in their judgments of it. Well-designed formations, graceful pictures, tastefully chosen music, and unique set designs assured this ballet a brilliant destiny.[13]

Sebastien Gallet, Les Circonstances Embarrassantes, *Ballet Roman, 1796, at the Grand Théâtre de Bordeaux*

Set far from a French border town, the next *livret* takes its exotic African theme from popular romantic novels of the period. Like *La*

Realistic Ballets

Fille Mal Gardée, this work, *Les Circonstances Embarrassantes*, or *Distressing Circumstances*, was produced in the port city of Bordeaux.[14] Though distant from the stages of Paris, and therefore ostensibly outside of this discussion, the influence of this ballet cannot be ignored. Both the exotic plot and the dancers brought Paris new choreographic material; Bordeaux presented remarkable ballets at this time, largely due to the influence of Dauberval. The great choreographer of the boulevard theatres, Sebastien Gallet, composed the scenario of *Les Circonstances* in 1796.[15] It was inspired though indirectly, by Bernardin de Saint-Pierre's *Paul et Virginie* (1788), whose sentimental story, set in the French isle of Mauritius and filled with Rousseauistic feelings, was very widely read.

Important elements from this book inspired Gallet's ballet, such as the search for an idyllic life in a faraway land, but the tragedy of *Paul et Virginie* is not repeated. Another significant influence on the plot may be found in the eighteenth-century preoccupation with slavery and human bondage. In *Candide* (1759), Voltaire paints the barbarity of slavery in the encounter with "Le Nègre de Surinam." In Marivaux's *L'Ile des Esclaves* (1725), Marivaux treats the problem of servitude between masters and their servants on an island where the roles are reversed. Social satire and moralizing sentimentality are threaded through this charming drama. In *Les Letters Persanes* (1721), as mentioned earlier, Montesquieu describes the intrigues in a harem in Ispahan, where the inhabitants fight, bicker, and revolt in the setting of a luxurious prison. The serious problem of slavery in *Les Circonstances Embarrassantes* serves as the motive and framework for the escape scenes that are so important to the action.

The ballet opens in a town on the coast of Africa where a young French couple, Céphise and Séricour, are on their way to the New World. They are seized, then separated, by pirates off the Barbary coast, who steal their ship and sell them as slaves to a rich pasha. His harem of jealous and cantankerous concubines, overseen by the Moor Jago, a crippled eunuch, presents a picture of a less-than-happy sultan. Jago falls in love with Céphise, promising her jewels and freedom if she will run away with him. Caught between the frying pan and the fire, Céphise chooses escape, and she and the deformed Jago flee by canoe to a neighboring isle. Séricour cleverly arrives by ship on the

Rediscovery of the Commonplace

same isle and, in "tempest-like" environs, the lovers rediscover one another. With Séricour and Céphise come the slaves and harem girls, who are also escaping from the sultan. There, on the isle, they all decide to travel to the New World to seek their freedom and a new life. Jago is disappointed but relinquishes his love for the promise of an adventurous future free from bondage.

Onstage, different kinds of dances such as the *pas de Nègre* and typical court dances of the eighteenth century highlight the drama by contrasts between the Oriental and European worlds. To perform these difficult, intricate steps, Gallet brought dancers to Bordeaux from the Paris Opéra and the Cité-Variétés troupes: Beaulieu, Simonet, and Laborie. It could be said that the dancers played the role of messengers of the goddess Terpsichore, carrying movement and ballet ideas to the cities where they performed. In *Les Circonstances*, the exotic locale highlights and adds interest to a story that expresses the values of the middle class—true love, and passion for new beginnings, and freedom. Revolutionary principles are also reflected in the concern for liberty, adventure, and free choice.

Jean-Georges Noverre, Annette et Lubin, *Ballet-Pantomime, Revived 1797, at the Opéra*

New productions were rare during the harsh times of the Revolution, and the Opéra administration chose to replay the old pastorals rather than to invest in new "exotica" that might cost 100,000 livres. Large sums were spent on spectacles that pertained to the Revolution, extolling the ideals and heroes of recent history, but with government politics so intimately tied to the arts, this was basically a waiting period. Choreographers at the Opéra could hardly indulge in subjects of their own choice. In 1797, consequently, Gardel revived Noverre's *Annette et Lubin*, a pastoral ballet-pantomime that had been created for the Opéra in 1778 when Noverre was *maître de ballet*. Having returned to Paris from London in 1797, Noverre was "broken in health, his savings lost in the Revolution, his pension stopped because of his association with the old regime and the lack of funds at the Opéra."[16] He spent much time at the Opéra watching rehearsals and the progress of the newcomers and made biting comments about their training, especially the fact that no male dancers were being schooled, with the

Realistic Ballets

result that the *danseuses* exceeded the *danseurs* in large numbers. Women were not always easy for Noverre to deal with, and in his original production of *Annette et Lubin* in 1778, La Guimard had refused to dance and suggested disdainfully that Noverre should give the role of Annette to Mlle Cécile, a second subject at the time. According to Deryck Lynham, "Much to the disgust of Guimard, who suddenly saw in Cécile a rival capable in Noverre's hands of threatening her popularity, the ballet was an outstanding success."[17] In 1789, in Bordeaux, Dauberval had also restaged *Annette et Lubin*, which gave his wife, Mme Théodore, a triumphal performance about which the critics raved.[18]

The ballet evidently spoke to audiences of the late eighteenth century and reaffirmed Noverre's artistic brilliance. The original tale by Marmontel had its source in a true story told by a friend one evening in Marmontel's summer home in Bezons. Later, Marmontel wrote it up as a *Conte Moral*, then as a *pastorale* that Favart and Rochon de Chabannes made into an *opéra comique* in 1762.[19] The true story concerned a young peasant girl, Annette, who lived with her first cousin Lubin in Bezons. When she became pregnant, the problem of marriage proved extremely complicated. Neither the curé nor the village officials thought their marriage was possible without a special dispensation from the pope, as they were cousins. Eventually, with the proper influences brought to bear, the couple received the dispensation, and they were married. When the comic opera was performed, the real young couple were invited and given fine seats. They applauded very loudly at the end of the show.

In the ballet-pantomime, as the *Journal des Théâtres* notes, the dancer was required to give extreme care to his gestures, using a heightened sensitivity inherent in Noverre's choreography and in the training of the dancers as mimes by Gardel.[20] Set in a peaceful, charming farm village in France, the ballet shows Annette and Lubin as they brave the adversity that rests in the powers ruling their tiny hamlet. Not only does the bailiff pose an obstacle to their future together, but he tells Annette that she is living in sin. He actually wishes to be the one to marry Annette. Interestingly enough, so does the seigneur of the entire canton, the supposed protector of the inhabitants. He, too, tries to grab more than just a kiss from the shy and lovely girl. When Annette and Lubin appeal to the seigneur for his assistance, he "decides that he must possess her; he orders the bailiff to call his henchmen; they hasten to carry out his orders to seize Annette and carry her off. Lubin becomes like a furious madman when he sees them take his loved one."[21] Without any hesitation, Lubin, the true French peasant who can bear no more abuse, attacks all the king's men, knocking them flat, and then does the same to the bailiff. The aristocrats and the public servants emerge as foolish, greedy figures, while the shepherd-peasant remains his stalwart, courageous self, an obedient but wily man who can be pushed just so far. A trial at the end of the ballet emphasized the enduring power of the ruling classes, however. The seigneur decides that right and good rest on the side of Lubin, while the bailiff is deemed guilty of cupidity. The seigneur, like Jupiter in the myth ballets, joins the hands of the couple and refuses to pardon the bailiff, whereupon Annette and Lubin fall to the seigneur's feet in gratitude.

Filippo Taglioni, Le Jour de Noce, ou L'Enlèvement, Ballet-Pantomime, June 24, 1800, at the Théâtre de la Gaîté

Pastoral ballets have their settings in rich agricultural areas, most often in France. But on June 24, 1800, at the Théâtre de la Gaîté, Citoyen Taglioni placed his ballet-pantomime in Naples, Italy, the country of his origin. Filippo Taglioni,[22] the renowned teacher of his daughter, Marie Taglioni (the lead in *La Sylphide*), also drew much of his story, it seems, from Marmontel's short story "Annette et Lubin," adding what he felt was native to Italy. In consequence, Taglioni's treatment of pastoral subject matter is very different from Noverre's. In the *avant-propos*, or preface, Taglioni exclaims that he wants "to depict the manners, customs, and violent passions of the Neapolitans." Like other pastoral pieces, *Le Jour de Noce, ou L'Enlèvement* (*The Wedding Day, or The Abduction*), appeals to our sense of the fresh outdoors—the peasants carry baskets, build grape arbors, repair thatched huts, and busily and dutifully go about their everyday work.

The ballet opens with dances of southern Italy and focuses upon Annetta, who, because she loves Lubino, refuses to dance until he arrives. Annetta's mother, Susanna, plays the understanding and patient woman, kind to the simpleton, Georginot, who follows her every-

Realistic Ballets

where. A threatening figure enters as the chief of the armed police force, Gugliermo, who also loves Annetta and tries to plot against Lubino in order to gain her. The stereotypes in ballets such as this are striking and obvious: the fun-loving peasant hero; the villain, usually powerful or rich; and the young peasant girl threatened with kidnapping, treated as a pretty object who can be lifted up and transported where her would-be owner wishes to place her. In this case, Gugliermo decides against having Lubino drafted. The villain chooses to steal Annetta away from her home just before her wedding to Lubino. At the time of danger to Annetta's life, Taglioni brings the simpleton (*imbécile*), Georginot, onstage for comic relief, giving him all sorts of childish antics such as ineptly plucking a melody on the guitar, eating and behaving badly, and falling asleep inebriated on a large table while the kidnapping is taking place. Annetta, in a faint (this, too, was traditional), carried off by Gugliermo and his small army, awakens to find herself in a mountain hideaway, dispirited by Lubino's failure to save her. In the dark mountains, Gugliermo attempts to make love to her, an advance she bluntly repels. Though she heroically plots her own escape, Lubino and his peasant friends arrive in time to rescue her from the abductor. At this point, directions are given for a *tableau vivant*. Posed onstage is a picture of Lubino's peasants overcoming Gugliermo's soldiers while the women help Annetta. The villain, Gugliermo, is defeated and his reputation ruined forever. Annetta and Lubino celebrate the nuptial day soon after.

This plot, concerned with the real-life anguish of a couple whose marriage is threatened, demonstrates the traditional theme of a wicked and wealthy man against the "little" guy. Unlike the Opéra, which tended to lag behind in its presentation of character and circumstance, class distinctions were more clearly defined in boulevard theatres. With sympathy slanted in favor of peasants and shopkeepers, ballets there expressed revolutionary principles. After all, the boulevard theatres had less expensive seats and catered to the general populace.

At the Opéra, on the other hand, old and cynical views of the aristocracy and upper classes were toned down and presented as parody. For example, Pierre Gardel fashioned a comic ballet similar to the sort of successful scenarios that his brother preferred; he created his ballet comedy of character, *La Dansomanie*, in 1800, a time when

41. M. Beaupré in the ballet,
La Dansomanie. Bibliothèque de l'Opéra.

Realistic Ballets

the Opéra audiences were finally ready to laugh and enjoy a joke on themselves.

Pierre Gardel, La Dansomanie, Folie Pantomime, June 14, 1800, at the Théâtre de la République et des Arts

Pierre Gardel choreographed his *folie* pantomime, to music by Etienne Méhul at the Opéra, then called the Théâtre de la République et des Arts.[23] It was his first full-length piece in six years, the most recent having been *Le Jugement de Paris* in 1793. Considered Gardel's most popular ballet, *La Dansomanie* in which different dance forms and styles are satirized was often used for benefit performances.[24] It is one of the few ballets with over 100 performances, having had 244 showings. In *La Dansomanie*, Gardel makes fun of the *genre noble*, or the ballet dancing often seen in mythological scenarios. This is an interesting switch, as Gardel had been one of the greatest dancers and choreographers of the *genre sérieux* in heroic ballets. He loved to perform the roles of the great heroes of mythology with elegance and grandeur. The famous Noverre was taken aback by the strange *Dansomanie*, not because of Gardel's newfound creative talent, but rather because he thought it demeaned and dishonored the art:

> This ballet which offers all the different genres of dance is filled with gaity and charming variations; but the choreographer ridicules "la danse noble." Couldn't one compare this act to the child who strikes back at his nursemaid? Gardel abandoned this style for lack of great funds; although it has been the genre in which M. Gardel excelled.[25]

In his *avant-propos*, Gardel excuses the title, which might have displeased the public because it was not French. But he maintains that the subject of this ballet has the precise meaning of *La Folie*, the same as contemporary plays called *La Métromanie* and *La Mélomanie*.[26] *La Manie*, which is defined in a long scientific article in the *Encyclopédie*, may be reduced to the Greek word meaning "fury." The fury of loving dance obviously only hurts the characters in the ballet. In the "Réflexions de l'auteur," Gardel also speaks openly of his distress

Rediscovery of the Commonplace

at not being creative: "I was in despair a thousand times; my friends complained about it and other people denounced me as being artistically sterile." With this new production, Gardel hopes to keep working (as he did, creating sixteen new ballets after *La Dansomanie*). He calls the work a fantasy, not a ballet. He mentions that, under the mask of gaiety, he wishes to display that grace and talent the public has always cherished. *La Dansomanie* was played for two decades after its premiere; it spoke directly to the emerging bourgeois audiences who went to the Opéra.

The names in the cast of characters indicate the tone of the satire. M. Duléger, Mr. Light Step, is the *dansomane*. It is interesting to note that the men are all *Citoyens*, but the women regain their prerevolutionary titles, Mlle, Mme, etc., rather than *Citoyenne*. Castagnet, which sounds like castanet, plays the little brother of the ingenue lead; the slightly simpleminded valet is called Pas Moucheté (fleabitten step); and, best of all, the dancing master is called M. Flic Flac. Today, this is a ballet step in which the dancer is on his toes, or *demipointe*, and flicks his foot out and then in, this action motivating him to turn. It means a whipcrack, which the dancing master figuratively uses all the time.

The aristocrat, M. Duléger, lives in a large chateau with his family; he is seemingly similar to all men of his kind except for one idiosyncrasy—he has a mania for the dance. As the ballet opens, M. Duléger is carrying his five-year-old son on a morning promenade through the countryside near the chateau. But he does not just walk; he jumps, swings, and twirls. When he reaches his home, he performs a dance in front of his son and then with him. The valet, Pas Moucheté, imitates the master of the house with exactly the same steps, proving that servants are often the monkeys of their masters. When Mme Duléger asks the valet to bring lunch, he executes some *petits ronds de jambe* from time to time, which his master carefully notes. The *livret* is filled with similar small bits.

The subplot concerns a young lover, Demarsept, a colonel in the infantry, and the Dulégers' daughter, Phrosine. Demarsept begs Phrosine to be his wife and implores her to write down what she feels about him. At this moment, Pas Moucheté jumps by with a tray of dirty plates. He trips and the dinner plates land on the floor. Begging everyone's forgiveness, he explains that he was practicing his *jeté battus* and *entrechats* when his foot got caught. Of course, M. Duléger forgives him. Then, Duléger also tries those difficult steps, and his legs get all tangled up. The lovers continue their courting; a dove with a letter alights near the colonel; he kisses the dove and Phrosine. Mme Duléger, exasperated by her husband's constant practice of his dance steps, cannot succeed in getting his attention. The father's weird interest in dance is considered completely acceptable, so long as it does not interfere with everyone else's plans. When the dancing master enters, things become both serious and funny. Like M. Jourdain in Molière's *Bourgeois Gentilhomme*, Duléger knows that the key to happiness is dance. The new steps are complex and require all Duléger's concentration to learn: "cuisses doubles, triples, and quadruples, pirouettes, temps de flêches, etc." Duléger, with his valet skipping in front and behind, tries to find a way to look as fine as the dancing master while doing these new movements. Amusingly, the valet often trips his employer. When Phrosine is given a dance to learn, it is Vestris' new gavotte.[27] This is the only moment when Duléger seems to notice his daughter.

During the lesson, the colonel enters and declares his love for Phrosine. He explains that he can take care of her in fine style, but the father only asks if he, too, knows Vestris' gavotte. Then, because the young man answers indifferently that he does not know or care to learn this dance, he is refused Phrosine's hand. Only an excellent dancer will be judged worthy. Since the father's will is law, Mme Duléger dreams up a marvelous scheme in which Turks, Chinese, and Basques will dance for the hand of Phrosine. In the meantime, as a divertissement, the Savoyards, known for their fine dancing, execute their country dances while Duléger and the valet try to imitate their figures. The joke continues when a shoemaker arrives with dozens of pairs of shoes to try on. Duléger sees the name of Vestris on one pair, which unfortunately is far too small. He struggles to push his poor feet into them; then he proceeds to try to do the big jumps for which Vestris was famous.

The fête, the central pretext for marrying off Phrosine, has to be carefully organized. The dancing master will play a Turk (like Lully, the famous musician who played the dancing Turk in *Le Bourgeois*

Rediscovery of the Commonplace

Gentilhomme); the *prévôt* will play a Chinese; and the colonel will do a Basque piece. The colonel has been thoroughly rehearsed with a Savoyard group in the costumes of these foreign countries. Duléger, who immediately agrees to give his daughter in marriage to the best dancer, beats his shoes with a cane as he tries to make them fit better. The Turk's dance, though well performed, bores Duléger; the Chinese dance has some amazing steps; but when the Basque enters and vivaciously does his variation, Duléger is entranced. The gaiety, the grace, and the lightness all conform to Duléger's strict standards of great dancing. Phrosine has also learned some tricky movements, which she does with the colonel, and "The poor Duléger is on the verge of going mad. The agreeable and sprightly moves, these appealing designs and this perfect ensemble work are so absolutely charming; the two Basque dancers are so amazing that Duléger cannot possibly recognize his daughter." Duléger looks everywhere for Phrosine, and when he returns to the celebration, the Turks, Chinese, and Basques have disappeared and in their wake remain M. Flic Flac, Phrosine, her lover the colonel, and the savoyards who assumed the roles of *corps de ballet*. The plan becomes eminently clear, and Duléger unites the young couple with great enthusiasm, provided that everyone continues to dance.

Louis-Jacques Milon, Les Noces de Gamache, *Ballet-Pantomime Folie, Music by Xavier Lefebvre, January 18, 1801, at the Opéra*

Les Noces de Gamache, or *Gamache's Wedding*, brought pantomime, ballet dancing, and, once again, *folie* to the Opéra boards. It remained in the Paris Opéra repertoire until 1841, having played more than 160 times. Placed in a Spanish village, a stop in Don Quixote's adventures, the ballet depicts one of the many vignettes used for theatre pieces ever since the book was published in France. Don Quixote and Sancho had been beloved figures in dance as well as in drama ever since 1614, when *Le Ballet de Don Quichotte* was performed.[28] Milon, Gardel's assistant, knew a good story when he saw one and embellished this episode from Cervantes' picaresque novel.

Many choreographers enjoyed the escapades of the Don, Sancho, and his horse. Philip Astley, an Englishman, created a mime drama

Realistic Ballets

42. *Costume design from the early nineteenth century, artist unknown. Bibliothèque de l'Opéra.*

called *Don Quichotte* in 1792 that featured the talents of horses; Astley later joined the famed theatrical horse trainer, Franconi. Hilverding in (Vienna, 1740), Noverre (France, 1768),[29] and Didelot (Russia, 1808) used fragments of Cervantes' *Don Quixote* as sources for their ballets. The comedy in Milon's *Les Noces*, inspired by the success of *La Dansomanie*, initiated a change in the opera-house stories, which had tended to idealize situations. In the past, the public rarely roared but did titter lightly at a funny bit. The comic ballets changed that, and genuine laughter must have rocked the audience. Thanks to music by Lefebvre and dancing by Vestris as Basile, Jean Aumer as Don Quichotte, and Beaupré as Sancho, the ballet had opening receipts of 7,684.77 livres. The ballet's story revolves about the beautiful young peasant girl, Quitterie, her father, Laurenzo, and her lover, Basile.[30] Unfortunately, like many fathers in pastoral ballets, Laurenzo would rather that his daughter marry Gamache, a rich man from the area. The ballet opens with Quitterie in a hide-and-seek game looking for Basile, her suitor. When she finds him, she dances as he strums the guitar, both are thoroughly amused and content with each other's talents. Lorenzo spots the young upstart and sends him away, admonishing Quitterie. The two throw themselves as his feet, but even this symbol of their humble respect is rejected, and Basile finally slumps off. In Lorenzo's cabin, the rich, fat, and ugly Gamache signs a contract promising riches to the family. Tableaux of working women and children on farms, with husbands returning from the fields and embracing their wives, enhance the country scene, painting a more realistic picture on the model of Dauberval's *La Fille Mal Gardée*. Small children excitedly announce the entrance of Don Quichotte and Sancho into their village. Since Lorenzo runs the inn, the newcomers naturally arrive at his door, seeking to spend the night. Thinking the inn a chateau, as he often does, Don Quichotte orders his squire to blow a trumpet. The door still does not open. When he knocks, however, Lorenzo reels out, tipsy from celebrating the lucrative contract with Gamache. Milon does not miss the more obvious moments of farce, and when Sancho watches his master swagger grandly into the inn, he tries to imitate him.

In the next scene, asked to play blindman's bluff with the villagers, Sancho agrees and then cheats the whole time, peeking out from under his kerchief and catching the villagers. When dinner is announced, poor Sancho never gets there in time; many obstacles prevent him from reaching the food, leaving a very hungry man behind. In the evening, Don Quichotte cannot sleep for thinking of Dulcinea; Sancho cannot sleep because he is starving. After wandering, finding the food bin, and eating heartily, Sancho seeks a wine barrel, sticks his head into it, and cannot get it out. At the same time, Don Quichotte had met Quitterie, who reminds him of Dulcinea. He stops to kneel and declare his love for her; Sancho flies by with the barrel over his head, bumps into Don Quichotte, and runs away in a fright.

Feeling challenged, Don Quichotte begins to fight imaginary enemies (after all, it's very dark out), and the commotion causes the villagers to come out and listen to Don Quichotte recount his victory over the brigands whom he sent off running. The next morning, when a large feast is being prepared for the wedding of Quitterie and Gamache, more comic buffoonery packs the action, especially when Sancho has a terrible time trying to steal food before the wedding takes place. Jousts and contests are the highlights of the celebration, and Don Quichotte agrees to duel the bravest person in the village. Even Sancho, dared by a fellow with a long nose, cannot turn down a fight. By accident, Don Quichotte knocks Sancho down; he rises in a fury, jumps on the squire with the long proboscis, and squeezes him in a tight embrace. A general melee ensues, with Sancho winning the prize for being the bravest warrior. Realizing that his master might be deeply insulted, Sancho offers the victory palm to Don Quichotte.

Curiously enough, a serious drama begins to unfold after all this buffoonery. Suddenly, a figure in black, Basile, crowned with cypresses, rushes through the crowd and sets himself in the center of the group. Basile, desperate, miserable, cannot believe that Quitterie has been untruthful and unfaithful. He pulls out a sword and plunges it into his chest. He collapses into his friends' arms while the crowd watches, shocked and trembling. Sancho blanches, but Don Quichotte looks at Sancho disdainfully. Basile, in Don Quichotte's opinion, has committed an act of heroism worthy of a great warrior, and he goes to congratulate him. Basile is ready to die, but asks for one consolation before his death—that he be united to Quitterie so that he may expire in her arms. Gamache refuses this absurd request, but the others, and especially Don Quichotte, who listen to the pulse of a dying man, beg Gamache to relent. After their hands are united in marriage, Basile reveals that his sword did not enter his chest at all; then he throws both parts of the sword in front of everyone. Gamache screams that the marriage is invalid and that Basile has no rights over Quitterie. Don Quichotte organizes an army of supporters and starts to battle Gamache and his men.[31] Sancho, not to lose a precious moment of self-indulgence, hides among pastries while drinking another barrel of wine. His stomach swells like a balloon as the combatants enter onstage for the last time. In the meantime, Don Quichotte has saved the day, and as he is on the verge of running a blade through Gamache's throat, Gamache gives in and agrees that the marriage may be validated. Sancho appears with a happy expression and a stomach so full that he cannot move, still trying to chew his last morsels of food. Though Don Quichotte sighs and bemoans his own chances as a lover, he brings gaiety and happiness to the star-crossed lovers, Quitterie and Basile.

Rediscovery of the Commonplace

Les Noces de Gamache finds its source in a well-known chapter of Cervantes' tale, and heightens its essential good cheer and visual interest. Traditional elements of broad comedy are displayed, especially in the low, vulgar humor of Sancho Panza, giving the common man an opportunity to laugh at himself. Don Quichotte remains the unlikely aging hero, a rare bird in an aviary of typical comic conclusions. The public is reassured that though love may not make the world go round, it is indeed the proper and best reason for marriage.

12
BOURGEOIS SENTIMENT ON THE BALLET STAGE

The ballets in the previous chapter reflect a newfound interest in the ordinary in addition to a novel way of treating normal troubles, that is, with farcical humor. So, on the ballet stage as in real life, the comic mood lightens the human struggles that are laden with potential castastrophe. These ballets, borrowing themes from the theatre, literature, and opera, presented to the middle-class audiences of the time a deliciously comic view of themselves. For the first time, ordinary people with all their foibles were the leading characters in the *ballet d'action*. They had funny names and funny behavior. The nastiness of Nicette's mother, Mme Madré, became muted, even amusing, by the ingenue's search for success. In Dauberval's *La Fille Mal Gardée*, suspense and joyful relief sifted through the illicit meetings of Lison and Colas, the lovers who hid from Ragotte. The widow Ragotte's open peasant style, her dealings with workers on the farm, brought a welcome earthiness to the ballet stage. Though audiences today might not find humor in a so-called simpleton's performance, I suspect the clownlike character Georginot prompted much laughter in Taglioni's scenario for *Jour de Noce*. He certainly cut the harshness of the villain Gugliermo's evil antics. In what might be Pierre Gardel's best ballet, *La Dansomanie*, nineteenth-century attitudes toward theatrical and social dances were satirized. Gamache of Cervantes' *Don Quixote*

Rediscovery of the Commonplace

suffered the extreme embarrassment of having a youthful and handsome rival in Milon's ballet *Les Noces*. Though his activities did not excite many smiles, Sancho's clumsy but innocent conduct certainly did.

Laughing in the face of disaster has its temporary rewards; the period of the Revolution witnessed many adversities that were reflected on the stages in Paris. Without the traditional Neoclassical rules, acts of murder or cruelty were no longer banned from the stage. Scenes of violence and imprisonment could be visualized and even prolonged. Of course, this was not the terror expressed in the classical verse of Racine's *Phèdre*, the kind that would please an audience who frequented the Comédie-Française. The violence of Racine's heroes and heroines was motivated by psychic or spiritual suffering, though the play's tragic ending may have brought an unseen death to the hero or heroine. In the ballet of the Revolution, women, the innocent, and the helpless were threatened, though in the end they managed to overcome the instruments of evil.

A device that heightened moments of drama on the revolutionary stage was the tableau. It was a stop-action picture of an important scene of danger or perhaps a victory over evil. In Taglioni's *Jour de Noce*, a tableau demonstrates the conquest of Lubino and his peasant friends over the villain Gugliermo and his soldiers—surely a common wish fulfillment during this period. Annetta's virtue is thereby saved for Lubino and their marriage. The same danger to Annetta is seen in Noverre's earlier version of *Annette et Lubin*. In *La Fête du Sérail*, the child becomes a hero when he successfully pleads for his mother's life. The ballet heroine Mirza recoils from the amorous attentions of a terrifying and unprincipled pirate. Fortunately, her lover, Lindor, rescues her from a worse eventuality, her own suicide. In *Les Noces de Gamache*, the unwanted Gamache accedes to Basile's marriage wishes on his presumed deathbed. Basile's trick suicide strikes a note of fear and trembling in the audience. Naturally, there is a happy ending, as not one of these ballets dared to be a tragedy. To please the spectator, big crowds, action scenes, and even horses were arranged so as to catch the eye as well as to move the plot along. Music was used more consciously than ever before as a way to provide suspense and to predict events in the ballet. Larger gestural techniques and

Bourgeois Sentiment

more truthful physical responses enhanced these scenic and musical effects. The clever use of the crowd onstage, with each person moving on a certain rhythmic cue, would later flourish in the choreodramas of Salvatore Vigano.[1]

The spectacle of fabulous stage settings, though traditional in ballet, projected a different kind of visual impression during the revolutionary period. The ballets described in the previous chapter attempted to be more geographically specific, more varied, and more truthful (in an imaginative way). There was a mixture of locales, with appropriate costumes from the rich farm homes of Mme Madré and M. Duléger and from the peasant lands in *La Fille Mal Gardée* and *Le Jour Noce*. The different nations of France, Spain, Italy, a North African country, and America were pictured in rich detail. The ballets of bourgeois sentiment broke new ground as they removed themselves from the intimate salons of the *ancien régime* as well as the airy regions of the mythic Olympus. Character dances introduced local color and emphasized regional costume and folk movements. Even the props and accessories onstage reflected a truthfulness and immediacy to the reality of the ballets. The capes, swords, and bales of straw clarified and furthered the plot and enriched its visual accuracy. Gone were the girdles of Venus and the arrows of Cupid that symbolized a dying value system.

Not only were the trimmings accurate to the new, compressed plot of the *ballet d'action*. Each of the protagonists also carried the image of the certain kind of person of a particular social class, whether that of the peasant, the bailiff, the mayor, the farmer, the bourgeois merchant, the slave, or even the pasha. Their gestures and actions echoed real behavior and truthful stories. There was a diminishing presence of the aristocracy (mythic or real) with its silk, brocades, and lace. Upper classes and their divine rights began to disappear. Increasingly, the bourgeois, monied, and landed classes took over and manipulated events, while their problems with each other and with the peasants took center stage. The common man and woman were glorified in the ballet as they seized the reigns of power in an extraordinarily eventful time.

13
BRAVO BALLET!

What, then, distinguishes the period of the French Revolution (ca. 1787–1801) as a singular time in the history of theatrical dance? The answer is that ballet changed its look and quality more dramatically and more notably than perhaps at any other time in its history. The cries for change and reform were heard! The demand by eighteenth-century dramatic theorists for a more human approach to the presentation of character on the stage, as well as for an authentic story, was heeded first by playwrights and then by choreographers. The writers of the *Encyclopédie* who propounded these theories, such as Cahusac, Grimm, Diderot, and Rousseau, would have been delighted by the *ballets d'action* of Maximilien and Pierre Gardel, Dauberval, Gallet, Didelot, and Milon. Not only did these choreographers create ballet *livrets* that had complete and well-knit story lines, but they infused their academic ballet vocabulary with expressive pantomime.

This new use of gesture in the evocation of character was perhaps the key to ballet reform. The dancers who executed the ballets of the revolutionary period learned to become pantomimes and actors, paying sincere attention to the roles they were asked to dance. The new aesthetics of the theatre as espoused by Garrick and Noverre, with their emphasis on a lifelike representation of human passions on the stage, brought both larger audiences and more serious prestige to ballet

Bravo Ballet!

than it had known before. Choreographers and dancers in Paris, who played at the boulevard theatres before they were employed by the Opéra, pleased a more popular audience with less attitudinizing and more honest dramatic or comic portrayals. Thus, the training of a dancer came to incorporate the use of expression as well as movement technique.

Opportunities to explore these new expressive styles increased after 1791, when the royal restrictions on the number of theatres permitted to show ballet and pantomime were removed. Also, change itself played a part—the introduction of new styles of dance tends to invigorate any movement form. In the late eighteenth century, when the theatres had a brief moment of freedom, pantomime, acrobatics, ropedancing, and character or folk dances could all be seen on the same stage. These opportunities enriched and revitalized the old Baroque dance forms, paving the way for a more exciting dance theatre. In addition, there was more work for choreographers on a steady basis and for practical experience in the training of future choreographers, such as Gallet at the Théâtre de la Cité and Taglioni at the Gaîté.

Observers of the time saw that pantomime spectacles at the boulevard theatres attracted larger audiences than the dramas or comedies, and large-scale pantomime productions proliferated in the boulevard theatres. Along with melodramatic tales, there arose a movement vocabulary that was already common fare across the Channel. For example, in London, as early as 1717, John Weaver wrote about the specific gestures of his actors in a ballet scenario called the *Loves of Mars and Venus*. "Indignation," he said, "is expressed by applying the hand passionately to the forehead, or by stepping back the right foot, leaning the body quite backward, the arms extended, palms closed and hands thrown quite back, the head cast back, and eyes fixed upwards."[1] The ballets of the revolutionary period are nearly all called ballets-pantomimes, and they tried to incorporate this language of gestures.

Perhaps as a result, ballets also attracted a large popular audience that seemed to have a new thirst for entertainment. The performance of a ballet often brought more spectators to the Opéra than did an opera showing. The highest receipts for any performance at the Opéra in the period occurred when the myth ballets *Psyché* and *Télémaque*

Rediscovery of the Commonplace

were enacted and when *Mirza* was revived. Evidence of ballet's growing popularity is the fact that two operas grouped together on a program usually had lower receipts than an opera paired with a ballet. The impressive salaries of choreographers, both at the boulevard theatres (Sebastien Gallet) and the Opéra (Pierre Gardel), suggested their importance as artists in demand. Also significant is the considerable number of dancers employed by a theatre as compared to the number of actors, musicians, and singers. In some theatres, there were twice as many dancers as actors.

Along with the addition of pantomime to the ballet vocabulary came a parallel change in the dancer's costuming. A new concern for historical accuracy guided the costume designer. Since shoes with heels did not look appropriate with the Greek and Roman draperies of the myth ballets and the *Fêtes Révolutionnaires*, much less with the bright regional costumes of peasant life, the dancers wore sandals or glove-fitting slippers, and thus the technique of *demi-pointe* was born. The new shoes increased the ability of the dancer to make multiple turns on one foot, to leap in the air and land without wobbling, and to beat one leg against the other in a series of startling *entrechats* and *grand allegros*. According to Ivor Guest, "More and more the public demanded to see dazzling tours de force that Duport and later Paul with their astonishing pirouettes and jumps were executing."[2] The audience relished the excitement of seeing the human body push beyond the virtuosity of a former age. With a freer body, no longer restricted by corsets and brocades, possibilities for dramatic expression emerged. This physical eloquence, in conjunction with the spectacles provided by developments in stage machinery, were the beginnings of what would later be the Romantic ballet.

But perhaps more important than any other change in the quality of its dancing, ballet began to flow across and throughout the stage rather than to continue the more confined, smaller, steppy sequences of Baroque movement. Ballet took to the air and to the notion of height, length, and grandeur of style and movement. The constrictions that limited the legs, arms, feet, head, and torso were released. Consequently, the male and female couple could work more closely, more intimately. The male dancer could lift the female and hold her in balances, prolonging physical pictures and designs.

Bravo Ballet!

Also, for the first time in ballet, as in our early silent films when strong emotional or dramatic scenes were presented, musical accompaniment accentuated the violence of passion, as did the expressive gestures of the dancer. Pathos and sentimentality were the rage. These qualities were heightened by the new device of the *tableau vivant*[3] in which performers froze into an affecting pose at a key time in the drama. This stage direction was meant to intensify the emotional impact of moments of touching anxiety before a father was reunited with his family or the triumphal union of peasant lovers.

Another feature of the stage picture of the period was the emergence of children who began to be seen more often and even to have importance in the ballet *livrets* as well as the revolutionary festivals.[4] The child became the hero, the sufferer, the *orphelin* who survived the destructive war created by the adults. Companies of children as dancers and actors might have been common on eighteenth-century stages, but the child's unique place in family dramas came about during the revolutionary period. Women, too, were represented as courageous participants in the Revolution. They were newly portrayed as defiant beings, not the fragile idealizations of court painters.[5] The physical and moral courage of Psyché and Mélide echoes the necessities of the time, while Mirza, Lise, and Nicette exhibit the feminine, wily shrewdness so feared, if admired, by Frenchmen. In the political epics, the focus fell squarely upon "La Liberté" and "La Raison," both female representations of France itself. These ladies served as the cynosures of outdoor festivals, where all eyes and actions were directed and riveted to their giant, puppet constructions. In these political interludes, women symbolized the power and fury one associates with a mother tiger whose cubs are in danger. They also represented the enduring gentleness and nurturing qualities of an earth mother. France truly discovered her feminine principle during the Revolution.

The ideology of political and social freedom invaded more than the aesthetics of the ballet. Into the theatre swept not just fresh ideas and a feverish desire for reform but a new sort of audience that was no longer content to sit passively and accept what was presented. During intermissions, the public in the theatres would often express its favor by singing "Ca Ira" and dancing "La Carmagnole." A broader section of Parisian citizens was able to participate in the boulevard

Rediscovery of the Commonplace

theatre, simply because the tickets were cheaper than at the Opéra. It is revealing that the price differential was immense—two sous for an evening of pantomime at the boulevard theatres versus forty sous at the Opéra.

The theatre was a microcosm of the political macrocosm and became the site—the forum—where audiences acted and danced out their feelings about the Revolution. They were the new acting troupes, whose performances began during intermission and ended with the finale. So, the theatre and the performing artist became linked to victory on the battlefields and the struggle against an insidious ruling class that continued to reign over the rest of Europe. Crowds in the streets, crowds in the audience, and crowds on the stage all echoed the agitations of this period. But there were paradoxes. The individual appears to have lost importance as the scale was enlarged and the single man or woman in the street was often frightened and diminished; at the same time, as a paradigm of the new heroic character, the ordinary person was the focus, his or her life emphasized as it took on dramatic and heroic proportions both on and off the stage.

There was during the revolutionary period, a growing theatrical trend toward the realistic evocation of particular types of middle-class people and their environs. Previously, the features and qualities attributed to mythological heroes and heroines such as Cupid, Venus, Jupiter, and Hades were depicted. But this psychological lexicon of dramatis personae began to bore the myth-weary Parisian public— they wanted to see themselves on stage. Though Gardel's *Psyché* and *Télémaque* were great hits at the Paris Opéra, they represented the swan song of the world of antiquity, the last lengthy, gorgeous gasps of the *ancien régime's* appetite for voluptuosity and careless loving. Though ballets continue to have happy endings, they were far more truthful in their descriptions of characters. Audiences relished watching middle-class ladies and gentlemen. After all, they had been defenders and heroes, so why not define their particular social importance onstage. Thus, individual professions and characters familiar to the common people filled the stages of revolutionary Paris. Gugliermo, the bailiff, M. Duléger, the wealthy landowner, Madame Ragotte, and Madame Madré brought a new view of class structure to the audience of the ballet stage. The characters now undergo changes in their actions

43. *Elisa Gougibus in the role of Petite Nichon,
a theatre piece. Cabinet des Estampes.*

Rediscovery of the Commonplace

and gestures, emotions befitting the new popular attitudes. M. Duléger symbolized the bourgeois or upper-class gentleman's mania for a societal attribute carried so far that it became a disease. The age-old theme of marrying off one's daughter to a good catch continued to occupy the thoughts of all the characters. The misplaced hopes of Mmes Ragotte and Madré, as well as Duléger and the parents of Mirza, entertained the new monied merchants of the growing middle class in Paris and other important urban centers.

Scenes borrowed from contemporary events were incorporated into ballets as the need for greater realism and scenery to protect this reality became paramount. Accustomed to the sight of bloodshed in the streets of Paris, the public demanded from the stage even more terror and bloodcurdling events. Ballet, while not normally the medium for such tales, nevertheless responded to these demands. The taste for exaggeration, violent death, and morbidity were the stuff of revolutionary *livrets*. A sense of mass, grandeur and large-scale scenery also characterized these productions. Inspired by the examples of Servandoni, stage sets became increasingly atmospheric, mammoth, and spectacular, a phenomenon we can compare with early movies of D. W. Griffith and Cecil B. De Mille. Scene designers of the revolutionary period, such as Moench and Martin, created elaborate productions with massive dimensions and casts of thousands. Visual excitement in the theatre, and especially decors with exotic landscapes, interested the eighteenth-century public. Pantomimes and ballets enchanted viewers' eyes with pictures of never-never lands in the Americas and other faraway places, particularly changes of scenery of specific national character. Local color and folk settings were enhanced by Native American Indian ritual dances, regional dances, and *danses de caractère*. They lent truth and specificity to stories and also displayed the individuality of peoples as well as the joy they expressed in performing what distinguished them from their neighbors.[6]

The revolutionary festivals, which stand out in dance history as oddities, emphasized mass movements and created grandiose spectacles. Closer rapport between the audiences and performer evolved during this time and encouraged popular approval of dance and the theatre. Naturally, the revolutionary authorities realized the power of this medium and sought to control and exploit it. They grasped im-

Bravo Ballet!

mediately that art could be used to foster their cause, and the politics of art affected the creative minds responsible for the ballet and pantomime. Robespierre gave large sums of money for his *Fêtes Révolutionnaires* and ordered patriotic plays and ballets to be performed. Such festivals, allegorical and pontifical in nature, were out of the mainstream of eighteenth-century dramatic theory. Hearkening back to Roman triumphal processions and simplistic posturing, they attest to a brief moment of political control in the arts.

It is evident that the vigor and excitement of ballet at the time of the Revolution contributed to its development. The qualities common to postrevolutionary ballet find their roots in the earlier tradition of this art form but were forever altered by the vitality of the revolutionary ballet. As has been stated earlier, most of the ingredients for the making of a Romantic ballet can be found first in revolutionary times: the significance of women as heroines, the new freer dance technique with more profound gestural movements, the melodrama with a villain of horrible dimensions in a story purporting to offer a moral message, the gigantic spectacle, and the importance of local color with regional dances emphasizing specific geographic regions. Other elements include the use of Gothic settings and the suggestions of mysterious forebodings (this was especially apparent in revolutionary pantomimes), the accuracy of costumes to the period, and the use of music to announce heightened or dramatic tensions. In short, Romantic ballet inherited a great deal from revolutionary ballet.[7]

After the Revolution, dancers—especially female dancers—demanded more respect and social recognition. The French Revolution was the hinge, the turning point for the dancer who increasingly argued for his or her career. Dancers served as agents who bargained with powerful theatre managers for good roles and good salaries. Political appointments by the court or the king who ran the theatres were replaced by zealous theatre impressarios with an eye for box-office personalities. The popularity of the ballet or ballet dancer rather than the whim of the aristocracy became the determining factor in playing power, although it must be said that these changes did not occur in all European countries and certainly not in Russia. But in France, because of the Revolution, dancers and actors and musicians and singers identified and sided with the powerful forces of democracy.

44. *Illustration for a prison design for the theatre. Cabinet des Estampes.*

They were no longer handmaidens of the court; they had their own minds and choices—they saw their future as tied to what should be, not what was.

Perhaps more touching and significant than any other aspect of this book is the choreographer's personal quest for beauty, truth, originality, and perfection as he often reveals these preoccupations in his *avant-propos* or *avertissement*. Schooled in the difficult dance vocabulary, he (alas, not one woman is represented) projects his fears and self-criticism so that the public might understand his intentions. One may deduce that in the midst of political disruption and discord, the choreographer remained disciplined and dedicated to his craft, offering his ideas to the new and larger public and thereby truly setting the stage for early nineteenth-century ballet and pantomime.

NOTES
BIBLIOGRAPHY
INDEX

NOTES

Introduction

1. Ballet and pantomime, both rapidly developing mute arts, became intimately related during the late eighteenth century. For example, a ballet dancer, Mlle Théodore, the wife of the choreographer Dauberval, played in a famous pantomime called *Dorothée* in 1788. Though the training for a pantomimist must have been quite different from that of a ballet dancer, these separate arts merged, so that ballets were called ballet-pantomimes and pantomimes were filled with ballet. Theatrical historians tend to distinguish ballet and pantomimes because of their different origins and techniques. Librarians in France keep books pertaining to pantomime with the dance books. In America, pantomime studies are often with books on the theatre, though the dance collection of the New York Public Library contains many pantomime *livrets*.

2. The following books have been immense help for an understanding of the period: Marian Hannah Winter, *Le Théâtre du Merveilleux* (Paris: Chez Olivier-Perrin, 1962); Marian Hannah Winter, *Pre-Romantic Ballet* (Brooklyn: Dance Horizons, 1974); Ivor Guest, *Le Ballet de L'Opéra de Paris* (Paris: Joly, 1976), Marie-Françoise Christout, *Le Merveilleux et le Théâtre du Silence* (Paris: Editions Mouton, La Haye, 1965).

3. I have summarized, the action of these *livrets* in some detail.

4. The unit of money in which box-office receipts are measured is called the livre or pound; the livre Tournois, or franc, was subdivided into sous, or sols, and deniers: 12 deniers equal 1 sou; 20 sous, equal 1 livre. See George

Rudé, *The Crowd*, 256. Also, the *Journal de l'Opéra* notes that as of May 1, 1798, the receipts were listed in francs, not *assignats*.

5. Rudé, *The Crowd*, p. 27.

1. The Ballet *Livret*, or the Moving Scenario

1. Raoul Feuillet, 1675–1710, French dancer and choreographer, became a member of the Académie Royale de Danse and claimed to have invented a system of dance notation that he published as *Chorégraphie ou l'Art d'Ecrire la Danse par Caractères* in 1704. In this *Recueil de Danses*, some of the dances at the Opéra were noted. Other sources for notation are: M. Magny, *Principes de Chorégraphie* (Paris: n.p., 1765); F. Rousseau (notator), *A New Collection of Dances . . . Composed by Monsieur Abbée* (London: n.d., n.p.); N. Malpied, *Traité sur l'Art de la Danse* (Paris, 1770, republished by Gregg in 1972). Malpied's was the last of the eighteenth-century works to reproduce almost exactly Feuillet's *Chorégraphie*. It also contains descriptions of arm movements and various steps. Pierre Rameau published *Le Maître à Danser* in Paris in 1725, which teaches the manner of executing all the different dance steps and the manner of holding the arms for each step. Six months later, he published *Abrégé de la Nouvelle Méthode de l'Art d'Ecrire ou de Tracer Toutes Sortes de Danses de Ville*. Gennaro Magri's, *Trattato, Teoretico-Prattico di Ballo* (Naples, 1779) is an interesting bridge between Baroque dance and ballet. Pierre Rameau's, *Abbrégé . . . Seconde Partie Contenant un Très Grand Nombre de Meilleures Entrées de Ballet de M. Pécour* (Paris: n.p., 1725) contains descriptions of many dance steps performed by *grottischi* and *mezzo-carattere* dancers. Mention must also be made of Mary Skeaping's fine re-creations of eighteenth-century Swedish ballets in the Drottningholm Court Theatre.

2. Michel de Pure, *Idées des Spectacles* (Paris: 1668; rpt. Geneva: Minkoff, 1972), p. 209.

3. Famous ballets by well-known writers: Pierre Ronsard's *Défense du Paradis* (1572), Isaac Benserade's *Le Triomphe de l'Amour* (1681), Pierre Corneille's *Andromède* (1650), Molière's *Les Fâcheux* (1661), Marmontel's *Céphale et Procris* (1775), Rousseau's *Les Muses Galantes* (1745), and *Les Festes de Ramire* (1745), Cahusac's *Fêtes de l'Hymen et de l'Amour* (1747).

4. Henry Prunières, *Le Ballet de Cour avant Benserade et Lully* (Paris: Henry Laurens, 1914), p. 193.

5. Ibid., p. 196.

6. Ibid., p. 193.

7. Claude-François Menestrier, *Des Ballets Anciens et Modernes* (Paris: 1682; rpt. Geneva: Slatkine Reprints, 1972), p. 292.

8. M. Dauberval, *Le Siège de Cythère*, "Grand Ballet-Pantomime de la composition de Dauberval, Donnée pour la première fois à Londres le 9 Mai

Notes to Pages 6–12

1791, sur le Théâtre de Roi au Panthéon. Décorations sont de M. Moench, Machines sont composées par M. Bénard de l'Opéra de Paris; les Habits sont dessinés par Mrs. O'Reilly, Lecour et exécutés par M. Lupino; la Musique est de divers auteurs et arrangée par M. Dauberval; La Symphonie est par M. Pozzi."
9. Ibid.
10. Gaspare Angiolini (1731–1803), Italian dancer, choreographer, and ballet master. In 1758, when he went to Vienna, he came under the influence of Hilverding and his theories about the *ballet d'action*. He was imprisoned in Italy in 1797 because of his sympathies for the democratic and progressive ideas of the French. He tried to develop a system of movement notation. Vicenzo Galeotti (1733–1816), Italian dancer, choreographer, and teacher, worked in many European companies; laid the foundations of the Royal Danish Ballet School; was influenced strongly by the *ballet d'action* of Noverre and Angiolini; and was the first to use Romantic themes in Scandinavian ballet. Franz Hilverding (1710–68), Austrian dancer, choreographer, ballet master and teacher, created more than thirty ballets for various Viennese theatres; pioneer in the *ballet d'action*; went to Russia where he was in charge of the ballet in St. Petersburg and Moscow from 1758 to 1764; returned to Vienna in 1765; taught ballet to Angiolini, the wife of David Garrick, Violetti, and others.
11. Jean-Georges Noverre, *Lettres sur la Danse et les Arts Imitateurs* (Paris, 1807; rpt. Paris: Editions Lieutier, 1952), p. 94.
12. Karl Engel, *Idées sur le Geste et l'Action Théâtrale*, 2 vols. (Paris: H. J. Jansen, 1795).

2. Ballet before the French Revolution

1. John Baron, "Les Fées des Forêts de S. Germain, Ballet de Cour," *Dance Perspectives*, (Summer 1975), 4; Abbé de Marolles *Mémoires*, 1754.
2. Louis de Cahusac, "Ballet," *Encyclopédie* 2:42–46. For a more focused discussion on the dance writing of Cahusac, Diderot, and Noverre, see my "Cahusac, Diderot and Noverre: Three French Revolutionary Writers," *Theatre Journal* (May 1983) pp. 169–78.
3. The precursor of the first ballet with a plot, or *ballet d'action*, was said to have been performed at the Chateau of Sceaux by the Duchesse du Maine in 1714, danced by Ballon and Prévôt, in a mimed scene from Corneille's act 4, scene 5, of *Horace*.
4. Louis de Cahusac, *La Danse Ancienne et Moderne ou Traité Historique de la Danse* (Geneva: Slatkine Reprints, 1971), p. 166.
5. "Jean-Georges Noverre is remembered in the history of music as well as dance for he was the Ballet Master who staged the compositions of Gluck. He shared this function with his rival Angiolini, parallel to Gluck's reform

of the opera, and vying with them in his austere administration for the antique" (Edgar Wind, "Noverre's *Horaces*," *Warburg Institute Journal* 4:128. Noverre wrote his *Lettres sur la Danse et les Arts Imitateurs* in 1760.

6. "Noverre was the creator of the ballet-pantomime, or the theatrical entertainment in which dancers attempted to recount a story by means of gestures and movements. Before Noverre, the ballet was a simple divertissement, and even his earlier creations such as *Les Fêtes Chinoises* and *La Fontaine de Jouvence* appealed almost solely to the sight by the beauty of their costumes and gracefulness of their figures. It was when he saw at London Garrick's animated acting in which the gestures of the hands, the expression of the features, and the posture of each part of the body were used to express the impulse and agitation of the heart and the mind, that Noverre conceived the possibility of choreographic drama" (F. A. Hedgecock, *David Garrick and His French Friends* [London: Stanley Paul, 1898], p. 144).

7. Denis Diderot, *Troisième Entretiens sur le Fils Naturel, Oeuvres Esthétiques* (Paris: Garnier, 1965), p. 162. Diderot has a fine quote calling for a brilliant choreographer: "The dance is awaiting a man of genius; it is mediocre everywhere because it is cliché-ridden."

8. Dauberval, or Jean Bercher (1742–1806), French dancer and ballet master, studied at the Paris Opéra Ballet School, joined its company in 1761, and became *maître de ballet* in 1771. He worked in Bordeaux, 1785–91, where *La Fille Mal Gardée* was performed in 1789.

9. Pierre Gardel (1758–1840), dancer and ballet master as well as choreographer, a pupil of Dauberval and his brother Maximilien. Pierre was *maître de ballet* at the Opéra, 1787–1820; director of the ballet school of the Opéra, 1799–1815. See article on Pierre Gardel by John Chapman, "Forgotten Giant: Pierre Gardel," *Dance Research* [London] (Spring 1987).

10. Denis Diderot, *Oeuvres Esthétiques*, p. 139.

11. Patricia Murphy, "Ballet Reform in Eighteenth-Century France: The Philosophes and Noverre," *Symposium* 30, no. 1 (Spring 1976):40.

12. Richard Oliver, *The Encyclopedists as Critics of Music* (New York: Columbia University Press, 1947), p. 77.

13. Castil-Blaze François, 2 *Tomes, De l'Opéra en France* (Paris: Janet et Cotelle Librairies, 1820), p. 136.

14. Baron Grimm, "Poème Lyrique," *Encyclopédie* 12: 834.

15. For biographies of famous eighteenth-century dancers and choreographers, see Emile Dacier, *Mlle Sallé* (Paris: Librairie Plon, 1909); Gabriel Letainturier-Fradin, *La Camargo* (Paris: 1908; rpt. Geneva: Minkoff, 1973); Deryck Lynham, *Chevalier Noverre* (London: Dance Books, 1972); Gaston Capon, *Les Vestris* (Paris: Société du Mercure de France, 1908); Albert du Bois, "Mlle Théodore," Extrait de *la Revue de Belgique* (Bruxelles: P. Weissenbruch, Imprimeur du Roi, 1896); Serge Lifar, *Auguste Vestris, Dieu de la Danse* (Paris: Editions Nagel, 1950); Mary Grace Swift, *A Loftier Flight: The Life and Accomplishments of Charles-Louis Didelot* (Middletown, Conn.:

Notes to Pages 16–32

Wesleyan University Press, 1974); Edmond de Goncourt, *La Guimard* (Paris: Charpentier, 1883); le Comte Fleury, *Jean-Etienne Déspréaux* (Paris Revue de la France Moderne, 1900).
  16. Adolphe Jullien, *L'Opéra Secret* (Paris: Edouard Rouveyre, 1880), p. 68.
  17. *Les Muses Galantes*, presented in 1754 before M. Le Duc de Richelieu, in 1747 in le Théâtre de l'Opéra, and in 1761 before M. le Prince de Conti. *Les Fêtes de Ramire*, given at Versailles December 22, 1745. Jean Jacques Rousseau, *Oeuvres Complètes* (Paris: Editions de la Pléiade, 1961).
  18. Jean Jacques Rousseau, *Julie, ou La Nouvelle Héloïse: Oeuvres Complètes*, vol. 11.
  19. Ibid., pp. 287–89.
  20. Marian Hannah Winter, *Pre-Romantic Ballet*, p. 115.
  21. Jules Lan, *Mémoires d'un Chef de Claque*, (Paris: Librairie Nouvelle, 1883), p. 105.
  22. Marian Hannah Winter, *Pre-Romantic Ballet*, p. 121.
  23. "The commedia dell'arte was an improvised theatre in which bodily expression, acrobatics and buffoonery took precedence over extemporaneous, sophisticated dialogue" (Michele Root-Bernstein, *Boulevard Theatre and Revolution in Eighteenth-Century Paris*, [Ann Arbor: U.M.I. Research Press, 1984], p. 88).
  24. Emile Dacier, *Mlle Sallé*, p. 133.
  25. Ibid., p. 54.
  26. Ibid., p. 134.

3. Theatres in Paris, or the Beset Stage

  1. Hallays-Dabot, *Histoire*, p. 139.
  2. Ibid., p. 152.
  3. Carlson, *Theatre of the French Revolution*, p. 75.
  4. Hallays-Dabot, p. 152.
  5. Winter, *Le Théâtre du Merveilleux*, p. 32.
  6. Hallays-Dabot, p. 200.

4. Ballet's Love Affair with Antiquity

  1. Marie-Françoise Christout, *Le Mervilleux*, p. 199.
  2. Alfred Cobban, *A History of Modern France*, vol. 1 (Middlesex, England: Penguin, 1957), p. 179.
  3. Selma Jeanne Cohen, "Freme di Gelosia! Italian Ballet Librettos, 1766–1865" *Bulletin of the New York Public Library* 67, no. 9 (November 1963):556.

4. Henry Prunières, *Le Ballet de Cour en France avant Benserade et Lully* (Paris: Henri Laurens, 1914), p. 33.
5. Gaspare Angiolini, *Dissertation sur les Ballets Pantomimes des Anciens Publiée Pour servir de Programme au Ballet Pantomime Tragique de "Sémiramis"* (1765; Milan: Achille Bertorelli, 1956).
6. Ibid., p. 47.

5. Ballets from Olympus, 1787–1801

1. Maximilien Gardel, *Le Premier Navigateur, ou Le Pouvoir de l'Amour*, ballet d'action, Juillet 1785, Opéra. I use the word Cupid for Amour as he's a real type and not an abstract symbol. Maximilien Gardel (1741–87) was a dancer and choreographer, the son of a ballet master. He made his debut at the Opéra in 1755 and was one of the first dancers to appear without a mask. He was ballet master at the Opéra from 1783 to 1787.
2. Karl Engel, *Idées sur le Geste et l'Action Théâtrale* (Paris: H. J. Jansen, 1795), p. 134.
3. According to the *Journal de l'Opéra*, which was an official handwritten account of the business transactions of the Opéra administration, setting forth operas and ballets. It presented receipts, replacements, promotions, salaries, and other pertinent information.
4. Pierre Gardel (1758–1849), a great *danseur noble*, pupil and younger brother of Maximilien; soloist of the Paris Opéra in 1780; *maître de ballet* of the Opéra, 1787–1820; director of the Opéra Ballet School, 1799–1815; choreographer, teacher of Carlo Blasis.
5. Pierre Gardel, *Télémaque dans l'Isle de Calypso, ballet héroïque*, music by Ernest Miller, in three acts, presented at the Académie Royale de Musique on February 23, 1790.
6. Ivor Guest, *Le Ballet de l'Opéra de Paris*, trans. Paul Alexandre (Paris: Flammarion, 1979), p. 64.
7. Jean-Georges Noverre, p. 304.
8. Baron Grimm, *Correspondance Littéraire* (Paris: Garnier Frères, 1880), 15: 601. *Correspondance Littéraire* was a periodical circulated to a very small but highly privileged list of subscribers. First edited in 1753 by Baron Grimm until the year 1780, it was then taken over by J. H. Meister. Thus, Grimm's criticisms of the ballets after 1780 were edited by Meister.
9. Ibid.
10. Valentine Gross Hugo, "Tableaux de la Danse Pendant la Révolution," *Revue Musicale* (Mars 1922), pp. 46–47.
11. Télémaque as a theme was used by Dauberval in London, March 19, 1791, and by Didelot in 1806 in St. Petersburg.
12. *Journal de l'Opéra* manuscript.

13. "Psyché" is the name for the soul in Greek; it mourns its own lost body. Psyché may last forever as an image in the underworld (the important underworld scenes in this *livret* reflect the Greek preoccupation), if its living owner has entered into mythology or history. The particular Psyché in the underworld is, of course, available to any neoromantic poet who cares to address it, but many have lost their individuality and are seen (in Greek art) in massed crowds or fly around anonymously to welcome newer dead. When the Psyché was corporeally conceived, it was a miniature replica of the individual endowed with wings to account for its swift demonic flight, retaining some powers of memory and emotion. See Emily Vermeule, *Aspects of Death in Early Greek Art and Poetry* (Berkeley: University of California Press, 1979).

14. Marie-Françoise Christout makes the interesting point that kings of Hell and devils were not easily believed by turn-of-the-century audiences in her *Le Merveilleux et le Théâtre du Silence*, p. 234: "Les Diableries sont froidement accueillies à l'Opéra. Sous l'Empire on juge celles de l'acte III de *Psyché* de Pierre Gardel fort démodées."

15. Baron Grimm, *Correspondance* 16: 135–36.

16. La Fontaine, *Oeuvres Complètes* (Paris: Editions de Seuil 1965), pp. 405–54. La Fontaine's narrative poem *Les Amours de Psyché et de Cupidon*, based on the classical myth (as taken from Apuleius' *Metamorphosis*), serves as an important source for the *livret* by Gardel. The family, Psyché's parents and sisters, have a significant role, as does the extraordinary beauty of Psyché. People from all over the world seek to cast their eyes upon her. Venus' cult is endangered by this graceful upstart as they turn their attentions to Psyché. Vengeance is sought by the goddess Venus; she asks Cupid to arrange a love affair for Psyché and to make sure that she falls deeply in love with the ugliest person in the world. Psyché's parents fear this fate, and she is left in mourning to die upon the summit of a high mountain. Zephyr swoops down and carries her to an enchanted palace, where she observes riches and luxury. Her husband in the palace is invisible, and Psyché, through the jealous suggestions of her sisters, suspects that perhaps her invisible husband is an evil monster. She takes a lamp and tries to get a look at him during the night. He is not at all the frightening creature of her imagination but a magnificent god. When a spark from the lamp falls upon the charming Cupid, who is asleep, he flies away and disappears in the skies. Then, Psyché submits to harsh tests instigated by the jealous mother, Venus. Finally, Cupid appeals to Zeus for his approval of Cupid and Psyché's marriage, which he gives with his blessing and the promise of Psyché's immortality. La Fontaine situates several of the episodes at Versailles and in a personal, ironic tone, recounts the story as if it took place in the seventeenth century.

17. *Ballet de Psyché.* 1656, Louvre; verses, Benserade; music, Lully and J. B. Boesset; choreography, P. Beauchamps; decor, J. Torelli.

18. Baron Grimm, *Correspondance* 16: 135–36.

19. Ivor Guest, *The Romantic Ballet in Paris* (London: Isaac Pitman, 1966), p. 20.

20. Jean-Georges Noverre, *Psyché et l'Amour*, ballet héroi-pantomime, printed by H. Keynell, Picadilly, Londres, 1788, originally performed in Stuttgart to music by Rodolphe in 1762. Dauberval, *Psyché*, February 16, 1788, Frères La Bottière, Bordeaux. Pierre Gardel, *Psyché*, ballet-pantomime, December 14, 1790, printed by Chez Ballard, 1804.

21. Auguste Bournonville, *Psyché*, a ballet in one act, music composed and arranged by Edvard Helsted, decorations by M. M. Christensen and Lund. Performed at the Royal Theatre for the first time on May 7, 1850.

22. Mary Grace Swift, *A Loftier Flight: The Life and Accomplishments of Charles-Louis Didelot, Ballet Master* (Middletown, Conn.: Wesleyan University Press, 1974), p. 52.

23. Jean-Georges Noverre, *Lettres sur la Danse et les Arts Imitateurs*, 1807 (Paris: Editions Lieutier, 1952), p. 277.

24. Jean-Baptiste Hus (1733–1805), second *maître de ballet* de l'Opéra National, pupil of L. Dupré; dancer and choreographer at the Paris Opéra, and later the ballet master of the Théâtre Français. Partisan of Noverre's theories, Hus was praised by him for knowing how to compose a good ballet. See Winter, *Pre-Romantic*, p. 33.

25. *Les Muses ou le Triomphe d'Apollon* "(Ballet anacréontique, en un acte, musique du Citoyen Ragué, décors et costumes de Fontaine et Porfillion) (Paris: l'Imprimerie de P. de Lormel, 1794)." See my article "Wine, Women and Song: Anacreon's Triple Threat to Eighteenth-Century Ballet," *Dance Research* [London] (Spring 1987).

26. *Journal des Spectacles*, December 17, 1793.

27. See Marvin Carlson, *The Theatre of the French Revolution* (Ithaca: Cornell University Press, 1966), p. 191.

28. *Journal de l'Opéra*, 1795.

29. Winter, *Pre-Romantic*, p. 169.

30. *Journal de l'Opéra* indicates opening night as December 4, 1799, with receipts at 7,161.25 livres; it teamed with *Oedipe à Colone*.

31. Louis-Jacques Milon (1766–1845), French dancer, teacher, choreographer, ballet master at the Opéra.

32. Jean-Georges Noverre, *Lettres*, p. 307.

33. Winter, *Le Merveilleux*, p. 127.

34. Guest, *Le Ballet de l'Opéra de Paris*, p. 73.

35. Louis-Jacques Milon, *Héro et Léandre*, "Ballet-Pantomime en un acte représenté pour la première fois le 6 frimaire, an 8 [Lajarte says the *livret* is wrong, the date is not December 4], Paris, de l'Imprimerie à Prix Fixe."

36. *Héro et Léandre*, p. 13.

37. Ibid., p. 18.

38. *Héro et Léandre*, p. 26.

Notes to Pages 63–79

6. An End to Suffering Psychés and Devilish Cupids

1. Carlson, *The Theatre of the Revolution*, p. 28.
2. Ibid., p. 247.
3. Winter, *Pre-Romantic*, p. 180. Also, in *Le Merveilleux et le Théâtre du Silence*, Christout says, p. 205, that one had to wait until Pierre Gardel choreographed *Le Jugement de Paris* in order to see the goddesses get rid of the heavier leather cothurnus for the lighter sandal.

7. Ballet as the Servant of Politics

1. Charles Dickens, *A Tale of Two Cities* (London: 1859; rpt. Signet Classic, 1960), pp. 275–76.
2. Honoré de Balzac, *A Study of Henri Beyle*, trans. Scott Moncrieff, Introduction to *The Charterhouse of Parma* (New York: Liveright Publishing, 1925), p. xxiii.
3. Louis De Cahusac, *La Danse Ancienne et Moderne, ou Traité Historique de la Danse* (Paris: 1754; rpt. Geneva: Slatkine Reprints, 1971).
4. Ibid., p. 142.
5. Claude-François Menestrier, *Des Ballets Anciens et Modernes* (Paris: 1682; rpt. Geneva: Slatkine Reprints, 1972), Préface.
6. Henri Welschinger. *Le Théâtre et la Révolution* (Paris: Charavay Frères, 1800), pp. 28–29.
7. Ibid., p. 150.
8. Jacques Herissay, *Le Monde des Théâtres Pendant la Révolution* (1789–1800) (Paris: Librairie Perrin, 1922), p. 16.
9. Carlson, *The Theatre of the French Revolution* p. 132.
10. Paul Ginisty, *Mémoires d'Une Danseuse de Corde, Mme Saqui* (Paris: Charpentier et Fasquelle, 1907), p. 41.
11. Roger Baschet, *Mlle Dervieux (Fille d'Opéra)* (Paris: Flammarion, 1943), p. 194.
12. Duchesse de Duras, *Prison Journals*, trans. Mrs. Carey (New York: Dodd, Mead 1892), p. 86. Mme Duras makes note of an interesting fact, that she was in prison with the famous Mlle Dervieux; she writes that Dervieux was sympathetic to the horrific *sans-culottes* and that Dervieux was a "Negress," which was untrue but an expression of the prejudices of the time.
13. Edmond de Goncourt, *La Guimard* (Paris: Charpentier, 1893), p. 296.
14. Adolphe Jullien, *L'Opéra Secret, 1770–1790* (Paris: Rouveyre, 1880). In this book, Jullien makes it clear that La Guimard was a powerful political figure and intriguer. In another letter to La Ferté (1787), Guimard thinks of

Notes to Pages 79–81

quitting the Opéra and retiring. She complains that the judges of the Opéra are lackeys and wigmakers. She asks to be permitted to go to London in order to earn some good money dancing. Her fears about the Opéra were justified. During the Revolution her retirement pension was often neglected or not paid. She and her husband managed to survive in hiding until their deaths.

15. Maurice Louis, *Danses Populaires et Ballets d'Opéra* (Paris: G. P. Maisonneuve et Larose, 1965), p. 192.

16. Gaston Capon. *Les Vestris* (Paris: Société de Mercure de France, 1908), p. 215.

17. On September 23, 1789, the *maîtres de ballets* attempted to assist the poor and the old during troubled times: "The group of dancing masters in Paris gave a gift of 4,000 livres that came from the furniture and silver of their chapels, as well as from their savings" (Ernest Lunel, *Le Théâtre et la Révolution* [Paris: Daragon, 1910], p. 27).

18. The Théâtre de la Nation was dedicated to playing all kinds of theatre: tragedy, comedy, opera, dance, and grand pantomime (Henry Lecomte, *Le Théâtre National et le Théâtre de l'Egalité*, 1793–1794 [Paris: Daragon, 1907], p. 16).

19. Ibid., p. 112.

20. Ibid., p. 83. All the dancers received a total of 155,000 livres, more than the actors, singers, or orchestra. Didelot and his wife each received 20,000 livres, more than anyone except Molé, a great actor.

21. One of the more important characters during the Revolution was a French general called Papa Charette, to whom many allegorical illustrations refer. Charette was an aristocratic French general during the Revolution who rose up against the patriots on March 1793. He was in charge of the Breton Marais, and "he even surprised Noirmoutier, which Haxo recaptured on January 3, 1794, thus the guerilla war was prolonged" (George Lefebvre, *The French Revolution* 2:84). On February 17, 1795, the pacification of La Jaunaye was completed with Charette and approved by the Convention. What had continued to spark uprisings in various pressure points was the destruction of the churches and the punishment of refractory clergy. Lefebvre asks the question, "How could other Frenchmen be denied the reestablishment of freedom of worship, which in theory had always existed," p. 141. The Convention on February 21, 1795, reiterated that the celebration of worship was not to be disturbed and confirmed the separation of church and state. Several months after *Les Royalistes de la Vendée* was presented, in July 1795, Charette tried to help the Count d'Artois, who had been involved in the Quiberon landing, where a surprise attack of men in English uniforms was thwarted by the republicans. Seven hundred forty-eight people were killed, of whom four hundred twenty-eight were nobles. This caused a new war in the Vendée. Charette was executed in 1795 by General Hoche, who pacified the Vendée.

8. Ballets of Political Passion, 1790–1796

1. See Mona Azouf's comprehensive discussion in *La Fête Révolutionnaire* (Paris: Gallimard, 1976).
2. August 18, 1794, *Journal des Théâtres*, Paris. Citing the fêtes of antiquity, Rousseau in his letter to D'Alembert insisted on the necessity of spectacles in a Republic to unite different elements of a populace in the open.
3. David Lloyd Dowd, "Pageant Master of the Republic, Jacques Louis David and the French Revolution," *University of Nebraska Studies*, 3 (June 1948): 129.
4. Marie-Joseph de Chénier (1764–1811), famous dramatist of the Revolution whose brother, the poet André, lost his life during the Reign of Terror. Chénier wrote *Charles IX* (1789), which became a *cause célèbre* and helped to fan the flames of the Revolution as a result of its portrayal of a spineless king and the intrigue in the court.
5. Carlson, *The Theatre of the French Revolution*, p. 43.
6. Dramatic plays in Paris had already inaugurated the ritual of celebrating some of these revolutionary dates, notably: *La Prise de la Bastille*, *La Fête de la Fédération*, and *La Fédération du Parnasse*, which brought playwright Cousin Jacques into the same position that Chénier, author of *Chant du Départ*, had at the Comédie. Cousin Jacques, the patriotic writer of *Le Retour du Champ du Mars*, saved the Beaujolais Theatre from bankruptcy in 1790.
7. Harold Parker, *The Cult of Antiquity and the French Revolutionaries* (Chicago: University of Chicago Press, 1937), p. 132.
8. Ibid., p. 129.
9. Winter, *Le Merveilleux*, p. 44.
10. Cobban, *History of Modern France* 1: 231.
11. Pierre Gardel, *La Contre-Révolution*, 1790s, Jacobin Club.
12. Boileau is referring to Louis XIV; he too had his troubles with internecine fights.
13. It is important to recall that Mirabeau represents one of the distinguished reformers of the theatre. In 1791, he submitted a revolutionary proposal to the Legislative Assembly.
14. Another joke! François de Montmorency de Lava was a seventeenth-century church dignitary.
15. Barnave, Péthion, and Robespierre—the famous young political authors of the new constitution of 1791.
16. These cryptic remarks would have assured Gardel's death during the Reign of Terror.
17. I do not know who this man was or if he ever existed.
18. Alfred Cobban, *A History of Modern France*, vol. 1 (New York: Penguin Books, 1957), p. 179.
19. In 1790, *assignats* were interest-bearing bonds issued by the Constituent Assembly in an attempt to secure much-needed revenue. Their security

was the National Treasury (*biens nationaux*) to which holders were to have a preferential right of exchange. The theory was that as *assignats* were returned to the state, the whole issue would be canceled. Later, the *assignats* became paper currency pure and simple, bearing no interest, constantly overissued and depreciating. The *assignats* in circulation were liquidated at a bankruptcy value in December 1796, and plates from which they were engraved were destroyed.

20. Mirabeau's politics represented a middle-of-the-road statement. He sought a new relation between king and people that attested the rights of both authorities. He insisted that the indivisibility of the king and the people would be safeguarded by the Constitution and was at the heart of the French nation.

21. It is interesting to see certain ballet steps mentioned, since movement vocabulary is rarely discussed in the *livrets*. In the *Dictionnaire de l'Académie Française* (1788), "couler signifie aussi en termes de danse, glisser doucement. 'Dans cette danse-là,' on ne fait que couler. Faites deux pas—et coulez," p. 327.

22. Suleau, (François-Louis) (1758–92), Royalist pamphleteer, journalist, son of a banker. His pamphlets reflected an ardent royalism; he was arrested and killed in the massacres of August 10, 1792.

23. Valentine Gross Hugo, "Tableaux de la Danse Pendant la Révolution," *Revue Musicale* (April 1922), p. 48.

24. Louis DuFranc, *Gossec, Sa Vie et Ses Oeuvres* (Paris: Librairie Fishbecker, 1927), p. 130.

25. Pierre Gardel, François-Joseph Gossec, creators of *L'Offrande à la Liberté*, premiered at the Opéra on September 30, 1792.

26. Winter, *Pre-Romantic*, p. 168.

27. Valentine Gross Hugo, "Tableaux de la Danse Pendant la Révolution," *Revue Musicale* (April 1922), p. 130.

28. DuFranc, *Gossec*, p. 132.

29. "Citoyen Gardel, Citoyen Gossec, et Citoyen M. J. Chénier, *Le Triomphe de la République ou le Camp de Grand Pré*, divertissement lyrique, en un acte; représenté par l'Académie de Musique, le 27 Janvier, l'an II, à Paris, Chez Baudouin, Desenne, Bailly."

30. *Journal de Paris National*, January 29, 1793.

31. Valentine Gross Hugo, *Revue Musicale* (April 1922), p. 132.

32. Ibid.

33. Declared July 11, 1792, in the manifesto of the Duke of Brunswick.

34. Frantz Funck-Brentano, *La Révolution Française*, (Paris: Flammarion, n.d.), p. 35.

35. Carlson, *The Theatre of the French Revolution*, p. 132.

36. Funck-Brentano, *La Révolution Française*, p. 35. See also George Rudé, *The Crowd during the French Revolution* (London: Oxford University Press, 1959).

37. Carlson, *The Theatre of the French Revolution*, p. 132.

38. "L. Jadin, Musique; Saulnier et Dutilh, Paroles; à Paris, Chez Maradan, *Le Siège de Thionville*, représenté le 2 Juin" (Carlson mentions the first performance on June 14), *The Theatre of the French Revolution*, p. 132.

39. André Grétry, the composer of many operas and ballets at the Académie, tells a story in his *Mémoires* that illustrates the fearful power of the crowd in the street: "Un jour traversant la Place de la Révolution, il entendit un orchestre et les cris de joie des danseurs. Au même instant, ses yeux rencontrent le couteau de la guillotine qui se relevait lentement pour retomber bientôt après" (Maurice Albert, *Théâtres des Boulevards* [1789–1848], p. 87). Also in July 1793, a new newspaper called *Le Journal des Spectacles* was inaugurated; it was the only paper dedicated entirely to the theatre, and its first issue sounded a manifesto: "Ce journal était d'autant plus indispensable que les mauvaises moeurs et le méchant goût faisaient au théâtre les progrès les plus rapides et les plus effrayants." See Valentine Gross Hugo, *Revue Musicale* (April 1922), p. 135.

40. Winter, *Pre-Romantic*, p. 168.

41. Funck-Brentano, *La Révolution Française*, p. 41.

42. Cobban, *History of Modern France* 1:231.

43. Mary Grace Swift, in *A Loftier Flight*, mentions *La Constitution de Constantinople*, p. 48: "To modern tastes the plot was a strange melange which centered around an acceptance ceremony of the new French Constitution in Constantinople wherein a Mohammedan Turkish damsel strove and won the right to marry a Frenchman. In the tableau depicting the feast of acceptance of the constitution, there advanced on the stage eight horses attached to a triumphal chariot. On it, tables of the new law were placed, preceded by a cavalry corps, infantry, old people, mothers, and white-robed virgins, who executed their march with wondrous precision. Above all this, the press extolled, however, the troops of fine dancers who performed a varied group of entries and steps under the inescapable Tree of Liberty. In particular, those émigrés from the Opéra Didelot, Rose and Laborie, were praised for giving great pleasure to the audience, wherever they deployed their talents."

44. Henry Lecomte, *Histoire des Théâtres, Le Théâtre National*, p. 26.

45. Ibid., p. 30.

46. Ibid., p. 53.

47. Swift noted in her *Loftier Flight*, p. 48, that dancers wrote to Robespierre after the assassination attempt, an obsequious message wishing him a long life: "Liberty, Equality, Fraternity or Death! The artists of the Théâtre de l'Egalité as representing the people to Robespierre: Permit the artist, always mindful of the important services that you render to our common motherland to share the frightful sadness they experienced at the first news of your assassination. You will easily be convinced of our profound and vibrant joy when we learned that Providence, protector of all happy destinies, has preserved you, so necessary to the health of the Republic, from the hands of the parricides. Accept this feeble tribute of our recognition and be assured that there is not

one of us who would not want to be your protector if the least danger would seem to menace you again. Long live the Republic and its defenders! signed: Didelot, Gallet and other artists of the Théâtre de l'Egalité." In the margin of the document, Robespierre inscribed scornfully, "Flatterers."

48. Théodore Lajarte, *Bibliothèque Musicale de l'Opéra* (Paris: 1878), p. 9. It is interesting that Lajarte says the *sans-culottide* played twenty-four times, whereas Mme Hugo, in checking the receipts, noted that it must have played thirty-eight times. "Citoyen Bouquier, membre de la Convention Nationale et du Comité de l'Instruction Publique, et Citoyen P. L. Moline, secrétaire-greffier attaché à la Convention; *La Réunion du 10 Août ou l'Inauguration de la République Française*, Sans-Culottide dramatique en cinq actes." My notes indicate that the work opened on July 16, 1794, and made 23,000 livres. However, the newspapers of the time and Lajarte report that it opened April 5, 1794. The *livret* was printed by the *Journal des Hommes Libres*, Chez R. Vatar et Asso.

49. *Journal de Paris National*, April 10, 1794.

50. Jules Michelet, *Women of the French Revolution* (Philadelphia: Henry Carey Baird, 1855), p. 200. We note that there were many ladies of the Revolution with extraordinary courage, notably Mme Roland, a woman of high intelligence and sincerity, and a generous enthusiasm, a lover of literature and an ardent admirer of Rousseau. She inspired the Girondins, and much of their policy was created in her salons. She hated Danton and Robespierre, and the enmity of the Montagnards brought her to the guillotine. Mounting the scaffold, she addressed the Statue of Liberty in a grave, mild, yet not reproachful tone: "Oh Liberty! How many crimes have been committed in thy name!"

51. Carlson, *The Theatre of the French Revolution*, p. 204.

52. Cobban, *History of Modern France* 1: 232.

53. Welschinger, *Le Théâtre*, p. 274.

54. "Cuvelier de Trye, et Othon Vandenbrock (cor de l'Opéra) Musique: *La Fête de l'Etre Suprême*, représentée la première fois le 20 Prairial, l'an deuxième de la République Française, une et indivisible sur le Théâtre de la Cité-Variétés, Scènes Patriotiques, Mêlées de Chants, Pantomimes et danses, à Paris, de l'Imprimerie des Ecoles Républicaines." *La Fête de l'Etre Suprême* was performed on the Opéra stage on August 10, 1794.

55. Carlson mentions that "despite the great effort already expended on the new location for the Opéra (formerly Montansier's on the rue de la Loi), the government arranged for further alterations before the Opéra moved in" (*The Theatre of the French Revolution*, p. 191). In my notes from the *Journal de l'Opéra*, I have the date July 27 when the company moved to the rue de la Loi, and I have the date July 16 for the opening of *La Réunion du 10 Août*, not July 27.

56. Carlson, p. 217.

57. Louis, *Danses Populaires*, p. 210.

58. "'Journal des Théâtres et des Fêtes Nationales,' Tome Premier, Par une Société de Gens de Lettres; à Paris Chez Barba l'An lll."
59. Carlson, *The Theatre of the French Revolution*, p. 206.
60. In all the books I have read, there is not one mention of a dancer having been killed during the Revolution. At that time, dancers' movements were not incriminating. But many actors, directors, and playwrights lost their lives: Grammont and Roselly from the Comédie; Jean-François Papillon, a former director of the Opéra; the dramatists André de Chénier, Fabre d'Eglantine and Collot d'Herbois; Mlle Leroy of the Feydeau; Olympes de Gouges, a playwright; Pascal Boyer, a writer and editor of the *Journal des Spectacles*. His crime was to use the word *Monsieur* before someone's name instead of the obligatory *Citoyen* (Carlson, *The Theatre of the French Revolution*, p. 206).
61. Valentine Gross Hugo, "Tableaux de la Danse pendant la Révolution Française," *Revue Musicale* (April 1922), p. 143.
62. Ibid.
63. Julien Tiersot, *Les Fêtes et les Chants de la Révolution Française*, (Paris: Hachette, 1908). The provenance of "La Carmagnole," though unknown, was thought by Tiersot to come from a Marseille *ronde à danser*.
64. Ibid., p. 192.
65. Carlson, *The Theatre of the French Revolution*, p. 235.
66. Famous artists did not fare well during the Revolution. The painter Fragonard was almost totally neglected when he died. No obituary appeared in the *Journal de l'Empire*. Greuze was practically penniless. In a letter of 1801, he complains of being destitute. See Richard Friedenthal, *Letters of Great Artists* (New York: Random House, 1963).
67. Ibid., p. 234.
68. Ibid., p. 236.
69. Winter, *Le Merveilleux*, p. 49.

9. The Tree of Liberty

1. Rouget de l'Isle (1760–1836), a French officer known as an excellent military man. Stationed in Strasbourg, he composed the war song for the Army of the Rhine in 1792 that became known as "La Marseillaise." Rouget de l'Isle composed the battle song of the Army of the Rhine in Strasbourg on April 25, 1792. People sang a lot in those days; according to Eugen Weber, they sang because they did not know French. Abbé Grégoire, who undertook a survey of the question in 1790, concluded that perhaps three-fourths of the people in France knew some French and that just a portion of these could sustain a conversation, perhaps three million (out of twenty-nine million), p. 162. See Weber's article. "Who Sang the Marseillaise?" in *Popular Culture in France* (Palo Alto: Stanford University Press, 1977). "During the Terror,

a revolutionary bishop, Grégoire, urged the National Convention to have dialects extirpated from France, telling that 'where language is concerned we are still, with our thirty different patois, back at the Tower of Babel, while in the matter of freedom we form the vanguard of nations.'" See Frederick Brown, *Theatre and Revolution* (New York: Viking Press, 1980), p. 61.

2. *Dance: A Very Social History*, Carol McD. Wallace, et al., New York: Rizzoli, Metropolitan Museum of Art, 1987), p. 19.

3. It is interesting that the Duchesse de Duras, nee Noailles, mentioned in her prison journals the kind of madness that took hold of the crowd as they sang and danced the song of the Revolution, "Ca Ira": "The Revolutionary army succeeded the National Guard, and made its entrance into the house in a manner suitable to the functions with which it was charged. At ten o'clock in the evening we learned that there were cannons pointed toward the chateau, and at the same moment we heard the grating open amid songs which sounded more like rage than joy. The vanguard was preceded by cannon, drums, and torches. Women mingled with the procession. The refrain of 'Ca ira,' les aristocrates à la lanterne!" was repeated with stubborn animosity. My neighbours were seized with terror, and rushed trembling into my apartment. I reassured them as well as I could without knowing why, except that the feeling of fear is one to which I do not readily yield. When the troop had finished its dances and songs in the courtyard, and gone through a sort of march, it placed its sentinels and retired. I had the full benefit of the performance, as my windows opened on the courtyard" (*The Duchesse de Duras: Prison Journals during the French Revolution* [New York: Dodd, Mead, 1892], p. 38).

11. Realistic Ballets, 1787–1801

1. Maximilien Gardel, *La Chercheuse d'Esprit*, "représenté devant leurs Majestés à Choisy, et à Fontainebleau en 1777 et par l'Académie Royale de Musique en 1778, Paris: P. de Lormel, 1778."

2. The censor's signature notes that he read the *livret* by order of the Monseigneur le Garde des Sceaux, and he found nothing that seemed to prevent its publication.

3. Moreau de Saint-Méry published a short book (1796) about the dance in Santo Domingo during that year, based on his experiences in that country: "There have been no religions which have not adopted characteristic dances to preserve and expand their faith, or to maintain the notion of their ancient origins; and the memory of the famous dances performed in honour of Bacchus is still with us" (*Dance*, trans. Lily and Baird Hastings [Brooklyn Dance Horizons, 1976], p. 9). See Lillian Moore's well-researched article "Moreau de Saint-Méry," *Dance Index* 5, no. 10 (1946).

Notes to Pages 141–46

4. The Panthéon, not a traditional theatre in Paris, used to be the Church of Ste. Geneviève, but was converted during the Revolution into a sacred place that held the mortal relics of famed revolutionary heroes. I have never read of another ballet performance there.

5. *Les Jalousies, ou Les Fêtes du Sérail* by Noverre was first performed in Lyons with music by Louis Granier; he revised it in 1771 in Milan to music by Mozart and revised it again in London in 1789. The story concerns a sultan in a palace surrounded by beautiful ladies, janissaries, bostanjis, dwarfs, and eunuchs. All the women strive to captivate the sultan's heart, but the choice was left between two women, Zaïre and Zaide. They both have enchanting qualities, but he chooses Zaïre. An emotional scene ensues with the rejected Lady Zaide who tries to kill herself in a fit of rage. She then attempts to murder Zaïre; finally, a fierce fight within the seraglio forces the eunuchs to make order and to restore the peace. Apparently, this satisfies everyone and the ballet ends in serenity.

6. *La Fête du Sérail*, "ballet-pantomime, Donnée au Panthéon pour la première fois, le Dimanche 9 Mars, 1788 (Paris: P. De Lormel, 1788)." It was danced by many of the dancers from the Opéra, such as Laborie, Despres, Colombe, and Deshayes.

7. Voltaire, in his play *Zaïre*, written in 1732, wrote about the clash of the Christian and Islamic worlds; this tragedy continued the tradition of the Chansons de Geste and stories about El Cid. *Zaïre* concerns a European girl brought up as a child in the seraglio of Orosmane. As she grows older, he falls in love with her and wants her to be his consort. In a complex series of events, Zaïre discovers that she is a Christian, and that she must convert back to Christianity before her father dies. Since she has been promised in marriage to the sultan, she postpones the marriage, which arouses his suspicions. When she tries to meet secretly with her brother, the sultan believes it is her lover and kills her with his dagger. When he learns of her sincerity and honor, he kills himself.

8. Nègre is the French word used in the *livrets* of this period when referring to any people of North African, sub-Saharan, or Caribbean decent. I have chosen to use the word "black" for the word Nègre.

9. Dauberval, *Le Ballet de la Paille, ou Il n'est qu'un pas du Mal au Bien* (Bordeaux: de l'Imprimerie P. de Beaume, 1789).

10. Ivor Guest, *La Fille Mal Gardée* (London: Dancing Times, 1960), p. 34. I disagree with Mr. Guest's assessment of eighteenth-century artificiality and sentimentality. Reading the ballets tends to refute these notions that historians of Romantic ballet assert. The classical heroes in myth ballets had as much vitality as Ragotte in *La Fille*. They were infused with human qualities; they lacked, perhaps, a sense of humor. The people in *La Fille* hold to the pastoral formulas, with a bit more horseplay and farce, also common to the French theatre before the Revolution.

11. Jean Aumer (1774–1833), dancer, choreographer, studied with Dauberval and was deeply influenced by him, made his debut as a dancer at the Paris Opera 1798, was ballet master of the Porte Saint-Martin and of the Opéra (1820–31).

12. Beaupré, comic dancer: "He was, for his comrades, the most profound protector. Connected to the powerful politican Hébert, who in jest told Beaupré that he was carrying in his pocket a hand-written list of twenty-two opera performers who were destined to go to the guillotine; Beaupré knew that two or three times a week Hébert would go to supper and drink far more than he ate. He was able to get the list away from Hébert during the course of one of these evenings" (Nerée des Arbres, *Deux Siècles à l'Opéra* [Paris: E Dentu, 1868], p. 153).

13. Henry Lecomte, *Histoire de Théâtres de Paris: Le Théâtre de la Cité, 1792–1807.*

14. *Les Circonstances Embarrassantes*, "Ballet Roman, De La Composition du Citoyen Gallet, Maître de ballet du Grand Théâtre de Bordeaux, 1796, De l'Imprimerie de Phillipot de l'an IV de la République." There is a wonderfully long, truthful, though stylized, *avant-propos* complaining of the incompetent and poor ballets in Bordeaux.

15. Sebastien Gallet (born 1753, died, Vienna, 1807), debut at Paris Opéra 1752, pupil of Noverre, rival of Angiolini, choreographed *Bacchus et Ariane* in 1791—quite a success (he was made assistant to Gardel as a result), in *Bacchus*, the costumes created history. Charles Didelot mustered the courage to wear flesh-colored tights with a tiger's skin thrown over his shoulder, grape leaves in his hair, and a staff of Bacchus in his hand. Didelot continued this daring pattern and wore a light, gauzy tunic in the opera *Corisandre*. Gallet also choreographed for the boulevard theatres, but he traveled extensively and finally settled in Vienna; in the spring of the violent year of 1794, Gallet produced a myth ballet at the Théâtre de l'Egalité, with the dancers Didelot, Laborie, Rochefort, and Rose—all dancers from the Opéra probably looking for more work.

16. Lynham, *The Chevalier Noverre*, p. 114.

17. Ibid., p. 96.

18. Louis, *Ballets d'Opéra, Dauberval et Théodore*, p. 202.

19. Marmontel, *Pastorale, Oeuvres Complètes*, vol. 7 (Geneva: Slatkine Reprints, 1968), p. 228.

20. Winter, *Pre-Romantic*, p. 169.

21. *Annette et Lubin*, (Paris: Chez Barba, 1804), p. 12.

22. Filippo Taglioni (born in Milan in 1777, died in Como in 1871) danced in Italy until 1799, when he went to Paris to study at the Opéra with Coulon. He danced there and choreographed in Paris until 1803, when he was appointed ballet master in Stockholm. He traveled and worked in all the European capitals. He returned to Paris, where he choreographed *Le Dieu et la Bayadère, Robert le Diable, Les Huguenots* (both by Meyerbeer), *La Juive*

(Halévy), *La Sylphide*, 1832, among others. He created a new style of lightness and elevation for the chaste purity of his ballets.

23. Pierre Gardel, *La Dansomanie*, "'Folie pantomime' en deux actes, représenté pour la première fois, sur le Théâtre de la République et des arts, le 25 Prairial, an 8, De l'Imprimerie de Ballard, Paris, 1799," cost, 75 centimes; opening night receipts, 6,025 francs.

24. Frustration and political strife caused an attempt on Napoleon's life near the Opéra where he attended that same evening a performance of Hayden's *La Création du Monde*. The *Journal de l'Opéra* indicates that the attempted assassination is mentioned, with receipts that evening reaching 23,974 francs. A benefit was held for the wounded who were injured in this attempt on Napoleon's life on January 5, 1801. The ballet *La Dansomanie* played with *Oedipe à Colone*. Receipts were 4,332.71 francs.

25. Noverre, *Lettres*, p. 304.

26. *Métromanie* by Piron in 1738, *Mélomanie*, comedy and ariettes by Louis Granier and Stanislas Champein) "C'est partout un père qui ne veut accorder à sa fille, qu'un gendre qui excelle dans l'art dont il à la manie. M. Gardel a su tirer de son sujet le parti le plus avantageux." See *Dictionnaire Générale de Théâtre* (1805–12), p. 80.

27. The "Gavotte de Vestris" notated by Thélour, and the "minuet de cour" notated by Zorn in another system of dance notation could have been that danced by Taglioni and Vestris in the Paris Opéra (Shirley Wynne, "From Ballet to Ballroom: Dance in the Revolutionary Era," *Dance Scope* 10, no. 1 [1975]: 72).

28. "Milon ne donnera dans *Les Noces de Gamache*, qu'une image bouffonne, totalement dépourvue de merveilleux de chevalier à la triste figure" (Christout, *Le Merveilleaux*, p. 253).

29. Long after he composed the ballet, Noverre's rendition of Cervantes' story was revised, according to the *Chronique de Paris*, on May 14, 1791, at the Théâtre de Monsieur: "On vient de remettre au Théâtre de Monsieur, *le Nouveau Don Quichotte*. La Musique, on le sait, est par M. Champein, qui sous le régime des privilèges, avait été obligé de cacher son nom sous celui de Nicolo Zingarelli. Le succès de cet ouvrage auquel on a fait beaucoup de changements, a été des plus complets. On assure qu'on va représenter à ce théâtre de grands opéras. M. Boulet, dont les machines ont été si admirées depuis trente années à l'Opéra, y porte ses talents. M. Noverre y fera exécuter des ballets de sa composition. M. Dauberval, sa femme et Mlle Hiligsberg y danseront. Il est certain que rien ne sera plus agréable qu'un beau ballet d'action, après avoir entendu la superbe musique, si admirablement exécuté par les virtuoses Italiens, et qu'en y joignant le grand opéra Français et l'Opéra comique, on réunira dans un emplacement avantageux, tous les genres de plaisir, tous les moyens d'enchanter les oreilles et de charmer les yeux. Ce sera encore au régime de la Liberté que nous devrons ces nouvelles jouissances" (Louis Péricaud, *Théâtre de Monsieur* [Paris: E. Jorel, 1908], p. 143).

30. In Cervantes' novel, the episode of Gamache, Basile, and Quitterie takes place in chaps. 19, 20, and 21 of part two. See *Don Quijote de la Mancha*, pp. 418–33.

31. A historic stage direction indicates "that the frightened women throw up their hands to the sky and run for the Mountains" (Louis-Jacques Milon, *Les Noces de Gamache* [Paris: Chez Dupré, 1801]).

12. Bourgeois Sentiment on the Ballet Stage

1. Salvatore Vigano (1769–1821), famous Italian dancer and choreographer, nephew of the composer, Luigi Boccherini. He usually composed the music for his ballets and choreographed in Vienna, Venice, and Milan. He married the Spanish dancer Maria Medina and worked with the Daubervals in the 1790s. His single greatest characteristic was his use of rhythmic pantomime, similar to normal imitative gesture and traditional dancing, with a strong subordination to the music.

13. Bravo Ballet!

1. Selma Jean Cohen, *Dance as a Theatre Art* (New York: Dodd, Mead, 1974), p. 55.

2. Ivor Guest, *Le Ballet de l'Opéra de Paris*, trans. Paul Alexandre (Paris: Théâtre National de l'Opéra, 1979), p. 77.

3. Tableaux common to the *livrets* of 1788–1801 are mentioned in *Le Jour de Noce*, *Les Muses ou le Triomphe d'Apollon*, and *La Réunion du Dix Août*.

4. Children appear in *livrets* of revolutionary ballet and pantomime in *Fête du Sérail*, *La Fête de l'Etre Suprême*, and *La Réunion du Dix Août*.

5. Heroic women in *livrets* of 1787–1801 include Céphise in *Les Circonstances Embarrassantes*. Women are celebrated in *La Réunion du Dix Août*, for their march to Versailles. For a more complete study of *livrets*, see also my dissertation "Livrets of Ballets and Pantomimes during the French Revolution, 1787–1801," University of New Mexico, 1981.

6. Character and regional or native dances are notable in the following *livrets* of this period: *Les Noces de Gamache*, *Les Circonstances Embarrassantes*, *La Fête du Sérail*, and *Le Jour de Noce*.

7. Ivor Guest, *The Romantic Ballet in Paris* (London: Pitman and Sons, 1966), p. 6.

BIBLIOGRAPHY

Ackerknecht, Erwin, M.D. *A Short History of Medicine.* New York: Ronald Press, 1955.
Aghion, Max. *Le Théâtre à Paris au 18 e.* Paris: Librairie de France, 1926.
Albert, Maurice, *Les Théâtres des Boulevards.* Paris: Société Française d'Imprimerie et de Librairie, 1902.
Allevy, Marie-Antoinette. *La Mise en Scene au 19 e.* Paris: Librairie Droz, 1938.
Angiolini, Gaspare. *Dissertation sur les Ballets Pantomimes des Anciens.* 1765. Milan: Achille Bertarelli, 1956.
Annales Dramatiques. *Dictionnaire Général des Théâtres, 1808–1812.* Geneva: Slatkine Reprints, 1967.
Attinger, Gustave. *L'Esprit de la Commedia Dell' Arte dans le Théâtre Français.* 1950. Reprint. Paris and Geneva: Slatkine Reprints, 1969.
L'Aulnaye, M. De. *De la Saltation Théâtrale ou Recherches Sur L'Origine, les Progrès et les Effets de la Pantomime Chez les Anciens.* Paris, 1790.
d'Auriac, Eugene. *Théâtre de la Foire.* Paris: Garnier, 1878.
Balanchine, George. *Stories of Great Ballets.* New York: Doubleday, 1975.
Balzac, Honoré. *A Study of Henri Beyle.* Trans. Scott Moncrieff. Introduction, *Charterhouse of Parma.* New York: Liveright Publications, 1925.
Baron, John. "Les Fées des Forests de S. Germain, Ballet de Cour, 1625." *Dance Perspectives* 62 (Summer 1975): 4.
Baschet, Roger. *Mlle Dervieux (Fille d'Opéra).* Paris: Flammarion, 1943.
Batteux, Charles. *Les Beaux Arts Réduits à un Même Principe.* Paris: Durand, 1746. Microfiche. Archives de la Linguistique Française, CNRS, 1972.

Bibliography

Beaulieu, Henri. *Les Théâtres du Boulevard du Crime, 1752–1862*. Paris: Daragon, 1905.
Beccaria, Cesare. *An Essay on Crimes and Punishments*. Stanford: Stanford University Press, 1953.
Bennahum, Judith Chazin. "Cahusac, Diderot, and Noverre: Three French Revolutionary Writers on Eighteenth-Century Dance." *Theatre Journal* (May 1983), pp. 169–78.
———. "Livrets of Ballets and Pantomimes during the French Revolution, 1787–1801." Diss. University of New Mexico, 1981.
———. "Wine, Women, and Song: Anacreon's Triple Threat to Eighteenth-Century Ballet." *Dance Research* [London] (Spring 1987).
Bernardin de Saint-Pierre, Jacques. *Paul et Virginie*. Paris: Classiques Garnier, 1958.
Bernstein, Michele Root. *Boulevard Theatre and Revolution in Eighteenth-Century Paris*. Ann Arbor: U.M.I. Research Press, 1984.
Binney, Edwin. *Les Ballets de Théophile Gautier*. Paris: Librairie Nizet, 1965.
Biographie Universelle. Paris, 1864.
Blasis, Carlo. *The Code of Terpsichore*. Trans. R. Baron. London, 1888. Reprint. New York: Dance Horizons, n.d.
Bonnet, Jacques [Pierre Bourdelot]. *Histoire Générale de la Danse Sacrée et Profane*. Paris: Chez d'Houry Fils, 1724.
Bougainville, Louis Antoine de. *Adventure in the Wilderness, 1756–1760*. Ed. Edward Hamilton. Norman: University of Oklahoma, 1964.
Brazier, Nicolas. *Chroniques des Petit Théâtres de Paris, 1783–1838*. Ed. Rouveyre et G. Blond. Paris, 1883.
Brown, Frederick. *Theatre and Revolution*. New York: Viking Press, 1980.
Cahusac, Louis de. *La Danse Ancienne et Moderne ou Traité Historique de la Danse*. Paris, 1754. Reprint. Geneva: Slatkine Reprints, 1971.
Campardon, Emile. *L'Académie Royale de Musique au 18 e*. Paris: Beger-Lenault, 1884.
———. *Spectacles de la Foire*. 2 vols. Paris: Berger-Lenault, 1877.
Capon, Gaston, *Les Vestris*. Paris: Société du Mercure de France, 1908.
Carlson, Marvin. *The French Stage in the Nineteenth Century*. Metuchen, N.J.: Scarecrow Press, 1972.
———. *The Theatre of the French Revolution*. Ithaca, N.Y.: Cornell University Press, 1966.
Castil-Blaze, François. *Académie Impériale de Musique*. Paris: Castil-Blaze, 1855.
———. *2 Tomes de L'Opéra en France*. Paris: Janet et Cotelle Librairies, 1820.
Cervantes, Miguel. *El Ingenioso Hidalgo Don Quijote de la Mancha*. Madrid: Espasa-Calpri, 1970.
Chapman, John. "Forgotten Giant: Pierre Gardel," *Dance Research* [London] (Spring 1987).

Bibliography

Chateaubriand, René de. *Oeuvres Complètes*. 12 vols. Nouvelle Edition, Précédée d'une Etude de Sainte-Beuve, vol. 3. Paris: Librairie Garnier Frères, n.d.

Chénier, André de. *Les Bucoliques*. Paris: Maison du Livre, 1907.

———. *Poésies Choisies*. Paris: Classiques Larousse, 1934.

Chinard, Gilbert. *L'Amérique et le Rêve Exotique*. Paris: Librairie Droz, 1934.

Christout, Marie-Françoise. *Le Ballet de Cour de Louis XIV (1643–1672)*. Paris: Editions A. and J. Picard, 1967.

———. *Le Merveilleux et le Théâtre Du Silence*. Paris: Editions Mouton, La Haye, 1965.

Cobb, R. S. *The Police and the People: French Popular Protest, 1789–1820*. New York: Oxford University Press, 1970.

Cobban, Alfred. *A History of Modern France*. 3 vols. Middlesex: Penguin, 1963.

Cohen, Selma Jeanne. *Dance as a Theatre Art*. New York: Dodd, Mead, 1974.

———. "Freme di Gelosia! Italian Ballet Librettos, 1766–1865." *Bulletin of the New York Public Library* 67, no. 9 (1963).

Critchley, M. *The Language of Gesture*. London: Arnold, 1939.

Dacier, Emile. *Mlle Sallé (1707–1756), Une Danseuse de l'Opéra*. Paris: Librairie Plon, 1909.

Desarbres, Nerée. *Deux Siècles à L'Opéra, 1669–1868*. Paris: Dentu, 1868.

Des Hayes. *Idées Générales sur L'Académie Royale de Musique*. Paris: Chez Mongie, Blvd Montmartre, 1822.

Dickens, Charles. *A Tale of Two Cities*. London, 1859. Reprint, Signet Classic, 1960.

Diderot, Denis. *Le Neveu de Rameau*. Paris: Gallimard, 1966.

———. *Oeuvres Esthétiques*. Paris: Classiques Garnier, 1965.

Dowd, David Lloyd. "Pageant-Master of the Republic, Jacques-Louis David and the French Revolution." *University of Nebraska Studies*, n.s. 3 (June 1948).

du Bois, Albert. "Mlle Théodore." *La Revue de Belgique* (1896).

Duchartre, Pierre Louis. *The Italian Comedy*. New York: Dover Publications, 1966.

Duchet, Michele. *Anthropologie et Histoire au Siècle des Lumières*. Paris: François Maspero, 1971.

Du Franc, Louis. *Gossec, Sa Vie et Ses Oeuvres*. Paris: Louis-Michaud, 1909.

Duthé, Catherine Rosalie Gerard. *Souvenirs*. Introduction and notes by Paul Ginisty. Paris: Louis-Michaud, 1909.

Encyclopedia Britannica. 11th ed. New York, 1911.

Encyclopédie ou Dictionnaire Raisonné des Sciences, des Arts et Métiers, Facsimile. Stuttgart Bad Cannstatt: Friedrich Frommann Verlag (Gunther Holz Boog), 1966.

Bibliography

Engel, Karl. *Idées sur le Geste et l'Action Théâtrale.* 2 vols. Paris: H. J. Jansen, 1795.
Fleury, Comte. *Jean Etienne Despreaux, Maître des Ballets de Cours sous Louis XVI.* Paris: Revue de la France Moderne, 1900.
France, Anatole. *Les Dieux Ont Soif.* Paris: Calmann-Levy, 1965.
Friedenthal, Richard. *Letters of Great Artists.* New York: Random House, 1963.
Funck-Brentano, Frantz. *La Révolution Française.* Paris: Flammarion, n.d.
———. *Scènes et Tableaux de la Révolution.* Paris: Editions Gautier-Langureau, 1934.
Gaiffe, Felix. *La Drame en France au XVIII siècle.* Paris: Librairie Armand-Colin, 1971.
Ginisty, Paul. *La Féerie.* Paris: Louis-Michaud, 1910.
———. *Mémoires d'une Danseuse de Corde, Mme Saqui, 1786–1866.* Paris: Charpentier et Fasquelle, 1907.
Goncourt, Edmond de. *La Guimard.* Paris: Charpentier, 1893.
Graffigny, Françoise. *Letters Written by a Peruvian Princess.* Facsimile. London: J. Brindley, 1748.
Grimm, Baron. *Correspondance.* Paris: Garnier, 1880.
Guest, Ivor. *Le Ballet de l'Opéra de Paris.* Trans. Paul Alexandre. Paris: 3 siècles, Théâtre National de l'Opéra, 1979.
———. *The Romantic Ballet in England.* Middleton, Conn.: Wesleyan University Press, 1972.
———. *The Romantic Ballet in Paris.* London: Pitman and Sons, 1966.
Hallays-Dabot, Victor. *Histoire de la Censure Théâtrale en France.* 1862. Reprint. Geneva: Slatkine Reprints, 1970.
Hedgecock, Frank A. *David Garrick and His Friends.* London: Stanley Paul, 1898.
Herissay, Jacques. *Le Monde des Théâtres Pendant la Révolution, 1789–1800.* Paris: Librairie Perrin, 1922.
Hillmacher, Frédéric. *Le Cirque Franconi.* Lyon: Imprimerie Louis Perrin and Marinet, 1875.
Hugo, Valentine Gross. "Tableaux de la Danse Pendant La Révolution, 1789–1795." *Revue Musicale.* Paris, 1922.
Jullien, Adolphe. *L'Opéra Secret, 1770–1790.* Paris: Rouveyre, 1880.
Kaplow, Jeffrey, ed. *France on the Eve of Revolution: A Book of Readings.* New York and London: John Wiley, 1971.
Kennard, Joseph Spencer. *Masks and Marionettes.* New York: Macmillan, 1935.
Kirstein, Lincoln. *Movement and Metaphor, Four Centuries of Ballet.* New York and Washington: Praeger Publishers, 1970.
Koegler, Horst. *Concise Oxford Dictionary of Ballet.* London: Oxford University Press, 1977.

Bibliography

Laffont, Robert, and Valentino Bompiami. *Dictionnaire des Oeuvres.* Paris: Société d'Edition de Dictionnaires et Encyclopédies, 1953.
Lahontan, Baron de. *Dialogues Curieux.* 1703. Baltimore: Johns Hopkins University Press, 1931.
Lajarte, Theodore de. *Bibliothèque Musicale de l'Opéra.* Paris, 1878.
Lan, Jules. *Mémoires d'un Chef de Claque.* Paris: Librairie Nouvelle, 1883.
Lecomte, Henry. *Histoire des Théâtres de Paris: Le Théâtre de la Cité, 1792–1807.* Paris: Daragon, 1910.
———. *Histoire des Théâtres de Paris: Le Théâtre National, Le Théâtre de l'Egalité, 1793–1794.* Paris: Daragon, 1907.
Lefebvre, Georges. *The French Revolution.* 2 vols. Trans. Elizabeth Moss Evanson. New York: Columbia Univeristy Press: 1964.
Letainturier-Fradin, Gabriel. *La Camargo.* Paris, 1908. Reprint. Geneva: Minkoff, 1973.
Levy, Darlene Gay, et al. *Women in Revolutionary Paris.* Chicago: University of Chicago Press, 1979.
Lifar, Serge. *Auguste Vestris, Dieu de la Danse.* Paris: Editions Nagel, 1950.
Louis, Maurice. *Danses Populaires et Ballets d'Opéra.* Paris: G. P. Maisonneuve et Larose, 1965.
Lunel, Ernest. *Le Théâtre et la Révolution.* Paris: Daragon, 1910.
Lynham, Deryck. *The Chevalier Noverre.* London: Dance Books, 1972.
Mander, Raymond, and Joe Mitchenson. *Pantomime.* London: Peter Davies, 1973.
Marmontel, Jean-François. *Oeuvres Complètes.* Vol. 7. Slatkine Reprints, 1968.
Marolles, le Comte de. *Mémoires.* 3 vols. Paris, 1754.
Mason, J. F. *The Melodrama in France from the Revolution to the Romantic Drama.* Baltimore: J. H. Furst, 1912.
McGowan, Margaret. *L'Art du Ballet de Cour en France, 1581–1643.* Paris: Centre National de la Recherche Scientifique, 1963.
Menestrier, Claude-François. *Des Ballets Anciens et Modernes.* Paris, 1682. Reprint. Geneva: Slatkine Reprints, 1972.
Michelet, Jules. *Women of the French Revolution.* Philadelphia: Henry Carey Baird, 1855.
Moore, Lillian. "Moreau de Saint-Méry and Dance." *Dance Index* 5, no. 10 (1946).
Mornet, Daniel. *Le Romantisme en France au 18 e.* Paris: Hachette, 1912.
Neidish, Juliet. "Whose Habitation Is the Air." *Dance Perspectives* (Spring 1975), pp. 7–9.
Nicoll, Allardyce. *The World of Harlequin.* London: Cambridge University Press, 1963.
Niklaus, Thelma. *Harlequin.* New York: George Brazillier, 1956.

Bibliography

Noverre, Jean-Georges. *Lettres sur la Danse et les Arts Imitateurs.* Paris, 1807. Paris: Editions Lieutier, 1952.
Oliver, Alfred Richard. *The Encyclopedists as Critics of Music.* New York: Columbia University Press, 1947.
Oreglia, Giacomo. *Commedia Dell' Arte.* New York: Hill and Wang, 1968.
Parker, Harold. *Cult of Antiquity and the French Revolutionaries.* Chicago: Univeristy of Chicago Press, 1937.
Pellison, Maurice. *Les Comédies-Ballets de Molière.* Paris: Hachette, 1919.
Péricaud, Louis. *Théâtre de Monsieur.* Paris: E. Jorel, 1908.
Pifteau, Benjamin. *Histoire du Théâtre en France.* 2 vols. Paris: Leon Willem, 1879.
Priddens, Deirdre. *The Art of Dance in French Literature.* London: Adam and Chas. Black, 1952.
Prunières, Henry. *Le Ballet de Cour en France avant Benserade et Lully.* Paris: Henri Laurens, 1914. Reprint. London: Johnson Reprint, 1970.
Pure, Michel de. *Idées des Spectacles Anciens et Nouveaux.* Paris, 1668. Reprint. Geneva: Minkoff, 1972.
Rousseau, Jean Jacques. *Confessions.* Bk. 11. Paris: Bibliothèque de la Pléiade, 1961.
Rudé, George. *The Crowd in the French Revolution.* London: Oxford University Press, 1959.
Sand, Maurice. *The History of the Harlequinade.* Vol. 2. New York, London: Benjamin Blom, 1915.
Schlundt, Christena. "Source Material for the Study of French Dance." *Dance Research Journal* 10, no. 1 (1979).
Schwartz, Judith, and Christena Schlundt. *French Court Dance and Dance Music.* New York: Pendragon Press, 1987.
Senninger, Claude Book. *Théophile Gautier, Auteur Dramatique.* Paris: Librairie, Nizet, 1972.
Smith, Patrick. *The Tenth Muse: A Historical Study of the Opera.* Libretto. New York: Knopf, 1970.
Swift, Mary Grace. *A Loftier Flight: The Life and Accomplishments of Charles-Louis Didelot.* Middleton, Conn.: Wesleyan University Press, 1974.
Tiersot, Jullien. *Les Fêtes et les Chants de la Révolution Française.* Paris: Hachette, 1908.
Tocqueville, Alexis de. *Democracy in America.* Ed. Richard Heffner. New York: Mentor Books, 1956.
Vereule, Emily. *Aspects of Death in Greek Art and Poetry.* Berkeley: University of California Press, 1979.
Wallace, Carol McD., et al. *Dance: A Very Social History.* New York: Rizzoli, Metropolitan Museum of Art, 1987.
Weber, Eugen, "Who Sang the Marseillaise?" *Popular Culture in France.* Stanford French and Italian Studies, 1977.

Bibliography

Welschinger, Henri. *Le Théâtre de la Révolution.* Paris: Charavay, Frères, 1880.
Wiley, William Leon. *The Early Public Theatre in France.* Cambridge: Harvard University Press, 1960.
Winter, Marion Hannah. *Pre-Romantic Ballet.* New York: Dance Horizons, 1974.
———. *Le Théâtre du Merveilleux.* Paris: Chez Olivier-Perrin, 1962.
Wynne, Shirley. "From Ballet to Ballroom: Dance in the Revolutionary Era." *Dance Scope* 10, no. 1 (1975): 65–73.

INDEX

Acrobatics, 20, 21
Age of Reason, the, 26
Anacreon, 54
Angiolini, Gaspare, 8, 33, 65, 133, 179
Apuleius, 33, 49
Aumer, Jean, 147, 194

Ballet: Anacreonitic, 54; Baroque, xxii, 144, 167, 168; court, of the 1700s, xvii; and opera, 17; and pantomime, integration of, 17, 166, 177; pastoral, 143–44, 152; before the Revolution, xvii–xviii, 10–28; Romantic, xvii, 26, 136, 144, 168, 173; schools, 17, 18, 19; technique, xix, 11–12, 19, 173. *See also* Gestural techniques; Pantomime
Ballet comique, 32, 145
Ballet d'action, xxiv, 8, 33, 163; innovative character of the, 14–15; invention of the, 16; and the use of mythic themes, 64–65

Ballet héroï-pantomime, 45
Ballet-pantomime, 15, 45, 167
Balzac, Honoré de, 71–72
Barnave, Joseph, 92
Baroque ballet, xxii, 144, 167
Baroque theatre, xxv, 144
Batteux, Charles, 3
Beaumarchais, Augustin Caron de, 13; *The Marriage of Figaro*, xxiv, 22, 104, 133–34
Benserade, Isaac de, 6
Bercher, Jean. *See* Dauberval, Jean
Bertaut, Jean de Caen, 5
Blasis, Carlo, 64
Bonaparte, Lucien, 25
Bonaparte, Napoléon. *See* Napoléon I
Bordier, François, 5
Bos, Abbé du, 3, 12
Boucher, François, 65
Bouquier, Gabriel, 112
Bourgeois, the, xxv, xxvii, 163–65, 172
Bournonville, Auguste, 54

205

Index

Bressoles, Chevalier Peicam de, 120–25, 126

Cahusac, Louis de, 3, 11–12, 13, 15, 133; on the relationship of dance and politics, 74
Camargo, Marie-Anne de Cupis de, 16
Carlson, Marvin, 56, 64, 125
Castil-Blaze, François, 15
Censorship, 20–26, 75, 129–30; and pantomime, 20, 135; before the Revolution, 4
Cervantes, Miguel de, 158, 159, 162, 163
Champagny, Jean-Baptiste, 25
Chapelier, Abbé, 22–23
Chardin, Jean-Baptiste-Siméon, 136
Chateaubriand, René de, xxvii
Chénier, Marie-Joseph de, 22, 24, 100, 116; *La Fête de la Fédération*, 84–86
Christout, Marie-Françoise, 32
Cobban, Alfred, xxvi, 30, 32, 116
Comédie-Française, the, 20
Comic bucolic myths, 32, 34
Comic tradition, Italian, 14, 15, 65, 134
Commedia actors, xviii
Commedia troupes, 18
Contredanse, 143
Corneille, Pierre, 5
Costuming, xviii–xxiv, 4, 63, 134, 165, 168
Court ballet, of the 1700s, xvii

Dacier, Emile, 19
Dances: Native American ritual, 172; regional, 172, 173
Danses de caracteres, 172
Danton, Georges-Jacques, 74, 111–12

Dauberval, Jean, xxvi, 8, 12, 77, 79; influence of Noverre on, 13, 19; *La Fille Mal Gardée*, 4, 144–48, 160, 163, 165; *Le Siège de Cythère*, 6–7; *Psyché*, 47–49, 50, 53–54
David, Jacques-Louis, 63, 82, 83, 106, 120, 123; innovations of, 126; *La Fête de l'Achèvement*, 86–87; *La Fête de la Fédération*, 84–86; during the Reign of Terror, 125
De Mille, Cecil B., 172
Demi-pointe, 156, 168
Desmoulins, Camille, 111, 112
Dickens, Charles, 69–70
Didelot, Charles, 19, 64, 77, 108, 159
Diderot, Denis, xxiv, 8, 166; dramatic works of, 11, 133
Drame bougeois, 13, 133
Dumouriez, Charles, 98
Duport, Adrien, 92
Dupré, Louis, 16

Engel, Karl, 9, 35
Entrechats, 168

Favart, Charles, 134
Fêtes Révolutionnaires, xxvi, 82–126, 168, 173
Franc, Louis du, 98
Frangonard, Jean-Honoré, 65
Funck-Brentano, Frantz, 106

Galeotti, Vicenzo, 8
Gallet, Sebastien, 76, 77, 108, 194; *Les Circonstances Embarrassantes*, 148–50
Gallini, Giovanni Andrea, 3
Gardel, Maximilien, 15; death of, 38; *La Chercheuse d'Esprit*, 137–39; *La Fête du Sérail*, 139–42,

206

Index

164; *Le Premier Navigateur*, 35–38, 61, 124; *Mirza*, 124, 142–44, 164, 168, 169
Gardel, Pierre, 8, 12, 15, 17, 38; choreography of, during the Reign of Terror, 76–77; *The Counter-Revolution*, 87–97; *La Dansomanie*, 153–54, 155–58, 163; *La Fête de l'Etre Suprême*, 116–20; *La Fête de l'Unité et de l'Indivisibilité de la République*, 106–8; *La Fête pour l'Inauguration des Bustes de Marat et Lepeletier*, 98–100; *La Réunion du Dix Août*, 112–15; *Le Jugement de Paris*, 57, 155; *Le Siège de Thionville*, 105–6; *L'Offrande à la Liberté*, 97–98, 102; myth ballets of, 64; and Noverre, 13, 19, 57; *Psyché*, 49–54, 57, 89, 124; *Telemachus on the Island of Calypso*, 38–45, 57, 124, 167–68, 171; *The Triumph of the Republic*, 100–104
Garrick, David, 13, 14, 18, 65, 166
Gessner, Salomon, 35, 37, 38
Gestural techniques, 164–65, 166–67, 173. *See also* Pantomime
Gluck, Christoph Willibald, 96, 135, 179–80
Gossec, François-Joseph, 96–97, 100, 116
Grand allegros, 168
Greco-Roman mythology, influence of, 29–34
Greuze, Jean-Baptiste, 136
Griffith, D. W., 172
Grimm, Friedrich Melchior von, 15, 16, 23; review of Gardel's *Psyché*, 49, 50; review of *Telemachus on the Island of Calypso*, 43

Guest, Ivor, 168, 193
Guimard, Marie-Madeleine, 16, 78, 79, 151

Hardy, Alexandre, 144
Haydn, Franz Joseph, 96
Henriot, François, 45
Hérissay, Jacques, 75
Hesse, Jean-Baptiste de, 18
Hilverding, Franz, 8, 64–65
Hugo, Valentine Gross, 121
Hus, Jean-Baptiste, 54–57

Improvisation, xviii, 15
Italian comic tradition, 14, 15, 65, 134

Jacobins, the, 91, 92, 95, 96, 120–21

La Fontaine, Henri-Marie, 49
Lajarte, Théodore de, 113, 118
Lameth, Alexandre, 92
Lavallee, Joseph, 108
Lecouvreur, Adriana, 18–19
Lefebvre, Georges, xxvi, 159
Lisle, Rouget de, 128
Livret, the, xxv, 3–9, 14, 22; and Greco-Roman mythology, 29; value of, for dance historians, 5–6
Louis XIV (king), xvii, xviii, 11, 14, 72; death of, 20
Louis XVI (king): in *The Counter-Revolution*, 94, 95, 96; execution of, 96, 100; flight to Varennes, 88
Lynham, Deryck, 151

Macklin, Charles, 63
Magri, Gennaro, 3
Malherbe, François de, 5

207

Index

Marat, Jean-Paul, 80, 104; death of, 106
Marie-Antoinette, 22, 80, 95; execution of, 96, 111; flight to Varennes, 88
Marivaux, Pierre de, 134, 149
Marmontel, Jean-François, 151, 152
Marolles, Comte de, 11
Marriage of Figaro, The (de Beaumarchais), xxiv, 22, 104, 133–34
Medici, Catherine de, 32, 72
Méhul, Etienne, 155
Melodrama, 48, 135, 167; *pantomime-lyrique*, 111
Menestrier, Claude-François, 3, 12, 29, 72, 74
Mercier, Louis Sebastien, 13, 134
Milon, Louis Jacques: *Héro et Leandre*, 57–62; *Les Noces de Gamache*, 158–62, 164
Minuet, the, xxiv
Mirabeau, Honoré-Gabriel, 76, 85, 89, 93, 188; death of, 96
Molière, Jean-Baptiste, 6, 50, 133, 138, 144; *Bourgeois Gentilhomme*, 157–58
Moline, Philippe, 112
Montesquieu, Baron de La Brède et de, 141, 149
Murphy, Patricia, 15
Muscadins, 120, 123
Music, use of, 8, 17, 83, 123, 164; prior to 1779, 3
Mythology, xxv, xvii–xix, 27–65, 96, 155

Napoléon I, xxvii, 25, 74, 127, 195
Noeuville, M., 79, 80
Notation, for ballet, 3
Noverre, Jean-Georges, xxiv, xxvi, 6, 8–9, 18; on Anacreontic ballet, 54; *Annette et Lubin*, 150–52, 164; and Gardel, relationship with, 13, 19, 57; innovative influence of, 12–13, 14, 19, 33, 64, 166; *Psyché*, 45–47, 49, 50, 53–54; remarks on Milon, 59; on the use of pantomime, 12, 13

Oliver, Richard, 15
Opéra comique, 14, 20

Pantomime, xviii, 14–15, 135–36, 172; and ballet, integration of, 17, 166, 177; censorship of, 20, 135; *folie*, 155, 158; of the Italian comedy, 13, 14, 65; nineteenth-century, 174; Noverre on the use of, 12, 13; Roman, 33; Rousseau on, 17. *See also* Gestural techniques
Pantomime-lyrique melodrama, 111
Paris Opéra, the, xxv–xxvi, xxvii, 11, 54; and censorship, 20–21, 22, 26, 56, 127–28
Parker, Harold, 30, 32
Passepied, the, xxiv
Petites pièces, 25
Petits ronds de jambe, 156
Pèyre, Antoine-Marie, 126
Plutarch, 86
Poetry, use of, 5, 12, 38, 83, 123
"Prise de la Bastille," the, xxvi
Prunières, Henry, 5–6
Pure, Michel de, 3, 5

Rabaut, Jean Paul, 86
Racine, Jean, 164
Rameau, Pierre, 3
Renaissance, the, xxv, 32
Restoration, the, xxvii
Révolte nobiliaire, the, xxvi
Reyer, Pierre de, 144
Robespierre, Maximilien-François de, 24, 74, 79, 90, 173;

Index

executions ordered by, 111–12; fall of, 119–20, 121, 129; after his election as president, 116–17
Romantic ballet, xvii, 26, 144, 168, 173
Ronsard, Pierre de, 6
Rousseau, Jean Jacques, 16–17, 57, 68, 126, 135
Rudé, George, xxvi

Saint-Mard, Remond de, 3
Saint-Pierre, Bernardin de, 149
Sallé, Marie, 16, 18–19
Saltation (dance), 33
Sans-culottes, the, 4, 55, 56, 106, 111
Sans-culottide, 23, 57
Sauteuse, 100
Set design, 3
Shakespeare, William, 14; *Romeo and Juliet*, 143
Shoes, heeled, xix, xxiv, 19, 168
Sieyès, Abbé, 90
Slavery, 108–10, 128, 149
Stage settings, 165
Swift, Mary Grace, 112, 189–90

Tableau vivant, 153
Taglioni, Filippo, 142, 194–95; *Le Jour de Noce, ou L'Enlèvement*, 152–55, 163, 164, 165
Taglioni, Marie, 152
Talleyrand, Charles–Maurice de, 85
Talma, François, 63
Theatre, the English, influence of, 14, 65
Théâtre de la Republique, 25
Théâtre du Monsieur, 21
Théâtre Français, the, 20
Théâtre Italien, the, 20
Tiersot, Jullien, 123
Tonnelet, xix, 13
Torelli, Jacomo, 30
Tragedy, 20, 33; "of the masses," 35. *See also* Melodrama
Tutu, the, xix

Variétés Amusantes, the, 21
Vaudevilles, 25
Vestris, Auguste, 77, 79, 159
Vestris family, the, 16
Vigano, Salvatore, 64, 165, 196
Vigarini, Carlo, 30
Voltaire, 18, 33, 63, 149, 193

Watteau, Antoine, 65, 147
Weaver, John, 167
Welschinger, Henri, 116–17
Winter, Marian Hannah, 126

Judith Chazin-Bennahum, a graduate of the High School of Performing Arts in New York City and Brandeis University, received a doctorate in Romance languages from the University of New Mexico and is an associate professor of theatre arts at the University of New Mexico, where she heads the dance program of the Department of Theatre Arts and teaches dance history, dance criticism, and ballet technique. A principal soloist with the Metropolitan Opera Ballet Company when Antony Tudor was director, Chazin-Bennahum also danced with the Robert Joffrey Company, Agnes de Mille in a Broadway show, and John Butler and Thomas Andrew in the Santa Fe Opera Ballet Company, which toured Europe under the musical direction of Igor Stravinsky. She currently serves as president of the Society of Dance History Scholars.